The Mind's We

Contextualism in Cognitive Psychology

Diane Gillespie

Southern Illinois University Press
Carbondale and Edwardsville

Library of Congress Cataloging-in-Publication Data

Gillespie, Diane, 1947–
    The mind's we: contextualism in cognitive psychology / Diane
Gillespie.
        p.   cm.
    Includes bibliographical references and index.
    1. Context effects (Psychology) 2. Cognitive psychology.
3. Knowledge, Theory of.   I. Title.
BF378.C72G55   1992
153—dc20   91-39988
ISBN 0-8093-1675-7   CIP

For Michael

To all my new friends
at Belmont, who provided
a rich context for thinking
about teaching and learning,
with best wishes,
Diane Gillispie
May 1994

Weave real connections, create real nodes, build
    real houses.
Live a life you can endure: make love that is loving.
Keep tangling and interweaving and taking more in,
a thicket and bramble wilderness to the outside
    but to us
interconnected with rabbit runs and burrows
    and lairs.

        Marge Piercy, "The seven of pentacles"

Contents

Preface

Twelve years ago, in a course on cognitive psychology, I sat struggling with my first set of research articles concerned with mediated generalizations, information flow systems, and internal knowledge structures. Confident and comfortable in their tone, these psychologists enthusiastically expanded a new enterprise: the study of complex intellectual processes. Behaviorism and its accompanying antimentalism lay gasping on the mat, still firmly pinned by Noam Chomsky's (1959) refutation of B. F. Skinner's theory of language. To warn against the study of mental concepts, Skinner had always called up the specter of the "unscientific" psychologist, who, in studying the unobservable, obstructed real scientific progress. Unfazed by such a potential charge, these new psychologists termed themselves "cognitive scientists." Adopting an information-processing model, they asserted that cognition could be studied indirectly, that is, inferentially and structurally. They used the analogy of the computer to argue that cognitive processes operated mechanically, proceeded formally, and functioned autonomously, even though invisible to the person using the computer.

As I finished the articles, I felt disquieted, confused. I rehearsed the objections that humanists had made to Skinner's behaviorism, but these seemed inappropriate challenges to the view of the mind set forth by this new anti-Skinnerian breed of psychologist. At that moment, my then three-year-old son pulled on my arm and said, "Mom, come here." He pulled me from an abstract world of formal procedures to a much messier one. How were we going to get the last block on his tower? Still thinking about the view of cognition laid forth in the articles, I watched him manipulate the concrete world around him, interact with me in an ongoing dialogue, and reflect to himself as he studied his possibilities. In this engagement with my son, I realized something essential was missing in what I had been reading—he asked me, for example, for attention and engaged me in his project. After years of further study, I now believe that for students of psychology this type of experience is frequent, deeply significant, and systematically ignored. At the time, I could hardly articulate the source of my disquietude. Now I recognize that my emerging project was to open a new path for myself as a student of cognitive psychology—one that honored not only the mechanical laws of the mind, its overarching structures, and its evolutionary growth over time, but also its social and historical situatedness, particularly its relational nature. I could see the use of extracting the formal and procedural aspects of my son's behavior from this event, but it was the social embeddedness of his behavior that seemed suspiciously absent from the concerns of the cognitive scientists I had been reading. Because of gender stereotyping, I kept my concerns hidden for a long time for fear that my thinking would be judged "irrational." But an even more deeply embedded experience kept me silent— there was no language to express what I found missing.

Putting too heavy a block on the teetering tower, my son cried out as the tower crashed around him. Was it possible, I wondered, to connect such ordinary, concrete experiences as this with the abstract, technical concepts in the readings? As a new student to the field, I did not realize that a similar blow had been delivered to the leading tower of thought in psychology—one built from associationism and reductionism. Although articles written during the 1960s were full of certainty about the scientific progress made in cognitive studies during that decade, new research in the 1970s had already questioned basic assumptions about the value of studying cognition through information processing alone. With the shift from behaviorism to cognitivism, psychology lost a conceptual framework that had riveted the thinking and research of a generation of psychologists. Yet as studies of cognition grew, the research became increasingly specialized; most psychologists simply stopped trying to reconstruct a tower. Somewhat ironically, many cognitive psychologists took blocks that had fallen from the reductionist tower and, in their own corners, started building on a smaller scale. By the 1980s students of cognition encountered specialized studies based on concepts taken from computer technology (e.g., inputs and outputs). Found in introductory texts, such terms as the fan effect in interference, recursive decomposition, and the Pandemonium model of pattern recognition illustrate the technical, abstract vocabulary that accompanied the rise of cognitivism.

As a student plunging into these highly specialized studies, I often felt adrift in this sea of arcane terminology. More often than not, such terms seemed to impose concepts onto lived experience and to restrict what could be taken as experience. Further, such specialization in the study of cognition resulted in the compartmentalization of cognitive functions. Each cognitive process had its own specialized literature, only weakly linked to that of others. As a student, I needed an interpretive framework to connect and integrate the various research programs, but most importantly, I longed for a theory that would address my concerns about the situatedness of cognition and its relational nature. Many of the models presented the individual "processor" as self-contained or, to use anthropologist Clifford Geertz's (1979) description, as "a bounded universe" with slots (senses) that let in bits of information from the world. Why did most researchers in cognitive psychology seem untroubled by the lack of discussion about context, not to mention consciousness, relationship, and subjectivity? Investigating my concerns, I soon learned that I was in search — not of towers — but of theoretical roots.

In an earlier study (1982) I undertook an exploration of the basic assumptions guiding the research of cognitive psychologists. There I identified a tiny cadre of nontraditional cognitive psychologists who took a critical stance toward the theoretical framework common in mainstream cognitive research — mechanism, the view that the mind is like a machine. With these new psychologists, I called for the expansion of alternative frameworks and metaphors to promote a healthier dialogue in the field. A particularly promising theoretical framework, called contextualism, had been espoused by James Jenkins (1974b) and Theodore Sarbin (1977). I endorsed it as a robust alternative that took into account the interactional, situational nature of cognition absent from what I could then identify as mechanistic accounts. As these psychologists espousing contextualism recognized, mechanism so dominated psychology that its constriction of knowledge claims and inquiry practices had become unhealthy. A longtime critic of psychology's scientific practices, Sigmund Koch (1981) humorously called this pathology of knowledge "epistemopathology."

In this book I describe how contextualism has become a more and more persuasive theoretical alternative in cognitive psychology. In the 1970s it was harder to see how concern for context, or ecological validity, had been suppressed by the merger of two different types of theoretical assumptions in artificial intelligence (AI), a project that lent important credibility to the scientific study of the mind. AI enticingly combined, as we will see, mechanistic processing with formal logic in a way that obscured other theoretical positions. Through its criticisms and concerns, contextualism not only guided the direction and shape of American cognitive psychology during the 1980s; it also arose as a viable and powerful alternative theoretical framework for the study of cognition in its own right (see Hoffman, 1986; Hoffman & Palermo, 1991; Shanon, 1990; Tiberghien, 1986).

Questioning the value of mechanistic metaphors, psychologists such as John Bransford, Jerome Bruner, Kenneth Gergen, James Gibson, Ulric Neisser, and Eleanor Rosch, to name a few, have turned to the metaphor of the event, with its emphasis on history and situation, as a more generative one for the study of cognition. As I argue, their work with this metaphor exemplifies, expands, and enriches the contextualistic worldview. In parallel developments, linguists such as George Lakoff (1987b) and Eve Sweetser (1990) and philosophers such as Mark Johnson (1987) have begun exploring theories of language that expand and support ongoing contextualistic work in psychology. But even these more recent contextualistic views have been powerfully opposed by mainstream psychologists, who historically have rejected the insights of more radical contextualists. (For example, James Gibson and Hubert Dreyfus met with considerable hostility and even rejection from the psychological community when they advanced their more radical contextualistic views.) The standard mechanist's refrain when replying to serious alternatives to mechanism has been "baffling" or "unscientific" (for a recent example of this defensiveness, see G. Johnson's, 1990, criticisms of both Penrose, 1989, and Dreyfus & Dreyfus, 1986), but such responses are losing their power to hold the contextualistic view in abeyance.

My general purpose in this book is to bring together the work of psychologists who are interested in telling the contextualistic story of cognition. I define contextualism and describe its vitality and generativity as a viable metaphor for understanding cognition. In exploring the resemblances of contextualistic thinkers, I hope to reveal and strengthen their insights and perspectives. Contextualism has emerged in the confines of a mechanistic milieu, and so it has been closely and critically involved in mechanistic projects. Understanding these two leading metaphors in cognitive psychology and the implications of these two ways of thinking about the mind can help students of cognition make better sense of research and debates in the field without sacrificing the subtlety and complexity of either worldview. Each more clearly defines the other as an alternative frame of reference.

My special interest is to make the field more invitational to women who have historically participated in alarmingly small numbers in the discussions. Recent feminist scholars point out that the way we think has been defined and described by male researchers promoting an objectivist set of assumptions that historically excluded women from science (Bordo, 1986; Harding, 1986; Keller, 1985; Wittig, 1985). A contextualistic worldview offers a different set of concepts about the mind, reality, and science itself, a view many women may find more hospitable. In seeking to understand cognition, it honors ordinary experience, embodiment, and events, "events so discriminately penetrated by thought that mind is literally at home in them" (Dewey, 1925, p. 161).

Mechanism can be a generative worldview, but it often ignores new perspectives and muzzles oppositional voices, as if diversity were incompatible with rationality (see Levin, 1986; Shweder, 1986, for fuller discussions of the need to recognize divergent forms of rationality in the contemporary social sciences). And to the extent that mechanism controls discourse, it limits rather than serves us. I wholeheartedly explore contextualism and advocate its potential. Whatever worldview a psychologist endorses, recognizing theoretical alternatives and encouraging diversity can only energize and enliven our discussions and broaden our understanding of the nature of cognition itself.

Acknowledgments

This book arose in a community of people whose thoughts and experiences are interwoven with my own, and I want to express my gratitude to all my colleagues, friends, and students who helped me as I wrote the book. In particular, I want to thank George McClure for his advocacy and steadfast mentoring and for his deep understanding of and abiding commitment to contextualism. I am also deeply indebted to Michael Gillespie and Missy Dehn Kubitschek for their detailed, sensitive, and thoughtful commentaries on the first draft. I thank Catherine Lacey, Carol Lloyd, David Paulsen, Greg Simpson, Mary Tourek, and Diane Wood for intense and engaging discussions over various sections of the book; their enthusiastic responses kept me going when the revisions got tough. Thanks too to Kathy Schroeder and Donadea Rasmussen-Hug for their careful readings of the first draft; they helped me to see cognitive psychology through students' eyes again.

For giving me the courage to be audacious about the importance of ordinary experience—to fall freely into it—I thank my writing group: Lynn Bjorkman, Kate Brown, Barbara Jessing, Judy Levin, Jeanne Schuler, and Bette Tarrant. I am grateful to Mary Walsh Jones, and Michelle Walker for their skillful editing in various stages of manuscript preparation. My gratitude also goes out to Don Dendinger and Dave Hinton, who actively encouraged this research project by offering much needed administrative support and encouragement.

And finally I thank my entire family, but especially Michael, Gannon, Gemma, and Adama Dieng for their patience, love, and support while I worked on the book. They provided the richest possible context for my writing and thinking.

The Mind's We

1

Introduction: Resituating Cognition

> We are trying . . . to open space for new thinking and modes of
> knowing; for heretofore suppressed voices to speak and be well
> heard in ways that may express and/or call for the creation of
> different epistemologies; for critique and reformulation of thought
> that has been entangled in unnecessary yet profound errors.
>
> —Elizabeth K. Minnich, *Transforming Knowledge*

Cognitive psychology poses fundamental questions about knowing and acting, about how we come to understand our experiences in
the world. How do we, for example, remember, use symbols, make logical connections, internalize other perspectives, and come to trust
our intuitions? To what extent are such cognitive abilities determined
by our neurophysiology, our unique histories, our cultural patterns
of engagement, our relationships with others, and our physical environment? Why is our knowledge usually trustworthy, and how does
it become distorted or lead us into trouble? Is our best knowledge
only objective and abstract, or is it also subjective and concrete? In
investigating cognition, should we construct abstract and formal
models of the mind, study specific mental processes in the laboratory, or observe cognition in natural settings? Are the formal,
transituational models created by cognitivists psychologically real?

Answers to these questions are currently being hotly debated in
cognitive psychology. Some of the more difficult dialogues disintegrate into simplistic polarizations, often motivated by commitments
to particular methods or technologies. Others, however, suggest
rich possibilities for interpreting cognition that have not yet been
fully realized. I begin by examining some of the more generative
controversies.

Psychologists have typically studied cognition by simplifying
its components and segregating its processes. In traditional labora-

1

tory experimentation, researchers isolated stimuli, such as dots or words, to study perception or verbal learning. Unlike traditional laboratory experimenters, information-processing researchers redefined stimuli in order to simulate abstract models of mental operations on a computer. Albeit very different from laboratory practice, such simulations also simplify and segregate cognitive processes. Assuming cognition is like computation, programmers commonly reduce experience to bits or units of information, treated as symbols. These enter the cognitive system via pathways supposed to be like the senses, and they can then be stored in memory. Having both physical and representational status, the units can be combined (or symbolically related) to simulate thought processes of varying complexity. The system uses these internal representations to solve problems introduced into it; any resulting actions are described as "outputs" of this system. Cognitivists assume that in our cognitive activities, we are simply unaware of this mechanistic processing; some assume further that processing mechanisms are unaffected by our behavior. During the 1970s, especially, information-processing theorists often equated information processing with cognitive psychology or cognitivism (see J. R. Anderson, 1980a, for a textbook typical of this merger). Cognitive psychologists working on information-processing simulations and other computational models of the mind rather pointedly began calling themselves cognitive "scientists."

This designation heightened awareness of what was at stake — the scientific status of cognitive science. (See Haugeland, 1978; Horgan & Tienson, 1990; Kintsch, et al., 1984, on definitional and methodological issues in cognitive science.) In an attempt to formulate assumptions different from those of traditional laboratory researchers, Herbert Simon (1980) defines cognitive science "as the domain of inquiry that seeks to understand intelligent systems and the nature of intelligence" (p. 35). Beyond this point, however, cognitive scientists differ among themselves in their assumptions about intelligence and the way to study it. Frequently, cognitive scientists believe that experimental psychology yields, perhaps interesting, but ultimately inadequate and fragmented results about cognitive phenomena and that broad theories or models are needed to study intelligence as an abstract, formal system. Cognitive science is more and more identified as a cross-disciplinary enterprise between computer science, neuroscience, philosophy, psychology, anthropology, and linguistics.

Closely allied to the development of information processing and cognitive science is artificial intelligence (AI). Historically, in "stronger" versions of AI, the mind is seen to be a digital computer or a symbol processor. In "weaker" versions of AI, the mind is seen to function like a computer in some domains. As a result of the influence of both types of AI, cognitive psychology has incorporated technical terms from computer science, some of which have formal and precise denotations (e.g., what is to be counted as "information") and some of which have vaguer connotations (e.g., "processing"). Some researchers argue that artificial intelligence is but a subdivision of cognitive science. Others such as John Haugeland (1984) assert that it is the most important theoretical alternative, "the first among equals in cognitive science."

Against this backdrop of heated discussions about the nature of information processing, its scientific status, and its relation to artificial intelligence, a new view of cognition has emerged: connectionism. Often traced back to Donald O. Hebb's (1949) neuropsychological research, this movement (which includes parallel distributed processing) views the mind as a computational machine, a network of self-organizing, interconnected "neurods," neuronlike units (see Allman, 1989; Bechtel & Abrahamsen, 1991, for general accounts of this movement; Rumelhart, et al., 1986, for a more technical one). What distinguishes connectionism from other computational models, notes Margaret Boden (1988), is that "concepts or representations are embodied in [the system] as *patterns of activity* across entire networks of computational units" (p. 7). Often defined in contrast to information processing, connectionism does not assume a central processor or sequential processing; rather, when representing information, the entire network is activated all at once in interactive patterns of associated connections. Some cognitivists argue that connectionism is a dramatic shift in the field (Schneider, 1987); others that connectionist models will become more like information processing over time (Massaro, 1988).

The field is rife with controversies, and recent theories such as Daniel Dennett's (1991) draw upon the contentiousness itself to further challenge positions that have seemed to others to be obvious. He argues against the localization and specialization characteristic of information-processing models (a practice he terms "boxology") and suggests alternatively that cognitive functioning is distributed throughout the cortex. In his metaphorical description of this view, little demons spread throughout the brain shout out and compete against each other for the right to say what is going on. They break open the neatly labeled information-processing boxes, ensnarl the rigid connections between them, and dethrone the central processor, a character essential in most information-processing dramas. As a result of the ubiquitousness of these demons, Dennett argues, cognition functions to distribute or smear meaning throughout the brain in what he calls multiple drafts of narrative fragments variously available to consciousness. His demons may work more to dismantle information processing, however, than to explain consciousness.

Dennett's theory indicates what has opened up for discussion in cognitive science, including, for example, methods of science, the use of metaphor in theorizing, and the nature of representation and the self. Such openness has been hard won and can produce tension, confusion, and complexity, but one pattern clearly emerges from cognitive psychology's recent history. Information processing has lost its power and dominance. In retrospect, the artificiality central to information processing could only approximate real life thought processes. Critics such as Hubert Dreyfus (1979) argued that it entered psychology, really, dead on arrival. As he pointed out, its fatal flaw was the inability to take abstract models and shed light on ordinary experience. Thus, it could never live up to the often grandiose claims of its advocates who promised that bigger and better machines would solve the problems raised by the absence of background knowledge and context in any given simulation. Progress will come with time, these programmers often maintained. But as Paul Churchland and Patricia Churchland (1990), defenders of the new connectionism, recently put it:

> Time was on Dreyfus's side as well: the rate of cognitive return on increasing speed and memory began to slacken in the late 1970's and early 1980's. . . . [The] relative slowness of the simulations was darkly curious; signal propagation in a computer is roughly a million times faster than in the brain, and the clock frequency of a computer's central processor is greater than any frequency found in the brain by a similarly dramatic margin. And yet, on realistic problems, the tortoise easily outran the hare. (p. 33)

The loss of faith in information processing has intensified the debates in the field, as the exchange between Churchland and Churchland and John Searle (1990), a well-known critic of artificial intelligence, illustrates. Recent discussions among cognitive psychologists, scientists, and philosophers are often dense and technical, a strange mixture of philosophy, computer science, and psychology. One does not have to read far into these discussions to recognize that the field is in flux — some claim even chaos. Although the confusion can be intimidating, new and exciting areas of dialogue about cognition have been opened. How one might respond to the confusion and what new possibilities have emerged are the focus of this chapter.

The next section is a brief history of cognitive psychology and an explanation of why people in the field need to reassess its metatheoretical orientation. Such a history is, of course, interpretive and selective. For those unfamiliar with the major themes in the rise of cognitive psychology, it will set the context for my major arguments throughout the book. Readers familiar with the field may want to bypass this history to the discussion of Stephen Pepper's (1961) reflections about theories, which reveal significant patterns in the literature on cognitive psychology.

Cognitive Psychology: A Field in Flux

There was a time when, so it seemed, American psychologists pursued with certainty and confidence a single, rational, and objective scientific enterprise. According to many historians of psychology, this "golden age" occurred between 1930 and 1960. Psychology was then centered around the methods and concepts of behaviorists such as Clark Hull, B. F. Skinner, and Kenneth Spence, a group of men in search of the laws that governed behavior. By no means a monolithic formulation, behavioral psychology evolved from classical or Watsonian behaviorism through what is commonly referred to as neobehaviorism and a more radical behaviorism associated with Skinner (see Kantor, 1968; Segal & Lachman, 1972, for concise histories). The golden age may be more mythic than real, however, since critics have always questioned the legitimacy of modern psychology's scientific status. These attacks against the myth became especially vigorous and more damaging in the 1950s and early 1960s (see Lashley, 1951; Chomsky, 1959; Epilogue in

Koch, 1959, 1964). In his history of behaviorism, J. R. Kantor (1968) argues that psychology's career as a science has been "tortuous" (p. 165). Skinner (1976) also argues in an article originally entitled "The Steep and Thorny Way to a Science of Behavior" that psychology has been plagued by digression and dalliance. Psychologists "have been drawn off the straight and narrow path," to one leading, he boldly asserts, away from "that heaven promised by a science of behavior" (p. 523). The golden age of psychology perhaps best refers to the beliefs of a group of men who hoped, their own differences notwithstanding, that a "hard core," empirically based science would dominate the field.

By the 1960s the attacks on their particular version of science were so persistent and damaging that, to keep critics at bay, behaviorists often insulated themselves and overdramatized their cause as sacred. Perhaps lent impetus by the insularity of the radical behaviorists or their conformity to a particular view of science or developments in other fields such as linguistics and philosophy of science, for these and other reasons, during the early 1960s, new winds blew through the heavens. Cognitive psychologists began to focus on what behaviorism had proscribed—the "unobservable." In trying to represent complex mental processes, cognitivists opened up psychology to the study of such common experiences as problem solving. Researchers carefully analyzed, for example, protocols of subjects solving problems (which they could then compare with computer simulations). Such methodology looked to many traditional experimentalists like introspectionism that, at the turn of the century, had been discarded as unreliable and thus unscientific.

In their histories of cognitive science, Howard Gardner (1985) and Pamela McCorduck (1979) note that models for formalizing intelligent behavior could be traced back to the 1940s. At first, the cognitivist influence spread slowly. But it began capturing the attention of more and more psychologists, so that by the 1960s, it was growing rapidly. The publication of Ulric Neisser's (1967) influential text *Cognitive Psychology* was a benchmark; cognitive psychology had attained institutional legitimacy. During the 1970s cognitive psychologists proposed a plethora of information-processing models. Allen Newell (1973), for example, counted fifty-nine different experimental paradigms current in the research literature. By the early 1980s, mainstream psychologists looked not to the animal laboratory, but to the computer and its simulations of cognitive processes.

Using Thomas Kuhn's (1970) analysis, some psychologists characterized the shift from behaviorism to cognitivism as a "revolution in scientific paradigms" (e.g., Palermo, 1971; Segal & Lachman, 1972). In his history Terry Knapp (1986), for example, asserts that cognitive psychology "won the revolution" and that by the 1970s it had become institutionalized "as mainstream academic psychology" (pp. 27–28). Such an interpretation is appealing. The growth of cognitive psychology over the last three decades has marginalized behaviorism in academia (as behaviorism had at one time marginalized cognition). Until his death, Skinner (1989) continued to nip at the heels of the cognitivist position, and those radical behaviorists calling themselves "praxists" have ignored the cognitivist challenge by restricting their research "to simple behaviors and simple stimuli" (R. Epstein, 1986, p. 105). But, by and large, processing terms such as *encoding*, *input-output*, *information flow*, and *representation* have replaced terms such as *reinforcement*, *stimulus-response*, and *response chain*. Diagrams of boxes through which bits of information flow have replaced discussions about the empty black box. More important, perhaps, the language and methods that cognitivists use to explain their scientific enterprise rely on reductions made through mathematics and formal logic (what Haugeland, 1978, has called systematic reduction), while the behaviorists, in their most radical form, rely on the reduction of psychology to "fundamental" physical laws (Haugeland, 1978; Secord, 1986). Did such a shift in discourse and methodology signal a scientific revolution?

Several cognitive psychologists (e.g., Boden, 1987; Schnaitter, 1986; Warren, 1971) convincingly argue that it did not. And in fact much of the confusion that has accompanied the rise of cognitive psychology centers around the nature of scientific practice in psychology generally. The paradigm shift analysis makes it look as if there were a viable scientific framework that had guided psychologists. But the diversity of philosophical orientations and scientific assumptions among psychologists make any claims to paradigmatic status suspect. Further, the shift to information processing did not involve a systematic or sudden reworking of a worldview in psychology. Its new research strategies only partially challenged traditional experimental practices. Even though, for example, Newell and Simon (1972) took very seriously their subjects' introspective reports about problem-solving operations, their theories maintained many of the assumptions of the behaviorists, such as the need to reduce behavior to its atomistic parts. Most important, this new "science" of cognition retained the central theoretical assumption that had been basic to the traditional view of scientific psychology—mechanistic descriptions. The recent shift from information processing to connectionism has also been called a paradigm shift for psychology (Schneider, 1987). But again, the diversity of experimental practices and programs does not support such a claim. Describing myriad disagreements, Boden (1988) states, "It is clear that computational psychology is a beast with many different incarnations" (p. 8).

Adena Rosmarin's (1989) metaphor of torque, of turning force, then, may more appropriately describe these critical junctures in the history of American psychology. Psychologists turned away from the more accustomed paths of studying behavior to paths that involved new customs. Such displacement usually involves negativity, which, Rosmarin notes, "ranges from subsumptive to adversarial to dismissive" (p. 13). Leona Tyler (1981) claims that the change in direction resulted, in part, from dismissiveness. "Strategies of ignoring new facts and questions, resorting to strict definitions of science, and confining separate groups of workers in separate cages, can be thought of as defense maneuvers designed to ward off challenges rather than to meet them head on" (p. 4). Certainly many psychologists, including learning theorists such as Albert Bandura (1977), criticized radical behaviorist tenets and incorporated cognitive concepts; yet others, spellbound by the digital computer and its possibilities, more quietly abandoned the neobehaviorist tradition and started to simulate problem solving on a computer. I argue the turn to cognitivism appeared more radical than it really was, and somewhat ironically, it affected the health of the whole field more than behaviorism itself. The implications for scientific American psychology were profound—during the 1970s psychology was catapulted into a crisis of multiplicity from which many feel it has yet to recover.

During the 1970s psychology and its status as a social science became the subject of extensive critical examination. With the decline of behaviorism and the rise of cognitivism, a growing number of psychologists challenged many generally held assumptions about the nature of psychological investigation, such as the common belief that the stimuli manipulated in laboratory experiments are meaningless. In a call for ecologically oriented inquiry, John Gibbs (1979), for instance, argued that traditional laboratory investigation had become so narrow and precise that it no longer yielded meaningful explanations of ordinary experience in real environments. Peter Manicas and Paul Secord (1983) criticized the "standard view" of science in psychology and advocated an alternative view. The trouble extended to other areas of psychology as well (e.g., Parker, 1989, on the crisis in social psychology) and to other social sciences (e.g., Bernstein, 1976). A separate crisis literature developed (e.g., Westland, 1978; bibliography in Fiske & Shweder, 1986a) that raised hard questions about the future of scientific psychology. These critics contended that without rethinking its premises, psychology could not go on as usual.

Cognitive psychology played a central role in this growing reassessment of theory and research (see Hilgard, 1980, for an extensive overview). In the sense that it explored terrain previously off limits to behaviorism, it stimulated general revisions of behaviorist theories and models and developed different assumptions about the role of cognition in behavior. As Tyler (1981) claims in her assessment: "The period in which we are now living is characterized by major attempts to extend boundaries, assimilate, reorganize, synthesize. . . . Of the many directions this effort is taking, probably the broadest and most significant is the construction of a *cognitive* psychology" (p. 4). In and of itself, however, the introduction of new cognitive models and approaches does not signal the rise of a new, competing view of human behavior. From a broader vantage point, cognitivism retained several fundamental assumptions of traditional scientific psychology. For example, it still reduced behavior to components seen to operate causally in a sequence of discrete processing stages. It also studied behavior objectively from the standpoint of an outsider and isolated it from its social and historical contexts.

But even as cognitive psychology has grown in influence, its presuppositions and views have often been hidden behind the excitement over new high-powered information processing and mathematical techniques. During the 1970s, many textbooks in the field simply explained in a few opening pages how "a human brain is seen as a 'midget computer'" and how "humans can . . . be thought of as possessing programs" (Loftus & Loftus, 1976, pp. 5–7). The multiplicity of miniature models about various cognitive processes often conceals questionable mechanical presuppositions and theoretical assumptions (see Jenkins, 1981; Palmer, 1987, for further criticisms along this line). Even as it has undertaken interesting experimental programs, connectionism (with its use of parallel distributed processing machines) also raises further controversies about preprogramming and learning.

In their histories Gardner (1985) and Boden (1988) remind us that the development of cognitive science has been so complex and its research programs so numerous that any historical, interpretive framework is bound to oversimplify the key issues. Minimodels have obfuscated underlying patterns and configurations in theory and research, especially since, as Newell (1973) argues, experimental procedures in the information-processing approach generated so many competing models that they could not be meaningfully tested before being displaced by other new ones. This overgrowth of models and approaches has resulted in a general rethinking of the nature of cognition, and a number of researchers have critically examined basic or fundamental concepts (e.g., Costall & Still, 1987; Dennett, 1991; Gergen, 1982; Varela, et al., 1991; Winograd & Flores, 1986). This book participates in that reexamination. I argue that the shift from behaviorism to cognitivism occurred not haphazardly but as the consequence of the way in which psychology had historically limned its theoretical boundaries. Such systemic shifts have been most telling in studies of perception, memory, and categorization, key subjects of this book.

The splintering of cognitive psychology has made a grasp of the literature difficult. In order to outline the development and patterns of thought in the study of cognition, I shall first draw back from the particulars of competing theories to take a broader, metatheoretical view. From such a perspective, basic assumptions in a given movement or school in psychology can be identified; for example, when faced with a particular theory, say of the role of context in categorization, such analysis helps us determine what counts as data, what occurrences can be legitimately studied, what kinds of generalizations are possible, and so forth. It also helps evaluate competing theories; for example, it helps explain why what a cognitivist judges as "substantive progress" appears to the radical behaviorist as "mere dalliance."

Pepper's Theory of Worldviews

Pepper's (1961) *World Hypotheses* has been one of the most widely used frameworks for understanding assumptions that go into theories. The *Journal of Mind and Behavior* devoted a special issue to Pepper's ideas as they applied to different fields, including historical psychology (see Efron, 1982). In psychology Franklin Berry (1984), Kenneth Gergen (1986), Robert Hoffman and James Nead (1983), James Jenkins (1974b), Theodore Sarbin (1977, 1986b), Leona Tyler (1981) and Joan Walls (1982) have found his work relevant and valuable in helping to expand what have been restrictive theoretical boundaries. Historically, mainstream psychologists resisted metatheoretical discussions. In his introduction to a volume on the history of metaphor in psychology, David Leary (1990a) points out that "a stoic, antimetaphorical view of science" typified American psychology throughout this century. "Data gathering— generally presumed to be an activity that can and should be pursued without any theoretical preconceptions—was frequently considered to be the source of psychological theory and practice" (p. 21). Pepper, too, recognizes and rebuts positivistic resistance to his theory of metaphor. Leary and the other contributors to his volume make clear that scientific psychology can no longer insulate itself from theoretical and metaphorical discussions. We have increasing evidence of the metaphorical nature of psychological theory and practice, and more important for our purposes here, we have increasing evidence that metaphor may be central to cognition. The latter claim comes from new developments in linguistics and philosophy (such as Langacker's, 1987, cognitive grammar, M. Johnson's, 1987, and Lakoff and Johnson's, 1980, work on metaphor, and Lakoff's, 1987b, work on categorization). Because of its detailed analysis of philosophical perspectives and because of its clear delineation of the implications of taking up a particular worldview, I adopt Pepper's framework as a heuristic in my interpretive analysis of cognitive psychology from 1960 through 1990. In contrast to other available metatheoretical frameworks, Pepper's gives the best account of a contextualistic worldview.

   The use of Pepper's framework reveals a pattern of dominance in cognitive psychology. Reliance on one worldview has admitted only certain types of investigation as scientific and counted only certain types of thought as intelligent. (See Fiske & Shweder, 1986a, for a call for pluralism in social sciences.) Such a pattern of exclusiveness, often hidden in the discourse of cognitive scientists, has resulted in the underrepresentation of women in the field. Almost solely emphasizing formal and objective criteria in its models, cognitivism has discounted shared intelligibility, mutuality in interaction, or "the communal basis of knowledge" that is often central to social and psychological experiences (Gergen, 1985, p. 272). For example, "the composition and arrangement" of Douglas Hofstadter and Daniel Dennett (1981), a collection of creative essays on minds, brains, and programs, is a score for an all-male orchestra. Such omission is not unusual. When asked to discuss gender issues in cognitive psychology in 1984, I analyzed my dissertation bibliography and found of about three hundred and fifty entries eight women's names: Barbara Hayes-Roth, Eleanor Gibson, Elizabeth Loftus, Katherine Nelson, Kathleen Nitsch, Eleanor Rosch, Janet Spence, and Leona Tyler. I find these numbers indicative of more than just the paucity of women in all the professions. Something forbidding to women exists in this field. A metatheoretical framework such as Pepper's allows us to raise questions about inclusivity and exclusivity, about what is made visible and invisible, controlled and uncontrolled, processed and unprocessed in mainstream cognitive psychology.

Gender, then, is a provocative thread that runs throughout my analysis of current debates in cognitive psychology. I believe that theoretical pluralism is central to degendering the field, which has been a largely male enterprise. To use a connectionist image, female perspectives need to be brought into the networks so that women's voices can become a part of the chorus. Toward this end, I include feminist perspectives where appropriate, including, for example, my review of Pepper's four world hypotheses in this chapter and in my choice of stories that I tell throughout the book.

Root Metaphors

In his characterization of worldviews, Pepper (1961) argues that different explanations about the nature of the world could not proliferate endlessly, that only a limited number can exist. Worldviews, he found, contain basic or root metaphors that organize and constitute how a person makes sense of his or her world.

A man desiring to understand the world looks about for a clue to its comprehension. He pitches upon some area of commonsense fact and tries to understand other areas in terms of this one. This original idea becomes his basic analogy or root metaphor. He describes as best he can the characteristics of this area, or . . . discriminates its structure. A list of its structural characteristics [categories] becomes his basic conceptions of explanation and description. . . . In terms of these categories he proceeds to study all other areas of fact. . . . He undertakes to interpret all facts in terms of these categories. (p. 91)

A commonsense metaphor, for example, used for understanding politics is to see the state as an organism—the body politic, the arm of the law, the head of state, and so on. At a more personal level, my friend Judy, who teaches composition, uses a commonsense metaphor to express her conception of women students and how they gain an authentic voice. She frequently talks about their growth and about the conditions that will nourish their liberation from stereotypic strictures that block or thwart their development as writers— she sees her students as seeds or plants. Such metaphors, Pepper argues, give us an overall organizing principle (a structure for current experience) and also a framework for interpreting new experiences. (Contrast Judy's metaphor with that of a teacher who sees students as empty vessels.) Metaphorical analysis also becomes relevant when the interpretations and the approaches conflict. What looks like progress from the perspective of one worldview appears baffling or nonsensical from another.

Pepper believes that the world affords a wealth of empirical knowledge that invites us to think hypothetically. To respond, we become metaphor makers. But not all commonsense metaphors have sufficient scope or explanatory power to guide our thinking across situations. Our common sense can fail and mislead us, or it can appear dubitable to other people, so cognition must work to expand its scope and achieve greater precision. Of the many hypotheses that might be proposed, Pepper claims that four have proved "relatively adequate." By "relatively adequate," he means that they continue to generate new theories, but none of them is totally adequate; that is, none of them can explain everything without remainder. The four hypotheses or worldviews he deems compatible with science—formism, organicism, mechanism, and contextualism—are rooted respectively in the craftsperson's form, the living organism, the machine, and the historical event. Each provides a frame of reference for understanding the world.

Formism

Formism is the root metaphor for the worldview that assumes entities in the world can be organized on the basis of their similarities and differences. The process of classification best exemplifies the organizational principles found in formism. As a scientist, the formist very carefully observes and classifies the empirical world and defines truth as correspondence or, more specifically, "as the degree of similarity which a description has to its object of reference" (Pepper, 1961, p. 181). Some formists want to uncover basic forms, formalisms, or structures that generate language or other schematic cultural practices. If such underlying forms undergo transformation in the generation of new structures, then such theories participate more in the organic root metaphor. Systems theorists such as Ervin Laszlo (1972), for example, emphasize forms within a system and focus on wholeness and dynamic integration of these forms in complex systems. If, on the other hand, a theorist thinks forms generate like kinds (say, under superordinate categorial structures or in mathematical discovery), then the theory participates in formism, as demonstrated by Roger Penrose's (1989) discussion of "contact with Plato's world" (pp. 426–29). In psychology, theorists interested in structures or dimensions of areas such as mental processing or enduring personality traits (learning styles, for example) work within formistic hypotheses.

Let me be more specific by turning to the literature on the psychology of women. Here, formism is represented in much of the research on androgyny. In this research tested experimentally by Sandra Lipsitz Bem (1974, 1978) and defended philosophically by Ann Ferguson (1977), "an ideal androgynous being" is a combination of the most desirable masculine and feminine traits. According to this view, both men and women can, for example, be compassionate and assertive, sensitive and forceful. Such an ideal, these feminists argue, makes it possible for human beings to transcend gender. By measuring masculine and feminine traits, researchers tried to correlate androgyny with a normative ideal for mental health. Interestingly, these psychologists worked from essential distinctions between the sexes to construct their nongendered, ideal human being.

Organicism

Organicism, with a root metaphor of the living organism, differs significantly from formism. While formism is a more analytic theory (i.e., it looks for the component parts of, say, masculinity), organicism is synthetic. It is concerned with process organically conceived that leads to integration and to the new structure that such integration yields. The organicist believes that events in the world appear as fragments — containing contradictions or gaps — that belong to an organic whole. Once this whole is discovered, the coherence of the fragments, in retrospect, becomes explicit; and when the fragments converge into the whole, the whole transcends the fragments that had seemed contradictory and incoherent in their isolation. Facts do not exist outside the whole; they both work toward and lead up to integration which occurs progressively, sometimes in stages or series, but always within a completely determined system. For the organicist, truth is a matter of coherence.

In psychology the recent developmental work of Mary Field Belenky, Blythe McVicker Clinchy, Nancy Rule Goldberger, and Jill Mattuck Tarule (1986) on women's ways of knowing represents an organicist hypothesis, as do most developmental theories in psychology. (See Overton & Reese, 1973; Reese & Overton, 1970, for applications of Pepper's theory to research strategies in developmental psychology.) Belenky and her coauthors found that as women gained their own authentic voices, they gained a firmer sense of self and of themselves as knowers. Women tend to grow or develop, for example, when they are asked to speak or when they have people who hear them out. Thus, the researchers recommend educational experiences that "encourage students to evolve their own patterns of work based on the problems they are pursuing" (p. 229). Women who actively construct their own knowledge used terms such as "integration" and "space" for growth. In contrast, women in disempowering environments describe themselves as "deadened" and thus unable to grow. The researchers structure epistemological development as occurring in coherent phases so that the final position, "constructed knowing," represents a kind of organic unity which has evolved out of the others.

Mechanism

In contrast to formism and organicism, mechanism takes the machine as its root metaphor. One of the dominant worldviews in Western culture, mechanism has been well documented as *the* worldview in psychology (see Hoffman & Nead, 1983; Marshall,

1977; Shotter, 1975, for historical discussions). As John Marshall (1977) notes in his history of the machine metaphor in psychology: "Whenever a particular machine analogy has been found wanting (either through direct disconfirmation or because it had too limited a domain of application) it has always been replaced (or supplemented) by another machine. As the little old lady might have replied to William James, 'It's machines all the way down' [or up, depending on one's view of science]" (p. 484). In the mechanistic worldview, a particular inhabits a time and place. Elementary units — atoms, for example — combine to form aggregates or clusters but do not, in the process, lose their individual autonomy. Any system of particulars can be reduced back to its most basic constituents. "The universe is thus conceived as a huge aggregation or system of essentially separate individuals. These individuals have specific potentialities of association. But the form of an association of individuals never actually takes over the autonomy of the individuals that make it up" (Pepper, 1956, p. 37). The machine metaphor entails parts that have specified, precisely defined locations. Each part can be expressed quantitatively, and the parts function according to laws which describe the machine's functioning. Truth resides in statements expressing cause and effect relationships between the parts. Lacking in the description of the machine, it is important to note, are sensory qualities; their absence becomes the impetus for a debate which I note here only in passing, the famous mind-body problem.

Walls (1982) argues that the assumptions of the mechanistic worldview for psychology were worked out early by David Hartley (1749) in the first part of his *Observations on Man*. "The overall effect of his assumptions about the nature of the material world, when translated to his beliefs about body and mind, was to materialize, atomize, and mechanize mental life more extensively than ever before" (p. 271). The longstanding availability and refinement of mechanistic assumptions contributed to their realizations in the research methods of classical behaviorists and neobehaviorists. Mechanism pervaded the attempts of psychologists to lift their field to the realms of the physical and biological sciences. For example, mechanistic assumptions include the following: the environment can be reduced to particular stimuli which can be isolated in a laboratory; only observable behavior can be taken as legitimate psychological subject matter; and the results of objective experiments, which establish efficient causation, constitute evidence and knowledge for psychology (i.e., laws of behavior). This metatheory employs systematic empirical assumptions that characterize the philosophy of empiricism and logical positivism, topics of the next chapter.

Because mechanism masks gender through its claims of neutrality and objectivity, feminist philosophers and psychologists have devoted considerable attention to its biases. In traditional, orthodox mechanistic research, gender remains invisible because the elements studied in laboratories are physiological or physical (not social). Thus, gender supposedly does not arise as an issue since empiricists claimed their studies are "objective" and "value free." But Carolyn Wood Sherif's (1979) analysis of psychological research revealed how traditional research practices were "loaded" with sexist bias (see Keller, 1985, pp. 75–94, for a provocative discussion of the association between objectivity and masculinity in scientific practice; Bordo, 1986, for a philosophical and historical account of the masculinization of scientific thought). As psychological research incorporated statistical design procedures, components of experience became abstract variables in statistical studies, and sex generally became an independent variable. Psychologists, then, could test for significant sex differences.

As a feminist philosopher who has worked extensively in the philosophy of science, Sandra Harding (1989) argues that traditional empiricism (historically closely associated with what I am terming mechanism) offers troubling ambiguities for the study of women in the social sciences. One cannot uncritically adopt empiricism's promise of objectivity; but she asks, "Isn't it important to try to degender science as much as we can in a world where scientific claims are *the* model of knowledge" (p. 23)? Feminist empiricists argue that once researchers remove bias in methodology, women will be seen to operate (as mechanisms) in the same way that men do (see Harding, for a range of feminist research possibilities). In cognitive science, descriptions of mental processes have typically been isolated from social context. For example, Dennett (1981) defines the emerging view in which the mind is "as an abstract sort of thing whose identity is independent of any particular physical embodiment" (p. 15). For mechanists, this abstraction offers possibilities for equal treatment (a possibility proponents of other worldviews strongly contest).

The Mind's We

Contextualism

The fourth viable root metaphor Pepper identifies is the historical event, the source of the worldview he calls contextualism. For
the contextualist, experience consists of total events that are rich in
features. Each event has a texture and quality—or "its intuited
wholeness or total character" (Pepper, 1961, p. 238). The resulting
felt quality of the event becomes primary to the contextualist; any
analysis of experience always starts from that given quality and
works down to particulars. Because the event takes up the knower in
the known, contextualism is an interactive, dynamic worldview.
Moreover, nothing in the event is permanent or immutable because
each particular changes with the flux of time. The contextualist
focuses on the richness of experience and on shared meanings that
arise out of interaction with others. Truth lies in the process of
taking up the whole context of the event, in its "thick description,"
including its complexities, ambiguities, and contradictions (Geertz,
1973). And so meaning is embodied in our experience of the world.
"On the one hand, cognitive activity is intimately tied to the
organism's being and acting in the real world. On the other hand,
cognitive activity cannot come into being and proceed without the
cognitive agent being part of a social world" (Shanon, 1990, p. 163).
In psychology contextualism has been identified with the func-
tionalist school (e.g., Dewey, Angell, and Carr), and unlike the
other three worldviews it developed fairly recently. Sarbin (1977)
points to contextual elements within Kurt Lewin's field theory and
George Kelly's personal construct theory (see Kirkland & Anderson, 1990, for an application of Pepper to Kelly's personal construct
theory). Most recently, Sarbin (1986b) has identified contextualism
with narrative. Although they do not refer to themselves as contextualists, Jerome Bruner's (1986) and Mark Johnson's (1987) work on
narrative and metaphor illustrates contextualistic thinking about the
mind.
   Because contextualism has only recently begun to be well
articulated as a worldview in psychology, it is difficult to associate it
with a particular school of thought about the psychology of gender.
Overall, however, contextualism and feminism have worked to
expand psychology's boundaries by including more complex contextual effects, such as those of gender, in both theoretical and
methodological discussions (see Hawkesworth, 1989; Wallston &

Grady, 1985). One of the best examples of a theorist's being influenced by contextualistic concerns is Bem's (1981, 1983) shift in thinking about gender. She recently abandoned her former theory about androgyny, a framework I identified above as formistic, to explain sex differences from a more contextualistic viewpoint, namely, that of gender schema theory. "The concept of androgyny is problematic from the perspective of gender schema theory because it is based on the presupposition that there is a feminine and a masculine within us all, that is, that 'femininity' and 'masculinity' have an independent and palpable reality and are not cognitive constructs derived from gender-schematic processing" (1983, p. 616). Bem's move to a cognitive processing theory is evident in her concern that social context has a critical and determining influence on engenderment and in her emphasis on individuals' active participation in and construction of their gender identity. How completely she will situate gender remains to be seen, but her theoretical shift exemplifies the recent influence of contextualism in psychology, especially in its emphasis on what the subject brings to experience.

Pepper claims that the four world hypotheses he describes stand as equally adequate. "We need," he states, "all world hypotheses, so far as they are adequate, for mutual comparison and correction of interpretive bias" (1961, p. 101). The root metaphor never becomes a fixed referent, but undergoes change and refinement in the course of interpretation and analysis over time. Since all four world hypotheses have worldwide scope and a high degree of precision, any assertion that one is more adequate than another is simply dogmatic. On the other hand, Pepper argues that attempting to combine world hypotheses results in confusion. "Through our study of their factual conflicts, their diverse categories, the consequent differences of factual corroboration, and—in a word—their distinct root metaphor—we become aware of their mutual exclusiveness" (p. 105). Up to a point, categories from within different worldviews can and do overlap and stimulate the development of one another. But Pepper warns that attempts at mergers ultimately produce eclectic stances that are theoretically incoherent. Each worldview must remain loyal to its scope (or metaphorical space). Its integrity lies in the elaboration of its own root metaphor (see Hoffman, 1986, p. 217, for a slightly different discussion). Once a root metaphor has set out its categories and its own criteria for truth, Pepper notes, the metaphor itself becomes less prominent, its premises buried.

Devoted proponents of any of the worldviews often claim to handle the categories of the others. Formists, mechanists, and organicists all explain context, for example, just as contextualists explain similarity, habit, and coherence. Just because a given theorist addresses the ways context affects memory, for instance, does not mean the theory participates in a contextualist worldview. As we will see throughout this book, cognitivists have been increasingly interested in the role of context in cognition, but not all discussions of context actually employ the assumptions of contextualism. We should keep in mind that each worldview attempts comprehensive explanations by reinterpreting strengths of opposing views in terms of its own categories.

Pepper's view assumes an eclecticism and tolerance that may be too idealistic given the combative realities of academic discourse where metaphors do become fixed. So reified, they become repressive epistemologically and socially. Each viable metaphor reveals the structure and coherence of our experiences, but each can also distort reality if held doggedly as the only worldview. Formism leads to stereotyping; organicism becomes globally vacuous; mechanism leads to mindless application of rules and systems; contextualism becomes parochial and overly relativistic.

In this interpretive history of cognitive psychology from the 1960s to 1990, I argue that mechanism in its dominance has become repressive. I use Pepper to identify the dogmatic adherence to the mechanistic metaphor and by extension to illustrate its social control beyond its theoretical persuasiveness (see critical interpretations such as Harré, 1990; Sampson, 1981, 1983; Shotter, 1987; Sullivan, 1984). People with questions and perspectives that fall outside the scope of mechanism are often excluded from public dialogues. Rarely do psychology students observe reciprocal exchanges between proponents of various worldviews. Most important, however, I argue that until the 1980s artificial intelligence seemed to combine formism and mechanism into a super worldview. This apparent merger historically buried alternates such as contextualism. But as mechanism's most pressing and consistent challenger, contextualism has been a catalyst in revisions, including the recent move to connectionism. Cited in William Allman (1989), David Rumelhart explains why he turned to parallel distributed processing: "The dominant view was that the mind was a very sequential, discrete-stage computing device. . . . I was trying to use this view to understand how *context* influences *perception*, but I just couldn't make it work from this stepwise point of view" (p. 102). In his book on consciousness, Dennett (1991) conjures up an imaginary debate with a petulant, but ultimately inconsequential, folk psychologist named Otto. Dennett rebuts Otto's objections, ones that concern ordinary experience. His attention to Otto's objections reveals his concerns with contextualistically oriented responses to his reduction of consciousness to mechanistic materialism, a strong version of artificial intelligence. A contextualist would, of course, immediately protest the artificiality of the staged debate. Dennett is right in pointing out, however, that the contextualistic folks have had trouble getting themselves heard.

Particularly problematic, as we will see, is the language needed to express contextualism's categories. "To those steeped in the traditions of mechanistic science," observes Sarbin (1986b), a longtime proponent of contextualism, "traditions that emphasize order, predictability, and causality, contextualism at first appears chaotic" (p. 6). Or as anthropologist Clifford Geertz (1983) has noted, "What to some, heritors of the social fact tradition and its pluralizing impulses, looks like the introduction of more profitable ways of thinking about thinking looks to others, heritors of the internal happening tradition and its unifying drives, like a blowing up of the foundations of reason" (p. 152–53). Contextualism has not until recently had eloquent spokespersons. John Dewey, for example, a prototypical contextualistic philosopher, has been inaccessible to many modern readers. Even Pepper's theory uses a somewhat awkward, esoteric terminology in describing contextualism. As a result of its own internal difficulties with language and its interplay with mechanism, contextualism did not emerge prominently and its spokespersons were ignored until very recently.

The most articulate voice of contextualism comes not from psychology but from anthropology in Geertz's (1973, 1980) interpretive research. His theoretical proposals, including his explication of "local knowledge" and "his call for ethnography of modern thought," are only now beginning to influence the social sciences generally and cognitive psychology particularly. Bruner (1986) states that Geertz's work, which "emphasiz[es] the irreducibility of meaning, has not had much hearing in psychology. Psychologists (even cognitive psychologists) like to think of worlds that people create as 'representing' a real or aboriginal world" (p. 98). Recently expressed views such as those of Francisco Varela, Evan Thompson, and Eleanor Rosch's (1991) are well informed about cognitive science but sensitive to the significance of broader issues such as the importance of enhancing our understanding of ordinary experience through the achievements of cognitive psychology.

An Overview: The Emergence of Contextualism

Throughout the book, I recognize that mechanism is a generative worldview and that it has often served psychology well. Having many eloquent spokespersons historically, it is already powerfully articulated and widely celebrated. Nevertheless, I also argue that it has dangerously overextended its boundaries. For example, it becomes dogmatic when it equates its own practice of science with science itself or when it defines what counts as intelligent behavior. This dogmatic adherence silences other perspectives. Even though I am critical of its dogmaticism, my intent is to be fair to its generative efforts. But the tension is difficult to handle; some will find my depictions of mechanism too critical, others not critical enough. In an effort to make contextualism more accessible and visible than it has been, I portray it enthusiastically.

My goal, then, is to bring forth and follow out the contextualistic worldview in cognitive psychology so that its categories and organizing principles can be more fully recognized and appreciated. I also argue that its emergence explains much of the crisis in psychology that surrounds the study of higher mental processes. (The other worldviews also offer challenges, but contextualism draws in mechanists who would like to expand their cause-effect laws comprehensively.) Contextualistic revisions have been especially important in the study of perception, memory, and categorization; I review current debates in these fields to illuminate the sources of mechanistic and contextualistic traditions, illustrate how each delineates itself in the study of cognition, and show how contextualistic thinking has been revitalizing these areas of research. Cognitive psychologists, for example, have increasingly focused on frames, schemata, and scripts as ways of including context in their explanations of how cognition operates in the real world. The connectionist movement has strong contextualistic overtones (although it is also claimed by mechanists). Additionally, contextualism has developed alternative research strategies (Hoffman & Nead, 1983; McGuire, 1983; Mishler, 1979, 1986) and theories based on narrative (Britton & Pellegrini, 1990; Bruner, 1986; Sarbin, 1986a). Recent work on metaphor (M. Johnson, 1987; Lakoff & Johnson, 1980) has significance for elaborating the root metaphor of contextualism by providing theories of language and its function in cognition. In all of these theories, there is a "growing conviction that cognition is not the representation of a pregiven world by a pregiven mind but is rather the enactment of a world and a mind on the basis of a history of the variety of actions that a being in the world performs" (Varela, et al. 1991, p. 9). These new efforts greatly expand and redefine Pepper's historically situated version of contextualism as historical event.

Given this larger perspective, the work of contextualistic psychologists in perception (e.g., Gibson, 1979), memory (e.g., Neisser, 1982), and categorization (Lakoff, 1987b; Neisser, 1987a, b, c; Rosch, 1978) can be seen as the beginning of a powerful alternative to the mechanistic study of cognition. Internal debates exist among mechanists and among contextualists. But the most heated, serious debates often occur between proponents of differing worldviews (e.g., the followers of Gibson against the cognitivists and Searle against artificial intelligence proponents). Through an analysis of the entailments of the mechanistic and contextualistic metaphors, we will see why a mechanistic psychologist such as Skinner can claim to walk on the straight and narrow path to the heaven of a science of psychology and why, according to Geertz's (1983) quotation from Wittgenstein, a contextualist "makes detours, goes by side roads; . . . one sees the straight highway before one, 'but of course . . . cannot use it, because it is permanently closed' " (p. 6). The questions, objects, and methods of inquiry of one worldview differ extensively from the other, and as we will see in chapter 2, contextualism's assumptions make it, in certain respects, a more tolerant worldview than mechanism. As the canonical worldview in psychology, mechanism has set the tone and the premises for scientific psychology. The contextualistic worldview which offers competing explanations of how the human mind works has remained, until recently, only intermittently visible.

In chapter 2 I characterize mechanism and contextualism in psychological theory and research, indicate their coherence as worldviews and their remainders (i.e., what they leave undone, unasked, or unanswered). I argue that formism and mechanism seemed to merge as worldviews in the development of artificial intelligence. For nearly a decade such a promise defined the way the boundaries of psychological thought would be drawn; thus, contextualistic thought was repressed. I discuss failures in the attempts to canonize mechanistic (particularly reductionistic) psychology as the only legitimate scientific approach. And, to expand Pepper's description of contextualism and update his terminology in light of present day formulations and possibilities, I identify new contextualistic research and its shared assumptions. Thus, the next chapter provides a basic understanding of these two worldviews so that subsequent chapters can elaborate their more specific applications in cognitive psychology.

The third and fourth chapters explore how perception and memory have been studied theoretically from the worldviews of mechanism and contextualism. The mechanist tends to isolate mental processes and to give primacy to memory in explaining meaningful experience. For the contextualist, "perceiving is the basic cognitive activity out of which all others must emerge" (Neisser, 1976, p. 9). Moreover, perception is inextricably linked to memory. My method in both chapters will be to trace the mechanistic assumptions that have historically dominated each area of study and then present experimental and theoretical evidence suggesting the development of contextualistic assumptions such as Neisser's. Although employment of Pepper's theory has not been extensive in the field of perception, many of the developments, particularly the debate between cognitivists (e.g., Fodor & Pylyshyn, 1981; Heil, 1979, 1981) and the ecological realists (e.g., Turvey, et al., 1981; Reed & Jones, 1981; Wilcox & Katz, 1981b), readily lend themselves to an explication within his framework. As one of the earliest cognitive psychologists to identify the need for an alternative worldview to mechanism, Jenkins (1974b) called directly for a contextualistic worldview in the field of memory, a view "still alive and well at both the empirical and theoretical levels" in human memory research (Horton & Mills, 1984, p. 362; Horton, 1991).

In the fifth chapter I show how the contextualistic assumptions behind memory and perception research culminate in categorization. Such an extension illustrates how basic philosophical assumptions about perception and memory influence more general cognitive theorizing. Recent work in categorization challenges both the mechanistic and formistic worldviews and suggests that "dramatic episodes," "narrative construction," and "mindfulness" better explain how we learn concepts. Contextualism emphasizes the centrality of shared meanings and thus gives language prominence because it alters our ways of being in the world and in relationship. Mechanism discusses an egocentric "one." Because contextualism opens cognition to lived experience and relationships with others in the world, I have termed contextualistic cognitive psychology the mind's "we," in recognition of its communal perspective.

In the final chapter I suggest, based on my analysis of the literature in perception, memory, and categorization, some of the implications of such a metatheoretical analysis for the field of psychology. My intent is to gather contextualist thought and piece together its quilt. The bits of cloth may not be in the right order as I will not have gathered all the possibilities, and they will undoubtedly take some eventual rearranging before they can be stitched together. But I want to place them over the metatheoretical backing developed throughout this book. So the conclusion will really be an introduction, especially to those who might gain entrance to the field through contextualism, to perspectives and forms of knowledge that were scraps discarded by the mechanistic worldview. And it is also an invitation for those mechanistically inclined psychologists (who have, by and large, been men) to consider a new viewpoint. Those researchers (e.g., Fiske & Shweder, 1986a) actively engaged in evaluating the social sciences stress that versions of psychological reality become more tolerable when they participate in a more liberating dialogue. Recognition of intellectual diversity and methodological pluralism brings relief. Such plurality may invite more women researchers to participate in constructing knowledge in the field of cognitive psychology: "It's good, you know, when you got a woman who is a friend of your mind" (Morrison, 1987, p. 273).

2
Contextualistic Alternatives to the Mechanistic Worldview in Psychology

Let us try to think of man as an assembled organic machine ready to run.

—John Watson, *Behaviorism*

An ideally adequate theory even of so called purposive behavior . . . ought to begin with colourless movement and mere receptor impulses as such, and from these build up step by step both adaptive and maladaptive behavior.

—Clark Hull, *Principles of Behavior*

Intuition, insight, and learning are no longer exclusive possessions of human beings: any large high-speed computer can be programmed to exhibit them also.

—Herbert Simon and Allen Newell,
"Heuristic Problem Solving: The Next Advance
in Operations Research"

[AI researchers] are concerned with developing a formalism, or "representation," with which to describe . . . knowledge. We seek the "atoms" and "articles" of which it is built, and the "forces" that act on it.

—Terry Winograd, "Artificial Intelligence and
Language Comprehension"

Leading behaviorists Watson and Hull and leading cognitive scientists Simon, Newell, and T. Winograd here assume that behavior is fundamentally machinelike—psychology can reduce behavior

26

to component parts to reveal a causal sequence of events that will explain human behavior. This way of thinking became more prominent during the early 1900s with psychologists trying to emulate the natural sciences, especially physics. The mechanistic metaphor seemed to many to reveal the structure of the physical world (see Koch, 1961; Converse, 1986). As interpreted by experimental psychologists, the methods of natural science obliged them "to search for some fundamental elements from which to build the mechanisms to mediate between our circumstances and our behaviour" (Shotter, 1975, p. 44). Historically, the insistence on the machine metaphor as the only viable one for understanding human behavior has condemned psychologists to investigate regularities in behavior through objective observation under tightly controlled circumstances. During the first half of this century, a mechanistic psychology overshadowed alternative metaphors, such as contextualism.

Contextualism frames our thinking about behavior along quite different lines. In following the extensions of its metaphor, the historical event, it orients us to an alternative way of seeing the world; for example, rather than stripping context away to isolate causal relations between artificial variables, it reconstructs context by emphasizing interdependent relationships and meanings. The emphasis on event contrasts with mechanism's emphasis on the ahistorical, atemporal particulars of experience. An event has temporal and spatial spread and occurs in a context that has overall quality that gives the event cohesiveness. A particular event is usually nested in other events (e.g., reading this section is part of taking a course), or it may fold into another event (e.g., reading this section while rocking a child to sleep). In its insistence on situational analyses, contextualism recasts psychological inquiry around dimensions that recognize the ongoing transaction between the organism and its environment, and so is often very closely associated with ecological psychology (e.g., Gibson's ecological approach to perception). It has emerged as a worldview during this century in an ongoing, often intense dialogue with mechanism.

In this chapter I examine these two root metaphors, illustrate their different orientations, and explore the significance of these differences for the study of cognitive processes. In doing so, I lay the groundwork for the discussion in subsequent chapters of perception, memory, and categorization. To provide the backdrop for contextualistic concerns and perspectives, I examine the mechanistic assumptions underlying both the behaviorist and information-processing approaches in psychology. These seemingly diverse approaches are tied together by their reliance on what philosophers and psychologists term an "objectivist" science (see M. Johnson, 1987; Gergen, 1985, for fuller discussions of objectivism; Leary, 1990a; Walls, 1982, for good historical analyses of the mechanistic metaphor in psychology). In his work on images that guide psychological research John Shotter (1975) explains that any form of mechanism needs objectivity: "Mechanical assemblages are constructed piece by piece from objective parts—that is, from parts that retain their character irrespective of the context of existence" (p. 52). Such objectification enabled mechanistically inclined psychologists to conduct experiments in the hope that they could build causal theories of human behavior based on universal laws (e.g., any given response is a function of stimulus factors and subject or organism factors). Discovering and explaining regularity in human behavior has been the central aim of a mechanist psychology in both the behaviorist and information-processing traditions.

Mechanism

In the mechanist tradition in psychology, one confronts not a single doctrine but a constellation of -*isms*: empiricism, associationism, reductionism, individualism, logical positivism, and operationism. Underlying all of these philosophic doctrines is an objectivist theory of meaning that, as M. Johnson (1987) explains, "assumes a fixed and determinate mind-independent reality, with arbitrary symbols that get meaning by mapping directly onto that objective reality" (pp. xxi–xxii). Some of these interconnected assumptions about knowledge, especially basic to psychological theories of learning, have also been retained in cognitive science. George Humphrey (1963) documents the emergence of empirical assumptions in his history of experimental psychology. Such a history is critical in understanding why later attacks—from philosophers of science, linguists, and psychologists—on such mechanistic doctrines as associationism had such profound effects on the field. The attacks led to the undermining of behaviorism as a viable explanation of human behavior and eventually to the increased interest in cognition and language.

Empiricism and Associationism

An empirical claim is one which can be justified by an appeal to sense experience. A problem, however, immediately arises: What is the evidence of experience? Although different thinkers have worked out answers that vary somewhat in detail, those philosophers who have come to be known as the British Empiricists, figures such as John Locke, David Hume, and John Stuart Mill, all take the same general approach. Experience can be reduced to the smallest units or elements ("atoms") of sensation, which are simple and invariant. These uninterpreted basic units do not change. They are the final evidence of the "known" and thus are claimed to be the ultimate indicators for what is "out there," what exists apart from the knower. Empiricist epistemology establishes the object of sensation as primary to what can be claimed as knowledge. It appeals to atomism, the claim that ultimate units exist, and reductionism, the insistence that all inquiry should lead to explanations in terms of smallest units (see Haugeland, 1978, for a discussion of the differences between types of reduction made in psychological research). Most experience, though, is not characterized by the particularistic quality of raw sense data, so another question arises: How do the units (simple ideas) come together in more complicated groupings (complex ideas)?

To answer this question, the British Empiricists developed the theory of association. Again, Locke, Hume, and Mill differ somewhat, but their aim is the same: to discover laws by which units form into larger complexes and regularities. The empiricists put forth a number of different candidates for laws, such as the law of contiguity, which states that elements are associated (undifferentially connected) by simultaneous or successive existence in space and time. Other laws are those of similarity, resemblance, repetition, and cause and effect. As Mill says in a statement typical of this kind of account, "Our ideas spring up or exist in the order in which the sensations existed of which they are copies" (cited in Humphrey, 1963, p. 3). Regardless of the specific laws asserted, the British Empiricists describe the formation of associations as a nonrational and mechanistic process. That is, the relation between the elements is based on their random and simultaneous (or successive) occurrence. The connections simply occur; there is no other explanation of that fact. The organism plays a passive role in the process. The elements are associated or mechanically grouped as they are registered in sensory apparatus.

In psychology, associationism provided an explanation of learning that complemented empiricist epistemology: it was the mechanism by which basic units came together. Complex ideas can be reduced to connected simple ideas, and the content of these simple ideas is ultimately rooted in sense impressions. Thus, meaning is generated by the external environment. The organism registers units passively, and the units that are stored in memory as ideas have no potential to organize or construe meaning. For the empiricists, factual observation of the external world became the basis of objective knowledge. "It is inherent in the root metaphor of mechanism that one must 'get hold' of a phenomenon before it is real, and there is uneasiness about everything that cannot be expressed as a 'particular' in a certain time and place" (Walls, 1982, p. 267).

Having a secure, independent basis for knowledge claims allowed empiricists to distance the knower from the known—what is known exists "out there," apart from the observer. The knower becomes generalized in that what he or she brings to the learning experience becomes irrelevant. One can participate in this objective way of knowing on separate (but equal) footing without regard, say, to one's social history, childhood memories, or gender. The mind alone experiences and knows. As Harding (1987) notes, "Empiricism, like the Liberal political philosophy which provides its metaphysical and political foundations, has no conceptual space for recognizing that humans are fundamentally constituted by their position in the relational networks of social life. For empiricism, humans appear as socially isolated individuals who are here and there contingently collected into social 'bundles' we call 'cultures' " (p. 128). Conceived of abstractly, the individual of empiricism stands isolated and cut off from the social world.

Although a complete history of experimental and behavioral American psychology during the twentieth century is beyond the scope of this book, it is important to note just how pervasive mechanistic doctrines, such as empiricism and associationism, have been in American scientific psychology. Until the 1960s almost all psychological investigations of complex behaviors, particularly of verbal learning, relied explicitly on the doctrine of association and its accompanying reductionistic method (see Greeno, et al., 1978; Jenkins, 1974a, b). Even Gestalt research, which raised serious objections to atomism and associationism in the study of perception, had only indirect influences on American psychology (Robertson, 1986).

Behavioral psychologists employed the concept of association to explain the occurrence of given physical reactions within the stimulus-response framework. Uninterested in the association of ideas, since ideas are unobservable, they could treat responses in the stimulus-response unit in terms of associationistic assumptions. By 1934, Hull had made the direct connection between English associationism and American behaviorism (Humphrey, 1963, p. 4). Observable responses could be strengthened, weakened, or maintained based on prior association with the stimulus.

The behaviorist reliance on associationism resulted from the commitment to reductionism which supposedly would enable the scientific study of behavior experimentally. Because of the exclusive focus on what was mistakenly assumed as necessary for laboratory science, S-R researchers abstracted the "unit of behavior" from ordinary experience. This is an ironic development because behaviorism did have the potential and was in part originally motivated to explain human behavior in its total environmental context. Early on, Dewey (1896) warned behaviorists against reducing behavior to a causal sequence of discrete units. In retrospect, since the works of Dewey and William James were widely available, one might think that the pragmatic theory of situations would have had a more powerful influence on the direction of academic psychology. But academic psychology by and large subscribed to a version of mechanism which promised prediction and control of human behavior.

No one advanced mechanism more in psychology than John Watson, who linked mechanistic doctrines together in fairly dogmatic formulations of behaviorism. (His formulations would prove troublesome to later behaviorists, such as Kantor, 1968, who significantly revised them.) Watson's 1924 book *Behaviorism* combines assertions about the ability of behavioral "science" to predict and control social behavior with a chilling, managerial objectivism (see, especially, Watson's description of the personality as a "shop ticket," p. 217). In his explanations Watson translated an old mechanistic set of terms into new ones. For example, "the unconditioned reflex takes the place of the sensation, while the conditioned reflex and its elaborations take the place of associationally derived elaborations of the sensation" (Humphrey, 1963, p. 6). Watson's reduction of all psychological activity to the senses delimited, on the basis of an empiricist epistemology, what counted as psychological experience and how it could be studied. The elements of this basic unit had to be observable. Thus, he could dismiss from the analysis of behavior any subjective conditions of the organism. "The time has come," Watson asserts, "when psychology must discard all reference to consciousness" (1913, p. 163). Such a position assumes that what is internal to the organism is what is associated "out there." For Watson, implicit habits (thought) are, like every other acquisition—a product of conditioned reflexes. And behavior, governed by external stimuli, is an effect, not a cause. It is often controlled and always potentially controllable by an outside observer-experimenter.

Watson influenced the kind of knowledge claims one can advance in psychology, often to appeal to the natural sciences such as the following: "Psychology as the behaviorist views it is a purely objective branch of natural science. Its theoretical goal is the prediction and control of behavior" (1913, p. 158). Reacting against the mentalism of introspective psychologists, Watson shifted the basis on which knowledge claims could be made, namely, from unobservable to observable events. Although the experimental method had already been employed in psychology before Watson, his call for objective and naturalistic views helped open the way for psychological investigation to emulate more directly investigation in the physical sciences. Watson's view was so influential that scientific psychological investigation came to be equated with "the objective method of experiment" (Broadbent, 1961, p. 35) and the laboratory test (Bakan, 1967).

Watson's early formulations of behaviorism, particularly his reduction of thought to sensory stimuli, could not account adequately for complex behaviors such as language acquisition. Neobehaviorists such as Hull and Spence revised Watson's assumptions in trying to account for more complex behaviors. But these revisions retained associationist and reductionistic assumptions about the connection between the stimulus and response in the learning process. The S-R unit continued to be studied mechanistically through controlled laboratory experimentation. Joseph Rychlak (1977) summarizes the assumptions underlying the experimental method that constrain psychological inquiry:

(1) antecedent Ss [stimuli] determine consequent Rs [responses] in the cause-effect terms of efficient causality; (2) experimental IVs [independent variables] define Ss and DVs [dependent variables] define Rs; (3) for all practical purposes IVs are Ss and Dvs are Rs; (4) the relationship between these two "variables" [is] therefore determinate, as proven by the statistically significant evidence of a predicted outcome; (5) the extent of this efficient-cause determination of an antecedent-to-a-consequent can be expressed mathematically as a(n) (S-R) law or function; and (6) theoretical speculations going beyond such empirically observed facts are unwarranted, unless they make direct reference to further variables which can be manipulated (i.e., efficiently caused to vary). (p. 173)

So strong was the emphasis on methodology that at its worst the basic scheme became an empty tautology: A stimulus is whatever evokes a response, and a response is anything produced by a stimulus. Further, as the language of behaviorism took over academic discourse, the stimulus-response unit was increasingly isolated (e.g., the use of nonsense syllables in memory studies) from meaningful contexts in the name of objectivity. (For accounts of the damage to psychological inquiry in adhering to mechanism as the only legitimate way to practice science, see Gibbs, 1979; Joynson, 1970; Mishler, 1979.) Watson's aggressiveness notwithstanding, behaviorists were on the defensive in formulating their practices as scientific. Thus, many subscribed to positivism and operationism as philosophic programs to justify their inquiry; unfortunately, they bought sight unseen.

The Allure of Logical Positivism

Why was this "lusty embryonic science" of science, to use S. S. Stephens's (1976) early description of logical positivism, so important to the development of a mechanistic worldview in psychology? From the 1930s to the 1960s, logical positivism profoundly influenced the thinking of psychologists. Many experimental psychologists looked to the logical positivists and to the principle of operationism for the justification of their epistemological and methodological assumptions. Positivists hoped they could provide the logical tool box for explaining the theories of scientists who, according to them, worked on controlling and predicting natural mechanistic processes. Psychologists hoped that if they followed the positivist program, their practices would be legitimized and psychology would be considered a rigorous natural science.

The description and discussion of laboratory experiments present serious problems for the empirical scientist. Generalizations emerge from scientific observation. How are empiricists to verify that these generalizations indeed do map onto the real world of empirical facts? The philosophers called logical positivists answered this question by claiming that all cognitively significant meaning is propositional. Psychologists extended this theory of language to their experimental work with stimuli and responses, which could be put in propositional statements. Stephens (1976), for example, states, "All such propositions are reducible to protocol-sentences — sentences relating to the simplest elements of experience" (p. 18). The positivist emphasis on objectivity in the definition of constructs and on the reductionistic process especially appealed to behaviorists who believed they could discover the basic stimulus-response building blocks making up complex behavior. In their description of neobehaviorism, Howard Kendler and Janet Spence (1976) note this critical connection: "Neobehaviorists adopted stimulus-response language because it represented important traditions from which their orientation emerged: British associationism, classical conditioning methodology, and a methodological commitment to objectivity" (p. 514). But how could an experimentalist be assured that language objectively mapped reality?

Theories of meaning and reference that developed around advances in mathematical logic contributed to the empiricist viewpoint. The large accomplishments in formal languages, symbolized by the work of Bertrand Russell and Alfred North Whitehead, led to the enthusiastic endorsement of formal symbolism as a possible characterization of the structure of all meaning. This valorization of formal syntax, especially when tied to analyses leading to simple components of complex propositions, became the key to interpretations of science. In addition, this logicism of the "logical empiricists," as the logical positivists liked to call themselves, was often assumed to provide a model for interpreting meaning in natural languages and for characterizing knowledge in experience generally, whether scientific or not. Aspects of experience that proved relatively difficult to fit the procrustean bed of formal logic, such as felt connections, metaphorical structuring of meaning, imagination, and historical process, were set aside. Hence, the cognitive was often put in opposition to other capacities, the emotive, for example. This preference for formal and syntactical approaches to meaning and the attendant claim that intractable elements of experience can be discounted continues as a prevalent attitude in recent discussions.

The concern with an empirical basis for theoretical terms (hypothetical constructs) inclined psychologists toward operationism. Terms one uses in research must be defined empirically, at the level of observation, or at least this was the ideal, as exemplified by Stephens's (1976) early and strict definition: "A term denotes something only when there are concrete criteria for its applicability; and a proposition has empirical meaning only when the criteria of its truth or falsity consists of concrete operations which can be performed upon demand" (p. 8). By the 1970s, operationism allows behavioral scientists to "shuttl[e] back and forth between the level of theory-constructs and the level of observation. [They do] this by operationally defining the variables of [their] theory that are amenable to such definition and then by estimating the relations between the operationally defined and measured variables" (Kerlinger, 1973, pp. 34–35). Although not synonymous with logical positivism, operationism's connections to positivism legitimized the study of complex phenomena in learning, especially for neobehaviorists such as Hull who wanted to account for social behavior.

In introducing different kinds of propositions and concepts at different levels of generality, logical positivism gave psychologists the option to study unobservable forces such as anxiety or motivation as long as they had empirical content in a given statement (see MacCorquodale & Meehl, 1948, p. 96 on the intervening variable). Measurement of variables (through interval or ratio scales) became equated with being empirical. Or, in the case of hypothetical constructs, one could use formal logic to show the relation of generalization to observed data through a process of reduction. Harry Redner (1987) has well characterized reductionism in classical scientific method: "Usually [simplest objects and models] were theoretical constructs devised by means of analytic restriction through the elimination of all parameters except the ones that could be subject to law-like regularity" (p. 23). Through such reduction, psychologists assumed they could build an objective account of human behavior without reference to any point of view.

The laboratory experiment brings to the forefront these inter-
locking mechanistic hopes and assumptions. Its aim is to obtain
knowledge about the objective (usually antecedent) conditions that
control behavior. In isolating the stimulus-response unit, experimenters employed a reductionistic method. (That is, they assumed
psychological activity can be reduced to observable behavior that is
reducible to a more basic unit.) In the process of isolating the basic
unit of behavior, the stimulus is extracted from its environmental
context and studied singularly. The stimulus, invariant and simple
(i.e., measurable and controllable), remains unalterable during the
establishment of an S-R unit. The subject cannot alter the stimulus
while processing it, either perceptually or cognitively, since that
would make objective, transituational knowledge claims about
psychological functioning impossible. The subject, then, plays no
causal role in the experiment and is usually assumed to process the
stimulus in a mechanistic way. Laboratory studies "render living
organisms into passive subjects who simply convert stimulus inputs
into correlated response outputs" (Zimbardo, 1969, pp. 237–38).

Seeking to build up explanations of behavior through experimentation, behaviorists minimized the role of theory. Skinner
(1950, 1956), in particular, continually advanced the nontheoretical
nature of scientific analysis of behavior. If functional relationships
(lawful ties) between stimulus and response can be established, then
these laws can be used to control and predict behavior. Those within
the neobehaviorist tradition who did set up complex and abstract
theoretical frameworks (e.g., Hull, 1943; Spence, 1957) concep-
tualized psychological activity reductionistically (using logical
positivism to buttress their claims to empiricism). K. Spence
(1957), for example, states:

> We have chosen to investigate simpler phenomena first because
> we are of the belief that progress in the formulation of psycho-
> logical laws and theories will be more rapid in this area than in
> the case of more complex behavior. We also believe that many of
> the variables and laws isolated in the study of simpler forms of
> behavior will be operative in more complex instances, interact-
> ing presumably with the additional factors introduced into
> these more complex situations. If such is the case it would
> appear to be more efficient in the long run to investigate the
> simpler phenomena first. (p. 103)

The role of theory in the neobehaviorist tradition, then, was relegated to a particular view of scientific progress, namely, that simple bits of behavior such as classical and instrumental conditioning could eventually be pieced together to explain complex processes. Theory did not deal with the content of the science, only with its methods.

The doctrines of empiricism, associationism, and reductionism gripped psychology during the first half of this century. Psychologists thought the mechanistic metaphor would advance their scientific status, and they longed for the kind of eloquent knowledge the metaphor had made available in physics: a description of lawful relations. The behaviorists repeatedly exhort one another to be "tough-minded" and "strong-headed," all in their pursuit of hard science. In this classic view, of course, behavior must be treated naturally; nature appears "as a scene of objects and events displaying regular and automated, or mechanical connections. . . . there are general procedures, techniques, and methods for discovering truths about nature" (Shweder, 1986, p. 176). The hardheads were not needed so much to study behavior objectively as to hold off the onslaught of culture. (Considerations of important issues such as the interrelation of thought and feeling fell outside the realm of objective inquiry.)

At its best the mechanistic root metaphor that informed behaviorism illuminated the regularities in human behavior that become habitual, automatically and unconsciously carried out, and it certainly broadened our understanding of the environmental conditions that maintain and support them. In the 1950s, however, its broader claims and programs (e.g., to predict and control all human behavior) came under attack. Like a building undergoing demolition, behaviorism's additional wings were torn down and then its foundation began to crumble. Noam Chomsky (1959) undercut verbal behavior theory; Michael Scriven (1957) denied deduction; Sigmund Koch (1964) found only empty, "ameaningful" knowledge claims in his extensive review of laboratory findings.

The Scientific Crisis

One of the crucial arguments leveled against the traditional behavioral approach is that its model of science is inappropriate and outdated. The program set out by the logical positivists has gener-

ally failed; as Paul Meehl (1986) recently argued, "[Logical positiv-
ism] is not an accurate picture of the structure of advanced sciences
such as physics, and it is grossly inadequate as a reconstruction of
empirical history of science. So it is dead" (p. 315). The key
methodological convention of behaviorism—operationism—has been
found epistemologically problematic (see, for example, in the philosophy of science the arguments of Hempel, 1951, 1954, 1966;
Popper, 1963; see Horgan, 1976, for difficulties with reductionism
in psychology). Philosophers of science such as Thomas Kuhn
(1970), Paul Feyerabend (1975), and Michael Polanyi (1958), all
coming from very different orientations, introduced the importance
of subjective and theory-laden factors in the acquisition of scientific
knowledge. Manicas and Secord (1983), nevertheless, point out that
even as the turn away from positivism in the philosophy of science
occurred, psychologists continued to refine their methodologies
and procedures on positivist assumptions. The methodological
sophistication did not stimulate theoretical coherence or cohesion.
As late as 1979, Elliot Mishler lamented the fact that "despite the
philosophical critique of this traditional model of science, its
application to human affairs has remained triumphant" (p. 3). It
was as if mechanistic explanations mattered more than original
insights.

These philosophical criticisms have recently had a growing
effect on psychological thinking (e.g. Putnam, 1981; Fiske &
Shweder, 1986a, b; Secord, 1986; T. Winograd, 1980). At stake in
these accumulating arguments is the appropriateness of mechanism
as the only metaphor for psychology. For example, the conventional
view of science has confined psychological investigation to closed
systems in laboratories; critics such as Secord (1986) point out that
in the natural everyday world, behavior occurs in open systems.
Generalizing from results obtained under artificial laboratory conditions becomes difficult, if not impossible (see Bronfenbrenner,
1977; Finkleman, 1978). The laboratory environment itself con-
stricts the kind of experimentation one can carry out and such
constraints distort data. Critics point to the trivial nature of the
phenomena that have been investigated (e.g., rat licks on a lever) and
the dearth of significant accumulation of knowledge (Koch, 1981).
Further, because of its commitment to the autonomy of the entity
under observation, classic mechanistic science cannot handle organized complexity; that is, it cannot account for transformative or

transactive relationships between entities at different levels in events or systems (see Redner, 1987, p. 24).

These criticisms of the ways that mechanism has been employed in psychology participate in what Richard Shweder and Donald Fiske (1986) call "the postpositivist intellectual climate of our times" (p. 16). They echo many concerns of Dewey (1930), who wrote, "There is something in the *contexts* of the experiment which goes beyond the stimuli and responses directly found within it" (p. 411). The ideals of the standard view of science can no longer be used to dismiss the challenges of other root metaphors. Contextualistic thinkers have been especially active in showing the inadequacy of objectivist and reductionist methodologies for understanding human behavior (e.g., Gibbs, 1979; Givón, 1989; Mishler, 1979), but they have also been actively producing different conceptions of science and theories of cognition (e.g., Bruner, 1986, Gergen 1985, M. Johnson, 1987; Manicas and Secord, 1983; Varela, et al., 1991; Winograd and Flores, 1986). These streams of contextualist thought have recently converged; discussions about context, subjectivity, open-ended systems, meaning and understanding, and ordinary language, to name a few, are no longer rare in the literature of the social sciences.

Critics of behaviorism have been especially severe on the behaviorist conceptualization of "the subject" in laboratory experiments — merely reactive, the subject supposedly played a passive role in the acquisition of knowledge. Cited in Richard Evans (1968), for example, Skinner described his view: "As a determinist, I must assume that the organism is simply mediating the relationship between the forces acting upon it and its own output, and these are the kinds of relationships I'm anxious to formulate" (p. 23). This objectivist view of behavior has been extensively criticized by humanists on the grounds that it denies a role for consciousness and the imagination in explanations of behavior; these debates are well known, but the most damaging criticisms came from within the ranks of so-called "cognitive behaviorists" and from cognitive psychologists during the 1960s.

"The Mind is Back!"

So Skinner (1989) identifies the battle cry of the cognitive revolution. And revolution it has indeed become. In the late 1950s and early 1960s several cognitive psychologists such as Jerome Bruner and Donald Broadbent began to question the behavioral views of association as the basis for learning; they looked instead toward structured forms of information (e.g., hierarchically nested concepts) and logical relations and their effect on, for example, long- and short-term memory and problem solving. Several began to study short-term memory and auditory and visual perception outside the stimulus-response framework. Early cognitivists began to model the way in which information flows through the mind — from sensory stimulation to processing (storage and retrieval) to consciousness. So complete was this shift in emphasis that many cognitivists came to insist that "every psychological phenomenon must be seen as a cognitive one" (Reynolds & Flaggs, 1977, p. 13). In the early 1960s, as the behavioral tradition was reeling from attacks on its theoretical and methodological coherence, psychologists began to look toward alternatives. The computer offered possibilities for building a science of the mind (while often still not granting that mind mattered in itself). According to Neisser (1976), "The coming of the computer provided a much-needed reassurance that cognitive processes were real; that they could be studied and perhaps understood" (p. 6).

Influenced by information theory, information-processing approaches attempt to describe the internal flow of information; that is, how mental operations take in and order bits of information sequentially (see Gardner, 1985; Haber, 1974; Knapp, 1986; S. Palmer & Kimchi, 1986, for fuller accounts of the origins and development of information processing). Such approaches are based on an analogy to a digital computer. Although information-processing psychologists do not represent all cognitivists in psychology (e.g., Tolman, 1932), Newell and Simon's work in information processing through computer simulation of cognitive processes quickly became very influential (see Newell, Shaw & Simon, 1958; Newell & Simon, 1961, 1963, 1972). George Mandler (1981), a well-known organizational theorist, for example, assumes that information processing is "synonymous" with cognitive psychology (cited in Aanstoos, 1987, p. 188). With the release of Neisser's textbook on cognitive psychology, published in 1967, the information-processing approach had become institutionalized. "The task of the psychologist trying to understand human cognition is analogous to that of a [person] trying to discover how a computer has been programmed. In particular, if the program seems to store and reuse information, he [or she] would like to know by what 'routines' or 'procedures' this is done" (Neisser, 1967, p. 6). Unlike the behaviorists, cognitivists stressed that the organism is an active processor of information. Neisser describes the organism as active in construing its environment. How a person processes the stimuli becomes more determinate of behavior than, say, the contingencies of reinforcement. But the type of activity proposed by the information-processing models, as we will see in subsequent chapters, is circumscribed, perilously so. In information-processing theory, the organism's activity is not open-ended; it occurs in a closed system—that of a rule-governed machine.

The Mind as a Machine

Contemporary cognitive psychology does not represent a radical departure from the empiricist and associationist foundations of behaviorism: "A 'cognitive' psychology that makes . . . changes *without repudiating the conceptual framework underlying behaviorism* (and its predecessors) is not more adequate than behaviorism" (Weimer, 1977, p. 268). Both behaviorism and information-processing models share a mechanistic root metaphor, but cognitive psychologists shifted the type of mechanism—from one based on the mechanical laws of the physical world governing behavior to one based on computational processing. The main principle in both endeavors, however, is mechanistic; for example, both assume objects can be decontextualized (either in the laboratory or the computer), reduced to a set of elementary terms for analysis, and then reassembled or reconstituted through a synthetic process. As Christopher Aanstoos (1987) observes in his comparison and contrast of behaviorism and information processing, each approach assumes that "psychology's subject matter must be treated as objects, in the sense of mechanisms for causal analysis" (p. 190).

Information-processing theorists such as Simon and Newell (1964) explicitly adopted the mechanistic metaphor to study the role that rational reconstruction plays in behavior, but their mechanism originates in assumptions very different from those of behaviorists (see Aanstoos, 1987). For example, the behaviorist directly observes behavior (S-R links) without reference to cognition; the cognitivist assumes behavior results from rational reconstructions of information. While the mechanism that characterizes behaviorist research objectifies behavior (as response outputs), the mechanism that characterizes information-processing research objectifies thought (as rationally reconstructed output). Especially evident in early information-processing models, which used set theory exclusively, the objectification of thought reinforced the primacy of the abstract knower in psychological explanations. That is, only cognitive operations that occur inside any and all individual minds become salient in the analysis of behavior; contextual nuances and subtleties between individuals and cultures become even more shadowy and less visible than they were in behavioral research. Thus, because they only process algorithmically, knowers-as-processors become strangely disconnected from their life worlds. Cognitive activity becomes disembodied and abstract.

Information-processing psychologists and those working in artificial intelligence introduce into behavioral accounts a formalism that behaviorists avoided (by not attributing causal powers to the mind). The cognitive operations that many cognitivists study are taken to be representational: "Information processing actually takes place in the concrete physical world of mechanical, electric, optical, and biochemical devices. . . . information is carried by states of the system (here called *representations*) and operations that use this information are carried out by changes in state (here called *processes*)" (S. Palmer & Kimchi, 1986, pp. 55–56). Representations mediate between the organism and its world. Shotter (1975) puts it this way: " 'We' are not there as agents in the conduct of these processes; seeing objects is not something that 'we' do, it is something that our cognitive processes do for us" (p. 59). But why this intermediate level of representation, this "middle level of functional description" (S. Palmer & Kimchi, 1986), or, even more dramatically, this special "language of thought" (Fodor, 1975)?

In information processing this level of representation consists of as "small-scale units (bits, individual percepts, single associations examined in brief periods of time)" (Gardner, 1985, p. 96) that get substituted for thinking (routines) or various parts of thinking (subroutines). These units are abstract, symbolic, well-defined, functional entities that can be put into computer simulations and be manipulated. Each of these entities can only be interpreted by a single given code. The processes or manipulations rely on predetermined rules and calculations expressed in terms of logical relations.

Logical symbols substitute for real world information, and we can ascertain that this information is represented accurately when our actions or the program's actions are successful. Stephan Palmer and Ruth Kimchi (1986) point out that the representations must be such that the symbols can be recursively decomposed. That is, in the flow process (which is itself rule-governed), the psychologist-programmer must be able to trace the components (as input, as operation, and as output) throughout the processing. They define the kind of reduction as "complexity reduction": "With each lower level of description the internal complexity of the component operations should decrease" (1986, p. 52). Information-processing theories, then, offer flow diagrams that present formal, abstract relations, usually hierarchically arranged, as simulations of mental processes.

The above description gives the flavor of the mechanistic assumptions in information processing. What is generally referred to as strong artificial intelligence (an extension of the information processing not just to problem solving but to thinking or intelligence generally) claims that the mind is a machine. Weaker AI proponents claim only that machine simulations of cognitive processes can be fruitful in understanding cognition. As I will illustrate more specifically in the subsequent chapters, information processing, like behaviorism, has held key mechanistic assumptions about the study of behavior—reductionism, objectivism, individualism. What changes is the nature of the commitment to empiricism; the physical world is exchanged for a formal one. According to Kevin Smith (1987), "Part of what it means for cognitive science to be cognitive is that it explains behavior in terms of *a rational process of inference* [italics added]. . . . Such inferences are not only unconscious and fast, they are qualitatively different from the inferences that go on when one engages in discursive, conscious thinking, as when one balances a checkbook, plays chess, etc." (p. 158). Unlike the behaviorist who wants to stipulate environmental contingencies, the cognitive scientist stipulates elements in logical relations. Human thought appears in most computational models of the mind as logical and rational, in the sense of formal set theory or propositional calculus, and systematic, in the sense of logistic systems.

In working with bits of information, processing theorists retained not so much the empiricism of behaviorism but its emphasis on reductionism. They analyzed information into basic elements that follow a logical calculus. This particular merger of the machine with the form or algorithm seemed to create a super metaphor. Dreyfus (1979) suggests a similar "confluence of two powerful streams" (p. 231) when he recognizes that "in psychology, the computer serves as a model of the mind as conceived of by empiricists such as Hume (with the bits as atomic impressions) and idealists such as Kant (with the program providing the rules). Both empiricists and idealists have prepared the ground for this model of thinking as data processing — a third person process in which the involvement of the 'processor' plays no essential role" (p. 156). Thus, the cognitive science movement, like the behaviorist movement, held psychology captive by claiming to be scientific through its use of formal procedure and mechanistic models. In discussing the progress of AI, for example, Newell (cited in Bobrow & Hayes, 1985) stresses the importance of AI as science: "One feature of progress in AI . . . is the spreading out of application to new domains. This doesn't look like integrated science or like accumulation in depth, but it is an essential feature of our field and it counts as progress. In particular, it counts as scientific progress, because AI is in the game of understanding how to represent knowledge about the whole world, and we find this out only as AI gets applied to new aspects of the world" (p. 384). Cognitivists are often so eager to be scientific that they often wildly exaggerate their claims (here in a non sequitur).

The conflation of the formist and mechanist root metaphor in the computing analogy legitimized a certain version of cognitivism as a science. For years, the seeming merger of formism and mechanism into a super science of the mind presented a formidable barrier to contextualistic thinkers. Forced into alleys and byways, contextualists appeared like shadowy, unthreatening figures or poor sports (see Churchland & Churchland, 1990, p. 33, for an account of H. Dreyfus's reception as an early critic of AI). But in the early 1980s, new concerns, even from those within the ranks of cognitive scientists themselves, emerged. "I found myself wanting to describe a path rather than justify its destination," writes T. Winograd (1980) in a story about his experience with cognitive science. His radical reframing of what psychology must pursue (Skinner's road led to heaven) can also be seen in his title, "What does it mean to understand language?" A practicing cognitive scientist well known for his computer program for natural language conversation (called SHRDLU), Winograd spoke here from a new perspective, an indication of the contextualist movement of the next decade.

Contextualism

"Believing . . . that man is an animal suspended in webs of significance he himself has spun, I take culture to be those webs, and the analysis of it to be therefore not an experimental science in search of a law but an interpretive one in search of a meaning" (Geertz, 1973, p. 5). Here, Geertz movingly chooses the contextualist metaphor for work in anthropology, where it was used earlier and more fruitfully than it was in cognitive psychology. Although it did not arrive as a fully articulated worldview in cognitive psychology until the 1980s, contextualistic concerns and criticisms certainly influenced the direction of cognitive research. Basing his interpretation in the phenomenological tradition, especially the works of Martin Heidegger and Maurice Merleau-Ponty, Dreyfus (1979; Dreyfus & Dreyfus, 1986) closely examines the claims and assumptions of theories of artificial intelligence as they develop from the late 1950s on. He has continued to inform psychologists who might have been otherwise bereft of such a perspective of the generative potential of understanding cognition as engagement in the world. Thus, his work kept open the question of the connection of cognitive theories to lived experience. Prompted to simulate more naturalistic thinking, researchers recognized the importance of situational events. During the middle and late 1970s artificial intelligence workers, cognitive psychologists, and linguists focused attention on scripts, frames, and schemata as ways to represent past knowledge in information processing (e.g., Schank & Abelson, 1977). But the presuppositions of information processing continued to prove too confining for researchers such as Rumelhart, who gave up writing a book on schema to "dig some new ground" (cited in Allman, 1989, p. 120) or, perhaps more aptly, make some new connections with neural networking. This movement continues to bring contextualistic concerns to the foreground.

Parallel distributed processing models, part of what I have called the connectionist movement that Rumelhart helped pioneer, "assume that information processing takes place through the interactions of a large number of simple processing elements called units, each sending excitatory and inhibitory signals to other units" (McClelland, et al., 1986, p. 10). Information goes into a system and excites the units. For example, think of a jury or a classroom of children that must reach a decision about a problem. All members (neurons) start talking to a neighbor, slightly changing their opinions as they hear the opinions of others. Eventually, as consensus is reached, the system settles into a decision (see Boden, 1988, for a fuller development of this analogy and its variations). Such models attempt to simulate more natural cognitive tasks and to take into account contextually appropriate actions and information. Although this movement is very diverse and controversial, it is often seen to differ significantly from information-processing approaches that relied on discrete bits of information and formal logic for its simulations.

When fully blown contextualistic theories develop, they do not just redraw mechanistic boundaries but alter the very principles of mapping (Geertz, 1980, p. 166). What is contextualism's history in psychology, and how does the world look through the categories and assumptions entailed by the contextualist root metaphor?

Contextualism in psychology and philosophy has not been as readily accepted as mechanism. In philosophy and psychology, C. S. Peirce (1931), William James (1890), John Dewey (1896), George H. Mead (1934), Kurt Lewin (1935), and George Kelly (1955) contributed to early formulations of a contextualist discourse. Gestalt psychology had strong contextualistic leanings, particularly its insistence on the functional role of parts within the whole. From more recent philosophy, Ludwig Wittgenstein's *Philosophical Investigations* (1953) questioned the kind of objectivity in language logical positivism (and a younger Wittgenstein himself) thought possible. His work did not really infiltrate psychology until 1970, however, when many psychologists became increasingly concerned about the contextual dependency of meaning. Maurice Merleau-Ponty's work, especially *The Structure of Behavior* (1963) and *Phenomenology of Perception* (1962), have become increasingly important as a "fecund source of insights for psychology" (Aanstoos, 1987, p. 187; Varela, et al., 1991). All of these contextualist influences "meandered, sluggishly and unobtrusively, for a long time. They had accumulated, slowly, leisurely, behind the dam of deductive logic. Somewhere along the way, the flow began to quicken. . . . And all of a sudden the entire dam is threatened" (Givón, 1989, p. 25).

We have seen that mechanistic psychologists assume that the mind, taken as a physical entity, operates like a machine behind closed doors. Predefined, reality is composed of basic elements that interact in such a way that mental activity can be controlled and predicted. This objective perspective separates mental processes from consciousness (through representations), and "[the person is viewed] as reactive to and dependent on . . . input elements [in the environment]" (Gergen, 1986, pp. 145–46). When the mechanistic root metaphor does its generative work, the mind, as a machine, hums smoothly along, reliably and dependably. Contextualism, by contrast, provides a different way of discussing and seeing reality and the mind. Instead of frequencies of isolated and simple units, it begins with complexity and interrelatedness. It brings the mind out from behind closet doors and into social spaces where meanings can be shared and constructed. The body and the world are not separated from mental experiences which are then rationally reconstructed; rather the body and the world intertwine with the mind in experience like threads from differently textured skeins. Unlike mechanism, which aims toward precision and values regularity, contextualism's focus on continually changing events honors qualitative richness and novelty. If the mechanistic mind hums along in isolation like a finely tuned machine, then the contextualist's mind knits up questions and casts them outward like a net into the social and physical world.

Contextualism commonly brings to psychology the following assumptions about cognition: (1) Thought is always engaged in the world. Contextualistic analysis begins in lived experience, in *this* situation, but finds structure and coherence in events (very generally, the incidents of life, such as one would find in a play). (2) Events have overall qualities that cannot be reduced, in any ultimate sense, to parts. (3) Because cognition is situated, thought, action, and sociality intertwine in experience in complex ways—no abstract, transhistorical, transituational perspective or system of thought can be superimposed over experience in advance. As situations and contexts shift and alter over time, meanings change. (4) The world and experience are constituted by novelty and change, as much as by habit and regularity. (5) Actively engaged, cognition brings to experience the capacity to generate frames of reference that provide understandings of events; some of these frames may be more permanent and others more fleeting. Through analysis of situations and shared dialogues with others, we refine and attune our thinking. Contextualism often emphasizes the resourcefulness of our reflective practice when we are faced with the difficulties of

ordinary experience. Let me illustrate these categories by telling
you a story.

I have been debating about whether or not to send my five-year-
old daughter Gemma to kindergarten. Several months ago other
mothers at a picnic announced confidently that they were "holding
back" their five-year- olds. Although I actually had subterranean
feelings and doubts, I hadn't consciously thought about not sending
her. So, as a conscientious mother, I began to question my thinking
about this situation. Holding back children had not come up eight
years ago when my five-year-old son started kindergarten.

I began to observe Gemma from a new perspective, from the
eyes of others who will gaze upon her in public schools. She still
sucks her thumb at night. Her only friends in the neighborhood will
be going to other schools. She recently had crying spells when we
left her at school with a particular teacher. Sometimes she skips
from twelve to fourteen when she counts to twenty. These threads in
my description of her enter my thinking as judgments, but immediately they intertwine with the overall quality of my relationship
with her.

She's very intense these days. Right now she asks *why* about
everything. "Why is that light yellow? Why can't you have more
babies? Why do people die? Why do worms stay in the ground?
Who owns the world?" She asked all these just today. Her hearty
laugh, her feisty assertiveness, her ability to express herself emo-
tionally, her whining when she's tired—all these enter into my
holding of her—not as a disembodied mental image in my mind's
eye—but as a being in-relation-to-me in the world. My experience
of her and the categorial, socially prescribed meanings of her as
"kindergartner" are in constant interaction. When I do manage to
hold her stably in my thoughts, her presence breaks through the
particular category or character delineation I have construed. Like
light from a prism, my thoughts cast outward in different directions
even as they are pulled back to the central lines of her character.

I also observe myself as her mother through those same public
eyes. We weren't notified about kindergarten roundup and missed it.
Actually, the principal said it was months ago. I know that glitch
would never have happened with my first child, because my husband and I were so intent to do it right. What does this mean, I ask
myself, that I forgot kindergarten roundup? And I also see myself as

a psychologist. My training should inform my parenting in just this kind of questioning and decision making. I should speak with authority and certainty and employ clear, rational processes. Instead of searching for algorithms, however, I find myself seeking out the stories of others. Which are the most important stories to tell and to think about? I remember Piaget writing down the stories of his children, and I can see how his stories fit Gemma's experiences. In my graduate school training, we superimposed his formal categories onto children instead of using them to explore children's experience intersubjectively. And I can overlay such outside structures on my daughter's behavior—momentarily. The forms too quickly disintegrate in the face of her presence and the flux of our experience together. I sense acutely that my public training stands distanced from my personal life, a chasm Madeleine Grumet's (1988) work on women and education has helped me bridge: "For the world we feel, the world we remember, is also the world we make up" (p. 65).

The teachers at the child care center vacillate when I ask them what they think about her "readiness," as they call it, for kindergarten. "She is intellectually ready," they say, "but she is emotional about leaving you sometimes." For me, mother and teacher, this remark is freighted with conflicting possible responses. I have tried to lick it down like a wayward clump of hair, but it always sticks back up. She's emotional; she can't separate. Grumet describes the loss of our subjectivity in schools: "Dominated by kits and dittos, increasingly mechanized and impersonal, most of our classrooms cannot sustain human relationships of sufficient intimacy to support the risks, the trust, and the expression that learning requires" (p. 56). Gemma's world as a kindergartner appears before me: "Keep your hands to yourself. Don't cry if your picture gets torn." Of course my daughter is emotional about some of our separations (as was and is my son—and I). My principles say that's a problem not for my daughter, but for our educational system that weeds out the self and subjectivity. Yet I know I cannot channel Gemma's experience along the lines of my principles—her experience will be situated in a larger, already existent context.

I carry this dilemma with me, not as a legal question, but as a fuzzy background or a kaleidoscope. Each time I bring it to the foreground of my thinking, I find its dimensions changed; new stories have arisen, new possibilities have emerged. For example, my friend Mary was the youngest in her class, and she told me stories, not about falling behind, but about always being last. "Awful," she concluded. Through Mary and others like her, I think within my social relations and my social contexts, through what Grumet describes as the dialectical interplay of my experience in the world and the symbolic orders of our culture.

I know, too, that the mothers holding back their children from kindergarten are members of a privileged class. As a teacher of underprivileged college students, my own membership presses into my consciousness daily. Said one mother, "We kept our older daughter back. As a result, she's been in all the top reading and math groups; we're so afraid Susan [the younger one] might get behind." David Elkind (1987) reminds us that hers is no passing concern: privileged parents are training their children to play instruments at early ages and to read by age four. Navigating through the worlds of other professionals' children, I try not to compare, not to judge, not to isolate performance; but the atmosphere is thick with the agenda: have a gifted and talented child—by first grade. This mother's comment lands into a field of recent discussions with my philosopher friend who has been teaching an honors seminar entitled "The End of Knowledge." In this larger cultural context, I realize that in their concern with their children getting behind, these parents are keeping alive the dream of being out in front. But where are these frontiers of knowledge? What kind of world do they imagine? If these held-back kindergartners get to the head of their classes, where will they go? The economically disadvantaged women I teach don't even have desks for their children.

In this way of moving toward a decision about my daughter, my thought is embedded inextricably in its social, cultural, and historical context. As Gemma's experience emerges, I retell the story based on what novelty and change have occurred; these transformations enter my thinking as qualitative shifts and not aggregated accumulations of observations. The flux of our experience together over time is as real as my pointing to the letter *T*, which she subsequently finds everywhere. Nevertheless, in the midst of this changing situation, my thinking is also anchored by what has become entrenched in her behavior: her ability to say the alphabet, recognize numbers and letters, and repeat her phone number. These remain constant over time, like her freckles and red hair . . .

Suddenly, in the midst of all of this thinking, I see why I have been troubled so by this decision. I recognize a difference in

Gemma's and my son's situations. My son walked to school with other children from our neighborhood and, on the first day, waved goodbye to me at our front door. My daughter has no one with whom to walk. Will she walk with me? What does this mean? Erupting out of this flow of thought and my interactions with others, this insight feels substantial, like a rope rather than a thread; I will hang on to it for transportation to another ground for potential action. In the context of such empathic engagement with others who care about her and in light of the environmental information (which includes her actual skills and behaviors), we construct our way into kindergarten. This is the mind's we of contextualism.

The Primacy of Context and Event

For the contextualist, thought begins with the world as perceived and given, the overlooked background of our actions. Merleau-Ponty (1962, 1963) calls this the worldedness, or situatedness of thought which is always perspectival. Thus, I construe my daughter's possible entry into kindergarten at the age of four as an opening for thought. This event has a quality, to use Pepper's (1961) description, "its intuited wholeness or total character" (p. 238), rich in features. For example, the overall quality of the event with my daughter enters into in my caretaking of her in this new situation — not as child-in-my-eyes but as child-in-the-eyes-of-others who will judge her in the public world. An event's quality can be characterized by its spread backward and forward in time, by changes in the textures of a situation (a new kindergartner moves into the block, for example), and by the relationships that bring textures together in an organizational framework (for example, she meets and likes the kindergarten teacher). A contextualist starts from an overall quality of an event and works down into the textures, which consist of "strands," "contexts," and "references" that constitute the experience of the event. Strands lie in contexts. Thus, my daughter's ability to recognize letters and state her phone number, strands of the situation, make sense against a background context (both social and cultural) that includes, for instance, books, phones, and Sesame Street.

When contextualists more closely consider strands in a context, they examine or analyze references. For example, my thinking becomes framed along certain dimensions when someone says that

Gemma is emotional about leaving me. Or in taking up a somewhat different kind of referent, I realize that, unlike my son, my daughter will have no one with whom to walk to school. This provides what Pepper terms an instrumental reference in that it leads to action towards an end: This summer I can invite children who will be in her kindergarten to play with her. All of these interwoven strands in a context construct the quality, and if they change sufficiently, then the overall quality changes.

Pepper's metaphor for contextualism, the historical event, does not completely capture in a dynamic way the interactive character of this worldview, nor does it evoke a specific, immediately apprehensible metaphor, such as the clock (mechanism) or the oak tree (organicism). One searches for another metaphor. For example, weaving is evoked from the terms Pepper uses, such as the strands and textures of an event, but the metaphor would have to be taken in the sense of a tapestry that weaves itself because in contextualism the weaver and the woven are inseparable. This activity of bringing together threads and strands from experience in the creation of meaningful thought corresponds to music making, storytelling, and weaving. It is also captured by the spider's spinning out a web; the self creates out of his or her own body the webs of meanings and relationships, even as a person works with materials from the physical and social worlds to create that home. But these referents can only partially capture the full work of contextualism.

In the event and its interactive features, thinking strives toward meaningfulness and action and so is often a social process. From the field of social psychology, a group of theorists such as Gergen (1982, 1985, 1986) are advancing social constructivism. As editors of a special issue of *Theory & Psychology* entitled "Cognitivism and its Discontents," he and Gerd Gigerenzer (1991) express concern about the individualistic focus of the research in current cognitive psychology. They find such an emphasis on the isolated individual as, for example, an information processor to be culturally idiosyncratic rather than methodologically universal. They describe the contributors to the special issue as especially interested in exploring cognition in its social context: "Rather than commencing analysis at the level of the individual mind and working out towards an understanding of social interchange, these theorists propose that social activity be viewed as logically prior" (pp. 404–5). Social constructivists remind us that our situations are full of complex social interactions rich with linguistic and cultural meanings. Such sociality contrasts mechanistic models of thought where processing occurs in an internal region of an individual's mind. Unlike the mechanist, the contextualist does not assume that there is a detached, objective, disembodied perspective from which, if I could only get there, I could authoritatively decide about my daughter's readiness for kindergarten. Instead I focus on social processes and meaningful interpretations which, in Gergen's (1985) terms, "may be suggested, fastened upon, and abandoned as social relationships unfold across time" (p. 268). Such a process, I am maintaining, can be systematic, open, and flexible without it dissolving into undisciplined investigations. In contrast, a dyed-in-the-wool cognitive scientist will "see any form of experience as at best 'folk psychology,' that is, as a rudimentary form of explanation that can be *disciplined* [italics added] by representational theories of mind" (Varela, et al., 1991, pp. 144–45).

Our sociality and engagement with others can result in a revisioning of our situations. Without other perspectives, we sometimes lose awareness of the social and political background that highlights or foregrounds our thought. For example, even entertaining the question about sending a child to kindergarten at all is culturally bound. For the five-year-old in my sister's project village of Saam Njaay in Senegal, West Africa, there is, yet, no possibility of formal schooling. For my child, in contrast, there are many possibilities, public or private, formal or informal. My thought processes reflect the opportunities that result from my social class and status. These strands weave my thinking into ways of conceptualizing our choices. One of my acquaintances quit her job so that she could stay home and give her five-year-old child a wide range of experiences in foreign languages and the arts. This brings a political context to social possibilities: I live in a society that does not yet provide flexible work times for parents, a situation that led this mother to leave her job to educate her child. For the contextualist, thoughts cannot be articulated in an objective way, divorced from social and political contexts. Because they are interwoven, they seem strangely detached when pulled apart for the sake of objective processing.

A contextualist analysis recognizes the importance of intersubjective meanings and shared and partially shared frames of reference such as that given by gender, class, or educational background. Dialogues with others about projects in the world open up possibilities and lead to new ways of thinking. Cognition, in the contextualist view, is interrogative rather than propositional. I do not present my daughter to you as a sequence of propositions, nor do you as reader see yourself as perceiving or engaging with sentences. To the extent that I engage you in the situation, you feel involved in a conversation that calls forth memories and experience, probably in the form of stories or events. In admitting imaginative and metaphorical language, for example, contextualistic analysis opens up questions about the way in which the metaphor gives insight as much as it describes situations. "In this sense, thinking launches itself beyond the sensible, toward latent possibility" (Aanstoos, 1987, p. 191, on Merleau-Ponty's approach to thought). Often mechanistic, predetermined and rule-dominated forms of rationality cut off the possibility of mutual exploration and block the potential for further thought and action.

Quite naturally, the contextualist uses metaphors often tentatively and conditionally. As M. Johnson (1987) notes in his theory of imagination, "Metaphorical projection is one fundamental means by which we project structure, make new connections, and remold our experience" (p. 169). Such thinking "transcends its bounds not only of the sensible givens, but also of any pre-established thought" (Aanstoos, 1987, p. 191). As we have seen, in most mechanistic accounts, the use of language restricts how experience can be represented. Had I not created a broad context for thinking about Gemma's going to kindergarten, for example, I may have never have reached the particular fact that I experience as an insight about her not having friends with whom to walk to school. And I have the possibility for more facts. Imaginative or natural language use provides opportunities for further exploration and reframing, not only opportunities for securing factual claims about states of affairs. In fact, the intersubjective exploration and the connections would be ruptured by such claims: "If your daughter fits the following standard classification, then you can send her to kindergarten." Standing at a distance as a disinterested observer of her behavior would provide a certain type of knowledge of objective things about her. But the contextualist points to what is missed: the particulars of this child at this time and meaningful, reciprocal exchanges between people engaged in her care.

As my thought is foregrounded and positioned, it participates fully in the specificity of the factual world. I know who Gemma's kindergarten teacher will be and can visualize the room where she will sit at a desk. I observe her growing cognitive skills and watch her cope with her own emotions and those of others. Others also interpret her behaviors, and so I have many stories about Gemma to use with or against mine. In all of this processing and interacting, I do not think representationally (although I can choose to) but engage, as Aanstoos (1987) states, "presentationally": "The term presentational is meant to indicate the emergence of meaning within the involvement of persons and the world. . . . Such a view differs from a representation model, in which rationality is a construction, indeed a reconstruction that is imposed by a detached and contextless Thought that is not primordially engaged in the world" (pp. 192–93). Much of our past knowledge is, as Polanyi (1966) describes it, tacit; that is, we may use it without consciously realizing we are going through such a process, and this very tacitness makes mutual exploration in relationship possible. How do we take all that we know and integrate it into careful thought and action?

The Role of Past Knowledge and Experience

I not only have knowledge that is specific to my daughter but also general knowledge of what it means to go to kindergarten. For example, I know that she will not ride wild horses or study the physics of black holes. This knowledge can be stated explicitly and formally. But the contextualist claims that my knowledge goes beyond detached statements; not all thinking can be rendered as propositions and logical inferences among them. I bring to my dilemma what Dewey calls "funding" from my past experience. Meaning and significance from past experience and learning are carried over into interpretations and actions in present situations. For example, I know that in our culture kindergarten is a transitional stage of childhood. Such products of past knowings control and enrich my particular experience with Gemma (see Dewey, 1951, p. 520). This funded background allows me to anticipate regularity, respond consistently, and predict accurately, but it also enriches present experience. Flexibly structured and interconnected, it allows me the possibility to respond creatively to uncertainty and novelty in this particular situation.

What the subject brings to bear from her experience is, indeed, central to cognitive psychology and to understanding differences among worldviews. In addressing how meaning systems become organized in cognition the contextualist eschews mechanistic explanations as leading to an overall adequate account, particularly their reductionism and their abstract reconstruction of experience (see Still & Costall, 1987, for a similar discussion, although not in Pepper's terms). Dennett's (1991) theory of consciousness challenges established mechanistic assumptions while nonetheless insisting on mechanism as the only adequate form of an acceptable account. For example, he wants to "[break] the single-minded agent down into miniagents and microagents (with no single Boss)" (p. 458). Although he attempts an account of cognition that unifies the brain's machinery and ordinary experience, he is entrapped in the argumentative framework that he inherits from the mechanistic tradition. He begins his study of consciousness by recounting a time when he was sitting alone in a room in a rocking chair looking out the window (p. 26). (He may have come out of Descartes' closet into the world, but he is still alone, thinking to himself). With an enlivening waggery that typifies his writing, he says toward the end of the book that he is getting back on his rocker (p. 406). But in the course of the book he has never really gotten off his rocker to engage in real situations with real people. He says of his rocking chair experience when he returns to it that his "task is to take [the] text [of his experience], interpret it, and then relate the objects of the resulting heterophenomenological world of Dennett to the events going on in Dennett's brain at the time" (p. 407). This is like the anthropologist in Northern Africa who sets up a tent in the middle of the desert outside a village, has the villagers line up outside, and then invites them one by one to come in the tent for an interview about what is going on in their village. Instead of choosing socially engaged situations (such as the one he footnotes about a confusing classroom situation for a Chinese student and himself, p. 435), Dennett takes on the problems of explaining consciousness by fabricating dilemmas, inventing strange situations, and talking about himself in the third person. At first he admits his self-consciousness about such manipulations; he says, for instance, "Officially, we have to keep an open mind about whether our apparent subjects are liars, zombies, or parrots dressed up in people suits" (p. 83). But eventually (in an imaginary debate, of course) he disparages the views of folk psychologists, those interested in starting with the concreteness and richness of ordinary experience.

He will have to be more mindful about how he dismisses the phenomenological account of Varela, Thompson, and Rosch (1991). Challenging the mechanistic tradition while appreciating its accomplishments, they argue for the importance of embodiment and situatedness in cognitive science, but not as remainders left over after "figur[ing] out the 'nature' of mental status and processes *first*" (Dennett, 1991, p. 462). By ignoring ordinary experience at the outset, Varela, Thompson, and Rosch suggest, "science becomes remote from human experience and, in the case of cognitive science, generates a divided stance in which we are led to affirm consequences that we appear to be constitutionally incapable of accepting" (p. 127). For example, they remind us that many cognitive theorists repeat the cognitive dilemma of Hume who "having brilliantly formulated the discovery of selfless minds . . . conceiv[ed] of no way to bring that discovery together with everyday experience" (p. 129–30). For cognitive science to progress, they argue, mind and world must "stand in relation to each other through mutual specification or dependent coorigination" (p. 150). Like Dennett (1991), Varela and his coauthors (1991) are anxious to show that dualism, the separation of body and mind in experience, is no longer a tenable theoretical outcome. But unlike Dennett, they preserve the importance and integrity of lived experience in relation to cognition on a coequal basis with the machinery of the brain. Nevertheless, for a mechanist, Dennett comes a good distance toward recognizing contextually significant phenomena. In contrast, other cognitivists simply live with dualism or claim an account of experience is not necessary for cognitive science. In traditional information-processing accounts, for example, meaning from past experience often sits in a disembodied mental space separated from the body and experience. It is understandable that mechanists would want to achieve what they take to be scientific rigor by emphasizing regularity and consistency (the mechanisms of thought), but the price may often be the elimination of the very experiences that they set out to explain.

In a contextualist worldview, by contrast, such regularity and repetition are often thought of as degenerative aspects of lived experience. If we begin with artificial or contrived situations, we frequently only caricature thought as, for example, mere calculation (see Neisser, 1976, for a recantation of his early mechanistic views along these lines). Even our routine "habits," Dewey (1922) argues, are skill-like and intelligent. Contextualism works to preserve the dynamic, integrative, and situated nature of past experience in cognition. As a result, it does not emphasize elaborate theories about where perception ends and memory begins or what objectively determined criteria might, in the abstract, determine category membership. In later chapters on perception, memory, and categorization, I describe how mechanism, to the contrary, works to simplify past experience in cognition through abstraction. It then separates each cognitive function to study it in isolation. A contextualistic psychologist such as Fredric Bartlett (1932) wants not simplification through isolation but simplification through integration, and so he begins with and recognizes simultaneous functioning and dynamic interaction. In pressing toward the recognition of the multilayered nature of past experience in the present, a contextualist leans toward narrative. Well-told stories contain the best traces we have of the creative processes of cognition itself.

It is this contextualistic insight that has continued to motivate new explanations about how past experiences infuse the present. In the 1970s a group of researchers began to develop alternative ways to represent knowledge in "schemata," a term used early by Bartlett that captures in some ways what Dewey meant by funding. David Rumelhart and Andrew Ortony (1977) define a schema as "the network of interrelations that is believed to generally hold among the constituents of the concept in question. . . . a schema [is] analogous to a play with the internal structure of the schema corresponding to the script of the play" (p. 101). Much in this research recognized the importance of everyday events (a theme central to ecological psychologists in perception), the interrelatedness of higher mental processes, and the active nature of past knowledge in the present situation. During this time, the work of Rosch and her colleagues (e.g., Rosch, 1973, 1975; Rosch & Mervis, 1975; Rosch & Lloyd, 1978) introduced to cognitive science the notion of category prototypicality. Rather than having fixed boundaries, categories have "best exemplars" which the subjects of their experiments judged to be more or less representative of a category. This freed cognitive theorists from using an objectivist model of categorization based on discrete properties that fit or did not fit into a category (Lakoff, 1987b). The responses to contextualistic concerns such as these have led researchers increasingly into the role of language and culture in cognition, as the recent work on folk models of the mind exemplifies (Holland & Quinn, 1987).

To sum up, confronting the problem of experience and context has, in part, led to dramatic revisions and new kinds of philosophical discussions in cognitive psychology. "Appreciation of the variation of meaning with context is . . . standard. What is not always appreciated, however, is how radical this variation may be. Not only are the interpretations of linguistic utterances in context not constrained, they exhibit unbounded novelty. Meaning seems, therefore, not to be selected by context but rather to be generated in it" (Shanon, 1990, p. 158). Many psychologists are rethinking how to investigate complex intertwinings of cognition and context. Mishler (1979) called for "methods drawn from ecological psychology, phenomenological research, sociolinguistics, and ethnomethodology." With the influx of these new approaches to cognition the question becomes how to sustain a dialogue that does not dissolve in dismissive, stereotypical, or trivial characterizations. How can both contextualists and mechanists bring to bear the insights from their respective root metaphors in ways that take advantage of their diversity and plurality for cognitive science? Perhaps no other concern separates cognitive scientists into warring camps more than that of subjectivity and its role in experience. How much is experience constituted by our perceptions, our memories, our mental faculties, our biological capacities, our culture, if at all?

Subjectivity and the Standard View of Science in Psychology

In considering the role of subjectivity in cognition, it is important to distinguish between those who talk about formal structures as universal characteristics of all human cognition and those who back away from any such claims. The former, often followers of Kant, believe that structures can be discovered that characterize human experience irrespective of time and place. The latter, to which contextualism belongs, believe that all appropriations of meaning are to an important degree contingent upon historical and cultural situations. The Kantian depiction of structures of possible experience remains a fertile source of insight in cognitive psychology, some of which moves in a strictly formal vein and some of which moves in a more contextual, situational direction. Piaget's work, for example, is often interpreted differently, depending on the emphasis the researcher or educator places on Piaget's formal, logical structures or his very contextualistic descriptions of knowledge acquisition (i.e., assimilation and accommodation).

Many historians have documented this Kantian legacy, a part of the rationalist tradition frequently present in cognitive psychology (for overviews see M. Johnson, 1987; Lakoff, 1987b). Gardner (1985), for example, describes the tension in psychology between the top-down approach, "which has rationalist overtones, [in which] the subject is assumed to bring to the task his own schemata, strategies, or frames which strongly color his performance" and the bottom-up approach, or empiricist approach, in which the situational details of the subject's task become the focus (p. 97). The cognitive movement drew psychologists back to the organism's construction of experience. But contextualism is not subjectivism. As I will show later, contextualists support the constructive role of the subject in accounts of cognitive functioning, but insist, as Gergen (1985) does, that the kind of constructionism current in cognitive science undermines its own potential to illuminate human interaction by adhering to an objectivist epistemology.

If we return to the story of my dilemma about kindergarten, the mechanist would want to "nail the meanings down to something fixed and stable, things you can point at, weigh, and measure . . . [in order to] eliminate all subjectivity from meaning" (Shweder, 1986, p. 184). Opposed to this kind of objectivity, the total subjectivist, in the most exaggerated form, "wants to argue that the meaning of any one thing in external reality is the totality of all the interior subjective associations it elicits in you and me" (Shweder, 1986, p. 184). And so from this totally subjectivist view, my decision would be seen as the result of an idiosyncratic and purely personal processing. Contextualism claims neither of these extremes is salient or generative in systematic, reflective thought. As science, it treads on what Shweder calls a "middle ground," a position anticipated by Bartlett's simplification through integration. The point of such practice is to retain, as much as possible, the dynamically interactive or transactive relationship between organism and environment. Continuous and integral, the contributions of the organism and the environment can only be differentiated, Dewey (1930) argues, by analysis and selective abstraction (p. 411). Here we see a cycle—reducible neither to subject nor object. The history and situation of the subject contribute to the process of inquiry but so does the environmental information which, in turn, shapes the direction of inquiry. In 1979, Gibbs writes that inquiry based on such a transactional perspective is avant garde in psychology. The 1990s find many psychologists more receptive to its aims than ever before (Shanon, 1990).

The overall diagrams and descriptions typical in information–processing models of cognition tend to mirror bureaucratic organizational structures and practices, such as the separation of conception (e.g., programmer/manager) from the execution (program/worker) and the fragmentation of thought (and work) into partial actions (see Sampson, 1981, for a discussion of cognitive psychology as ideology; Dennett, 1991, Chapts. 8 & 9, for a discussion of the shift away from such bureaucratic theories). Some cognitivists continue to refine ever more rational and rigidly structured knowledge representations. Like bureaucrats they endorse a scientific rationality that assumes there is a best solution (or program). Contextual modes of thought disturb this view of cognition (and standard bureaucratic practices). In its insistence on context, history, and sociality, it radically opposes impersonal, regimented forms of rationality. Contextualists point out that the simplification of experience for convenience (of programmer or administrator) can become stifling.

Mechanism tends to be reinforced in situations where formal and calculative forms of thought dominate. It is not surprising then that contextualism sometimes casts itself as challenger to the major cultural tradition:

> We are familiar with Hume's dictum that works which contain no quantitative analysis or causal reasoning should be cast upon the fire, but equally we are all too familiar with that kind of research which contains nothing else. Let us then counter Hume with a challenge to the drabness of mechanical research: if we take in our hand any research report, let us ask, "Does it contain any metaphor or idea which reveals a reality deeper than the conventional one? No. Does it excite you to a moral involvement in the affairs with which it deals? No." Commit it then to the flames, for it is nothing but information that will soon be superseded by more information. (Bolton, 1987, p. 248)

Thus, contextualists criticize mechanistic practices that have become oppressive. More recently their research also offers revisions of how we think about cognition and intelligibility.

Mechanism's grip on the field continues to loosen. Echoing T. Winograd's early theme, psychologists such as Sarbin (1986a) have explored the "storied" nature of cognition. Rationality itself is being recognized as "divergent" and "pluralistic" (Shweder, 1986), and emphasis is being placed on "negotiated intelligibility" (Gergen, 1985). Unlike more defensive traditional psychologists, contextualists have the opportunity to encourage new voices and perspectives, many of which have been repressed by the dominance of the objectivist assumptions in psychology. In the last ten years, contextualism has fast become a substantial, exciting alternative to a disembodied, impersonal, and overly rational cognitive psychology. In the next three chapters I examine what these new contextualist projects entail experimentally and theoretically in the study of perception, memory, and categorization, including their strengths and limitations; how contextualism may change the social, political, and cultural context of cognitive psychology itself (especially its exclusivity) will be the subject of the final chapter.

3

Visual Perception: From Machinery of the Mind to Interaction with the World

... we break the mirror and climb into our vision.

— Marge Piercy, "The Provocation of a Dream"

At 7:30 a.m. on a school day, I look across the breakfast table and know that my five-year-old daughter Gemma is getting sick. Because she's talking and responding normally, most others would probably not see the slightly red upper-left cheek and the droop of her left eyelid. (And paradoxically, as a working mother with a busy day planned, I do not want to see this.) How can we explain such ordinary perceptual experiences, those that involve seeing, knowing, and acting? Contextualists would say that in this experience with my daughter, perceiving, acting, and knowing fuse into one meaningful event: I see her anew, as "to-be-cared-for-differently." In my perception of her, I am attuned to her illness through my past experiences with her; that is, I have developed finely tuned perceptual skills as a result of taking care of her over time. I "home in" on information directly available to me for action. For example, as I look upon her, one hand automatically reaches toward her forehead to check her temperature as the other turns the pages of my appointment book to see what cannot be canceled. What I see is also culturally framed and socially meaningful. I see with and through social relations and practices; for example, my husband or I rather than a grandmother must care for our sick child.

In contrast, many mechanists would argue that I don't see my daughter as getting-sick, not directly at least. Fragmented, meaningless stimuli impinge upon my senses. These signals are then transformed into representations, usually linguistically rendered in the form of propositions. Through the aid of cognitive elaboration, a representation of her is constructed, one based on past experiences I have had with her and have stored in memory. At this point some mechanists have trouble explaining just who or what sees these internal representations. In such mechanistic accounts, I act from an inference *that* she is sick. Then I draw another inference based on past experiences of myself as a mother of a getting-sick child, and so forth. In most mechanistic accounts of perception, memory and inference are the workhorses of perception. Perceptions are judgments made through formal, abstract processing. This memorial and linguistic reconstitution of experience deeply troubles contextualists. Why do we need to separate the seeing from the seen, the knowing from the known? Why can't we, as Piercy poetically suggests, simply climb into our vision?

Using the exposition of mechanism and contextualism provided in the previous chapter, I illustrate in this chapter the way these worldviews have implicitly guided theory and research in the study of perception. Traditional mechanistic explanations of perception based on empiricism and associationism have been revised historically, and these approaches have continued as the dominant influence on the study of perception in psychology (see Rock, 1975, 1984, for thorough historical overviews of the perception literature and Swartz, 1956; Royce, 1974, for good discussions of special philosophical issues involved in perception).

During the last ten years, the theories and research of neo-Gestalt, phenomenological, and ecological psychologists have gained increasing influence in the study of perception. In terms of the framework provided in the last chapter, these perspectives utilize, in varying degrees, a contextualistic worldview in psychology. Furthermore, they have so effectively challenged the classic empiricist explanation (the eye is a camera) that it has, by and large, been abandoned. But the assumption that the environment contains specific information that is elaborated upon, sorted, and stored in a fixed memory has persisted in many modern mechanistic accounts of perception. Connectionists have recently questioned this assumption about memory, and their research has led to reconsideration of the nature of perception (e.g., Marr, 1982; Rumelhart, et al., 1986). In their attempts to capture dynamic perceptual interactions, these models have some affinity with Gestalt psychology (Robertson, 1986, pp. 178–79) and are motivated by dilemmas raised by contextualistic critics.

Until very recently, however, mechanism legitimized the scientific study of perception by rigidly adhering to the methods of laboratory research that isolated or stripped the object of perception from its context and encouraged analytic processing through focus on stimulus features. Generally speaking, this body of research assumes that perceptual processing occurs in an internal mind; sense organs serve as a screen or mirror for impinging, meaningless stimuli which undergo elaboration and construction by cognition; and the goal of perception is the apprehension of static objects. In these theories, perception is studied as if it were an intellectual process (e.g., an inference) occurring in an isolated spectator. As we will see, contextualists find that this mechanistic account buries perception in cognition and bifurcates the perceiver and the world.

After summarizing the traditional mechanistic account of perception, I describe the early Gestalt challenge to this perspective. Ultimately, however, Gestalt psychology only anticipated contextualism. Mechanistic psychologists responded to Gestalt criticisms by turning to information processing to avoid problems in traditional accounts (see Massaro, 1987, pp. 7–17, for a clear, brief summary of psychophysical and information-processing approaches to perception). In the last twenty years, this development has been so influential in the study of perception that Fodor and Pylyshyn (1981) dub it the "establishment" view. To illustrate the contrasting contextualistic approach to perception, I use an experiment on "event perception" (Johansson, 1973) as a more recent contextualistic challenge to mechanistic assumptions about perception. During the late 1970s, a group of psychologists advanced an ecological theory of perception that stands in opposition to mechanistic establishment or information-processing accounts (e.g., Gibson, 1979; Lombardo, 1987; Mace, 1977; McCabe & Balzano, 1986; Reed, 1987a, b, 1988; Turvey, 1977; Turvey, et al. 1981). Much in this line of theorizing has strong contextualistic overtones. The controversy that it has generated about the nature of perception illustrates some of the main points of contention between contextualistic and mechanistic assumptions. In viewing perception as a dynamic, interactive process, the ecological movement expands and develops contextualism as it offers an exciting alternative to mechanistic explanations. There are, however, unresolved difficulties in ecological theories which I discuss in the final part of this chapter.

Early Mechanistic Views of Visual Perception

The origin of the traditional approach to visual perception that Gibson (1979) and others have challenged can be traced back to the philosophies of John Locke, Bishop George Berkeley, and David Hume, especially to Berkeley's *An Essay toward a New Theory of Vision* (1910). As I suggested in the last chapter, these empiricists held that all knowledge is gained through experience and that what constituted experience could be derived from basic elements or units (usually of sensation) and then organized or structured through association. For these thinkers, perceptual experience originates in sensations. For example, Locke (1959) states: "When I say the senses convey into the mind, I mean, they from external objects convey into the mind what produces there those perceptions. This great source of most of the ideas we have depending wholly upon our senses, and derived by them to the understanding, I call SENSATION" (p. 123). Because he developed a specific theory of vision to explain perception of depth, Berkeley has been the most influential philosopher in the psychological study of perception, so much so that his theory of perception "is still very much present in contemporary psychology" (Rock, 1975, p. 14; see Earhard, 1974; Hochberg, 1978, for other summaries of his influence).

Generally, empiricists such as Berkeley claimed that ideas are copies of sensations available from the external world (and held in memory). The mind is viewed as the famed tabula rasa. Their description of perception begins with the registering of sensations such as color patches on the retina of the eye. These units of sensation, however, cannot explain our ordinary perceptual experiences of, say, size, depth, distance, and position. How does the perceiver acquire this information? Like the other British Empiricists, Berkeley answered, "through association." In this view, the retinal image of an object is only two-dimensional, so through other sensory experiences such as touch, one learns to alter the two-dimensional stimulus so that it can be perceived three-dimensionally. Not a given in perception, depth must be learned. Julian Hochberg (1978) summarizes Berkeley's empiricist theory in this way: "our experiences of visual space would . . . consist of three kinds of elements: (1) the 'purely' visual sensations such as color patches . . . which are nonspatial; (2) the kinesthetic sensations from the muscles of accommodation and convergence; and (3) those memories of the previous kinesthetic sensations of reaching or walking that had become associated with the specific accommodation and convergence sensations, and with visual depth cues, to lend *spatial* meaning to both of them" (p. 62). Our past experiences modify and correct incoming sensory stimulation, which is meaningless in and of itself.

In Berkeley's theory the appropriate objects of perception (sense data) combine to form sensory "experience"; such combinations build up or accumulate over time. As a result of his emphasis on units of sensation, Berkeley (1929) maintains that the organism registers sensations passively and that the sensations themselves are inert. "All our ideas, sensations, notions, or the things which we perceive, by whatsoever names they may be distinguished, are visibly inactive: there is nothing of power or agency included in them. . . . there is nothing in them but what is perceived" (p. 137). The sensations that result in perception do not in themselves contain meaning; they may be taken as signs or cues, but they must be supplemented, usually through past associations. The retina functions like a camera or "picture plane onto which the world's light rays are projected" (Mace, 1974, p. 139, for historical examples of the poverty of stimulation in theories of perception). In this way Berkeley's theory places singular importance on the retinal image as the determinant for what is perceived, but this image is only an equivocal sign of the external world. Assumptions such as these had considerable influence on subsequent psychologists, most notably Hermann von Helmholtz.

Spurred by criticisms about the inadequacy of empirical accounts and by their appeals to innate processes in three-dimensional space perception, von Helmholtz (1884) reasserted the empiricist view, basing it on atomistic units of analysis and the principles of association. He claims, much like Berkeley, that our memories of movement and information from touch (all associated through experience) provide the basis for perception of visual stimuli. Given his empiricism, some kind of operation had to explain the transformations of the retinal image, which contained inadequate spatial information, to the final perception that contained complete information. For such an operation, von Helmholtz appeals to "unconscious inference."

In perception, von Helmholtz postulated an inference process that adjusts or corrects otherwise meaningless stimulation by connecting it to information stored in memory. Richard Gregory (1974) gives the following example of von Helmholtz's inference: "This retinal shape has (nearly) always occurred when there is an external table. This retinal shape is present. Therefore there is (probably) an external table" (p. 275). Of course in normal perceptual experience the perceiver is not aware of such an inference; perceptions appear to be immediately given because associations are learned so well. According to von Helmholtz, perception is indirect and mediated; unconscious inferences intervene between sensations and perceptions (see Hochberg, 1978, p. 60, for a fuller account). Aaron Ben-Zeev (1988) points out that such inferentially based explanations intellectualize perception; that is, "perception is explained by the reasoning process typical of thinking" (p. 489). Furthermore, these thinking processes are causal, temporal, and rule-bound in that they begin in sensations caused by physical objects and result in mental percepts.

Grounded in empiricism and associationism, such sensation–based theories of perception participate fully in a mechanistic worldview. As Pepper (1961) reminds us, for the mechanist, "only particulars exist" (p. 214). And, indeed, these early mechanists so privileged the particular that they were willing to live with a troubling consequence of their assumptions: the mentally processed world of association comes to substitute for the world of experience. In psychology, such assumptions about the evidence of experience corroborated already standard laboratory practices. Seeking to uncover the laws governing perception, experimentalists isolated both objects (or their parts) and the subject from the environmentally rich contexts in which perception naturally occurs. Using simple stimulus features such as lines, dots, or letters in tasks involving recognition or discrimination, psychologists studied perception statically (see Johansson, et al., 1980, for implications of this approach). In these studies, the stimulus is taken to be pure and invariant. That is, in order to trace the causal relation between the stimulus and the resulting percept, the researcher assumes the stimulus cannot be altered by the subject in the act of perception. Additionally, different organizational configurations cannot change the particulars that result in perception. Early in the history of the psychological study of perception, this latter consequence of empiricism led Gestalt psychologists to abandon traditional views about perception. How, they ask, could one overlook the effects of organization and form in perception?

Gestalt Challenges to Mechanism

The research of Gestalt psychologists demonstrated that the nervous system was more responsive to configurations or patterns than to their individual parts. Arguing against Berkeley, for example, Kurt Koffka (1930) states, "Our space perception in all three dimensions is the result of organized brain activity and . . . we can understand our space perception only in terms of organization, i.e., in terms of actual dynamic processes, not in terms of mere geometrical stimulus-sensation correlations" (p. 185). In stressing the form of the objects of perception, Gestalt psychologists pointed to the relationships between configurations in wholes rather than to the reductionistic analysis of wholes into their constituent parts. If little mosaic pieces form the configuration perceived, they asked, how is it that we perceive shifts in patterns of continuity rather than shifts in pieces? As Wolfgang Köhler (1930) claims, "The hypothesis of independent little parts is unable to give an explanation" (p. 148). Thus, the Gestalt psychologists regularly attacked the atomistic reductionism in the empiricist tradition (see R. M. Anderson, 1974, on the holistic-atomistic controversy in neuropsychology).

Contextualistic psychologists have appropriated many of the Gestalt arguments against mechanistic assumptions about perception and used many of the perceptual phenomena studied by the Gestalt psychologists to describe perception. Gestaltists and contextualists share some assumptions about the perceptual process itself. For example, like contextualism, Gestalt analysis starts from the whole and works down to the parts. The whole is experienced as coherent, all at once, and does not, as Lynn Robertson (1986) notes in a thoughtful overview of Gestalt psychology, "occur indirectly through a set of preconscious calculations in which parts [are] interrelated to build a whole" (p. 181). Unlike the mechanist who starts with the rudiments of experience (bare sensations, for example), the contextualist starts with the dynamic event. Qualitative changes in the strands of a perceptual event affect its entire context since relationships between the strands change. As Robertson notes, "The properties of the overall form [of a perceptual event] can change the *quality* of the perceived elements" (p. 172). Take, for example, one of the famous figure-ground reversibility cases, the picture of the young woman's face that from another perspective can be seen as an older woman's face. The contextualist claims that as the perceptual experience changes from face to face, the felt quality changes.

Although Gestalt psychology underscores the importance of global structures and the irreducible interrelatedness of parts within a whole, several of its tendencies prove troublesome for contextualists. For example, many Gestalt psychologists emphasized a dynamic, interactive view of the object of perception, but did not extend this view to the biological, social, and cultural contexts of perception. In Pepper's terms, they narrowed the event of perception. Much more than the Gestaltist, the contextualist points to the relational nature of perception and the mutuality of perceiver and perceived. The Gestaltists remained too heavily focused on the form of the perceptual object in isolation.

As a movement, Gestalt psychology did not develop coherent theoretical perspectives. A number of psychologists have argued that Gestalt experiments only identified serious deficiencies in the empiricist tradition and did not ultimately offer a viable metatheoretical alternative (Gibson, 1979, p. 140; Hochberg, 1974, p. 204; Wertheimer, 1974, p. 87). Most psychologists back away from the early, extreme Gestalt claims about perceptual space and their reduction of mental states to vague physiological processes. Robert Shaw and John Pittenger (1977) make the case this way: "While there is good reason to agree with the Gestaltists' claim that the classical view of perceptual space as an inert, absolute space is woefully inadequate and must be rejected, we need not revert to their view of perceptual space as a field of mysterious forces in the cortex where isomorphic representations of physical objects act upon each other" (p. 107). Pepper (1961, pp. 219–20) points to the source of metatheoretical confusion in Gestalt assumptions: mixing contextualistic and mechanistic assumptions leads to incoherence. He felt some Gestalt thinkers did not reframe what were essentially mechanistic assumptions. If *Gestalts* are viewed as basic building blocks in a determined system and/or as physiological correlates of mental states, then they preserve the mechanistic focus. They simply consolidate the more basic constituents characteristic of a more discrete mechanism. Thus, Gestalt psychology did not fully articulate a theoretically consistent view. Perhaps as a result of this failure, recent theories of cognition, Robertson (1986) points out, do not retain a full blown Gestalt psychology; rather "Gestalt psychology has been fractured and applied piecemeal in contemporary accounts" (p. 160).

Recent Mechanistic Revisions

Mechanistic psychologists responded to the Gestalt challenges by revising earlier mechanistic approaches. For example, Hebb's (1949) theory, based on neuropsychology, tried to take into account the configuration problems identified by the Gestaltists; thus, his theory deemphasizes the importance of sensations but still posits a basic analytic unit to which perceptual experience can be reduced. Located in the central nervous system, these units, called cell assemblies, function as building blocks necessary to constitute the object of perception. Through repetition, various patterns of assemblies are excited, associated, and learned. Cell assemblies develop for perceptual elements such as lines and angles, and then combine to form increasingly complex visual forms that spread throughout the cortex. Hebb's theory exemplifies the mechanistic account of holistic structural features in perception. Moored to empiricism, reductionism, and associationism, mechanists had to appeal to other mental operations, such as conceptual activity, to explain perception. Once again, for the mechanist, the input into the perceptual system is, in and of itself, deficient and in need of cognitive elaboration.

Modern mechanistic theories take as their starting point "the structured forms" of perception identified in the research of the Gestalt psychologists (K. Smith, 1987). These forms can be represented though computation in neurological models (as in Hebb) or through linguistic units such as words that fit into propositions in information-processing models. Such representational theories avoid the atomism of early sensation based theories of perception by focusing on the symbolic units and the inferential possibilities they offer. John Anderson (1980b), for example, states that it is "typical to think of mental data as coming in *pieces* or *units* or *chunks*. These are the 'packages' of data which the cognitive processes treat in an all-or-none manner" (p. 123). Defined and elaborated by their capacity to be held in working memory, such units can be represented in hierarchical knowledge structures. Explanations of how data are assembled in perception vary from mechanist to mechanist.

Most information-processing models of cognition supplement the inadequate stimuli (percepts) through bringing memorial or conceptual knowledge to bear on it in controlled, serial processing. Between the phenomenological experience and the physiological activity, it assumes a middle level of symbolic description, usually linguistic and propositional. To use the introductory example of my sick child, information processors assume that the red patch on my daughter's cheek registers on my retina, and my past experience turns that into words, sentences, and eventually propositions about my experience with my daughter to make it meaningful. Such accounts, however, are often ambiguous in the definitions of just what "it" is that gets perceived; in addition, the intense interest in computer models of processing often obscured the act of perception. Especially in early simulations, researchers used stimuli (e.g., lights, bells, letters, words) that were usually isolated from their natural context; these stimuli were then shown to be reconstructed, linguistically and logically, in knowledge hierarchies. Using this model becomes cumbersome when applied to ordinary perceptual experience. Do I, for example, have symbolic representations not only of my daughter's cheek but also of my own hand as it reaches out to touch my daughter's forehead? The model insists on metalevels of symbolic representation to account for cognition of simple experience, like rococo decoration on a New England salt box home.

In an attempt to address such limitations, Hayes-Roth (1977) bases her "knowledge-assembly" theory of the evolution of cognition on Hebb's theory of cell assembly activation: "Perception of a stimulus," she says, "causes activity in the representative cell-assemblies" (p. 262). The basic analytic unit, termed a *cogit*, is activated directly and assembled with associations (p. 261). Her theory, however, provides an alternative to the linear, serial processing characteristic of Hebb's theory. She claims that "the identities of functional units (cogits) change as learning progresses and that any structure imposed on the to-be-learned information influences the evolution of cogits" (p. 265). Hayes-Roth's assumption that the elements (cogits) have an active construal capacity in higher organizational processes departs from the traditional associationist account of perception in which the elements have, to use Berkeley's phrase, "nothing of power or agency included in them" (1929, p. 137). The theory, however, still remains mechanistic in its insistence on basic units which alter their character along strictly associationist lines. This is in part the result of a commitment to a formal, objective view of language and categorization in representing knowledge (see Lakoff, 1987b, for a discussion of the limitations of the objectivist approach to language).

Hayes-Roth's theory is somewhat unusual (some connectionists might say foresighted) in the information-processing literature because it envisions a physicalist or neurological instantiation of mechanism when dealing with perception while it plays up formal and symbolic operations when dealing with other aspects of cognitive behavior. In contrast to information-processing theorists' linguistically based, usually indirect, approaches to perception, some researchers in artificial intelligence had tried to construct seeing machines. The memories needed for such machines were so overwhelming, however, that programs could only recognize simple scenes made, for example, of toy blocks.

David Marr's (1982) research on perception raised serious doubts about conventional views of perception, both from traditional information-processing and artificial intelligence perspectives. Since I later use Gibson's (1979) theory as the springboard for discussion on contextualism in perception, I only briefly note the impact of Marr's work. Marr challenged the notion of memory as a fixed storehouse necessary for recognizing either the bare sensations of perception or the basic linguistic units that entered as input into most computer simulations. First, he argued that perception is complex: recognizing a face, for example, is a different task from seeing in three dimensions. Second, he claimed some perceptual processing occurred independently of memory through computations. Indeed, as Boden (1988) notes, "The type of connectionism represented by Marr's theory is the most elaborate and psychologically relevant example that yet exists" (p. 78).

Israel Rosenfield (1988) recognizes the radical implications of Marr's departure from tradition: "He did show how a procedure could derive a three-dimensional image from the two-dimensional retinal image. That this can be accomplished without matching sensory images to fixed memory images is a major blow to the . . . localizationist tradition," (which coincides with what I have been calling the mechanistic worldview) (p. 136). Rosenfield argues that Marr simply did not follow out the more radical possibilities implied by his theory, especially about memory: "The computational view . . . [does not] take into account the ways in which our individual histories, the contexts in which we act, can affect *what* we see at a particular moment" (p. 144).

Marr's work stimulated researchers to adopt new perspectives about perception. In addition, parallel distributed processing models of perception were motivated by frustrations with serial processing and its inefficiency in handling complex real world perception, particularly context sensitive knowledge. For example, Geoffrey Hinton, James McClelland, and David Rumelhart (1986) state, "Existing artificial intelligence programs have great difficulty in rapidly finding the schema that best fits the current situation. Parallel networks offer the potential of rapidly applying a lot of knowledge to this best-fit search" (p. 109). These computational models attempt to encompass more naturalistic perceptual experiences. (See Ben-Zeev, 1988, pp. 507–8, for a discussion of how connectionism could explain the development of a schema.) Moreover, such network models continue to raise a critical question: Can perception be described as "neurons connected to other neurons and dedicated to specific functions" (Gardner, 1985, p. 320) without an "intervening" symbolic processing level (essential in information-processing models) between the neurophysiological and the phenomenological levels?

Symbolic processing models of cognition are currently under fire. Arguing against representational theories from within the mechanist camp, Dennett (1991) questions the hypothetical workspaces or structures characteristic of most cognitive models—where are they located in the brain? Instead he argues that "all varieties of perception . . . are accomplished in the brain by parallel, multitrack process of interpretation and elaboration of sensory inputs. Information entering the nervous system is under continuous 'editorial revision' " (p. 111). In proposing an alternative computational model, he radically recasts the temporal and spatial relations traditionally assumed to exist between perception and other cognitive processes.

Coming from a very different orientation than Dennett, Varela, Thompson, and Rosch (1991) also question any cognitive model that reconstitutes experience through formal representations. In describing the visual system they appeal not to a grand, distributed network model but to ones in which subnetworks can be patched together in flexible, heterogeneous collections. They believe that a very promising line of cognitive science research is Rodney Brooks's work in robotics. His "decomposition makes no distinction between peripheral systems, such as vision, and central systems," and in his system "there is no single place where 'perception' delivers a representation of the world in the traditional sense" (cited in Varela, et al., 1991, p. 211). Recent arguments such as these suggest that theories of perception requiring elaborate symbolic reconstruction may no longer be required or plausible. It may be that information processing (as rule-based symbolic computation) is the last picture show, or is it?

Among cognitive scientists, in any case, "there is violent disagreement on the importance of parallelism" or connectionism for better understanding cognition (Bobrow & Hayes, 1985, p. 401). Persuasive defenders of establishment or classical cognitive science feel that neurological analogies will not enhance understanding of how the mind works (Fodor & Pylyshyn, 1988). In contrast, others feel the ability to focus on specialized problems will advance such an understanding (see Boden, 1988). Generally, cognitive scientists have turned to parallel processing out of frustration with the limits of earlier mechanistic accounts and the desire to meet "the intractable problem of context" (Givón, 1989, p. 30).

Some mechanists might describe their history, from inside, as steady progress toward a complete account of perception (see Valsiner, 1991, for a review of the use of progressive narrative form in psychological science). A theoretical pluralism urges, however, that this history has been as much response to good contextualist criticism as development of a consistent research program. Like their predecessors, modern mechanists must restrict their account of human experience through reduction to basic units, whether symbolic or neurological. This produces a certain methodological sophistication, for example, explicit models and precise measurements, but such formality and technicality often constrict what can be taken as evidence of cognitive experience.

The mechanist, then, makes the following assumptions about perception. (1) Whether in laboratory experiments or in information-processing models, perception can only be understood through a process of reduction or simplification by isolation. We perceive static objects or parts of objects. (2) If the goal of perception is the accurate apprehension of an object, then under controlled laboratory conditions, objects can be identified and controlled. Such attributes of the object as size, form, hue, location, and brightness are independent variables. (3) From simple objects and their attributes, more complex aspects of perception can eventually be explained through laws. Based on experimental findings, laws that govern perceptual learning can be stated, if not in pure descriptive

form, at least in terms of probability. These laws express regularities of perception: through measuring the attributes of the object
of perception, laws of "the seeing machine" can eventually be discovered. (4) Finally, in the earlier mechanistic explanation of perception, the subject is assumed to be passive. In information-processing accounts, where subjects appear more active, what enters our
senses is transformed and supplemented by our past experience.
Models of where the stimulus (information bit) goes when it enters
the system—for example, in short- and long-term memory or hierarchically determined categorial slots—emphasize what the subject
brings to bear on the stimulus. What the subject brings is almost
always linguistic. As Edward Reed (1988) notes, the signs or cues of
information-processing models "reduce perception to a form of
language" (p. 213). And in these models a "homunculus" (a tiny
perceiver of retinal images in the head) actually directs the processing (Neisser, 1967) before the completed perception is experienced.
Furthermore, the input (say, the words *red cheek*) cannot change in
the processing; if it gets lost or integrated in the processing system
(say, into metaphors such as candle or apple), then how can it come
out as recognizable output? Such constraints on the subject's actions
make contextualists skeptical that symbolic information processing
will ever yield insight into ordinary perceptual experiences.

The traditional view of perception saw the eye as a machine, a
camera. Gibson (1979) finds that such a view has permeated the
study of perception in psychology, much in the way von Helmholtz
first stipulated:

> The intent of vision is to see as distinctly as possible various
> objects or parts of an object in succession. This is accomplished
> by so pointing the eyes that an image of the given object is
> projected on the fovea of each retina. The governing of the
> ocular movements is wholly subordinated to this end; both eyes
> are adjusted and accommodated together so as to permit this
> light absorptive pointing. Any . . . eye movement not having
> for its end the attaining of distinct imaging of an object cannot
> be performed. (p. 206)

By specifying the structure of the objects of perception and the
abilities of the machine (such as the capacities of fibers to conduct
light), mechanists hoped they could explain and predict perceptual

phenomena. To this end, they held the eye still in experiments: "Vision is studied by first requiring the subject to fixate a point and then exposing momentarily a stimulus or a pattern of stimuli around the fixation point. . . . What the brain gets is something like a sequence of snapshots" (Gibson, p. 1). Even in recent mechanistic revisions, the "object" of perception takes center stage.

Recent Challenges to Mechanism

The contextualist reimagines the plot and recasts the characters. What if perception is not a matter of a spectating mind apprehending a static object? What if it is instead a matter of an active organism apprehending as it participates in an unfolding event? Contextualists define events flexibly, as episodes, patterns, experiences, for example. Hoffman and Nead (1983) note, "Any description of an event is tied to the observer's purpose and method. . . . A critical aspect of events as contextualism defines them is the denial of permanent structures" (p. 518). There may be invariants in perceptual experience, but even these will change over time and with history. An event is never finally reducible to a series of movements by static objects. The participant in an event cannot easily detach him- or herself from the ongoing drama of the event.

Johansson's (1973) experiment on motion perception illustrates particularly well this principle of contextualistic interpretation of an event in perception. He attached small light bulbs to the main joints (ankles, knees, shoulders, elbows, and wrists) of people who were then filmed walking in a darkened room. Subjects unfamiliar with these patterns (school-aged youngsters) were presented a film of those light patterns for very short intervals. According to Johansson (1979), "[Forty percent] of the subjects perceived the dot pattern as a walking person at the 0.1-sec interval and no one needed more than 0.2-sec for this perceptual organization of the moving dots" (p. 100). The perception of the walking person is nearly instantaneous. In another part of the experiment, when some of the cues were removed, subjects still recognized the pattern but made adjustments. For example: "[When the camera followed the moving person so that there was no forward motion of the image] some of the Ss also spontaneously described the event as a walking on some kind of moving belt. The [invisible] ground then was experienced as

moving backward" (p. 209). The basic, original perceptual experience remained resilient in the face of cue modification.

The traditional, mechanistic image-cue model of perception
becomes extremely limited in explaining experimental findings
such as these. In studies of stroboscopic motion, the mechanistic
experimenter assumes that the perceiver views a series of static
images, each of which is stored in memory. As Michael Turvey
(1977) notes, in this approach, perception of motion is concep-
tualized as a deduction from sequences of static arrangements. A
traditional, associationist account of Johansson's findings would
have to assume the following stages: each element (dot) is registered
on the retina and its position held in memory; as each new dot is
added, a pattern emerges inside the perceiver (i.e., represented in
memory); this pattern has been experienced in the past and has
become associated with a certain body movement; a deduction or
inference is then made and the pattern recognized. But Johansson
wants to argue, on the contrary, that patterns of movements contain
instantaneously recognizable meanings. The tremendous mathematical complexity of the relations between dots, and hence the
extreme difficulty of representing what is going on, make the
mechanist's explanation—that a sequence of snapshots of dots of
light become joined together to form a meaningful perception (such
as a walking person)—implausible and ad hoc.

According to Johansson and his colleagues (1980), movement
creates an optic flow that can be seen as a perspective transformation. He and his colleagues studied, for example, the relations
between dots set into motion. In examining the motion in the
patterns, he found (based on vector analysis) that the transformations contain information about space and depth perception. Moreover, they argued, "the so-called projective properties, which
remain invariant under perspective transformations of a figure, are
abstracted" (p. 31). That is, one can perceive patterns in motion,
such as swinging. Simply stated, transformations are interrelated
into patterns, and such transformations give the organism considerable information in the experience of perception itself (as opposed
to the mediational theories that assume the source of perceptual
stimulation is somehow deficient). The dots are not just aggregates
of meaningless stimuli registered sequentially.

In interpreting this experiment, the mechanist comes up against
the problem of explaining the coherence of the perceptual experi-

ence. Certainly with simple types of motion patterns, association can be appealed to as a viable explanation of organization; however, given the tremendously complex nature of real motion mathematically, such an appeal becomes overwhelmingly complicated, particularly in accounting for new perceptual experiences. Consider even slight changes in the movement from walking to jumping or skipping, each of which produces distinct perceptual experiences. To be theoretically consistent, strict associationists cannot recognize any pattern or significant unit beyond the particulars they have stipulated.

Johansson thus broke with the traditional mechanistic world-view in psychology by shifting assumptions: What if the goal of perception is not the registering of such particulars in experience? What if, in this case, vision is attuned to spatial changes over time by an engaged and active organism perceiving an already meaningful world? Johansson's experiment points to the richness and meaningfulness of what we perceive as being immediately apprehensible and to the interconnection among the parts (see his 1979 summary of this experiment). In terms of Pepper's framework, this represents a metatheoretical shift from mechanism to contextualism. Characteristically, this new movement, called "event perception" or "ecological optics" (Gibson, 1979), turns to ecologically meaningful events, such as walking. The unit for analysis dramatically shifts from isolated objects to real life processes.

In mechanistic studies of perception, experimenters tried to reduce perception to its basic particulars or units (such as the spots in Johansson's experiment), regardless of their final composition. In contrast, the flow model assumes that perception begins with the recognition of interrelations among patterns (such as a walker's gait), especially those that are ecologically given in experience. Such a model goes beyond the Gestalt account of form perception in assuming that perception occurs in the flow of the event over time rather than in the apprehension of form in and of itself. The shift in the unit of analysis, Johansson (1979) and Gibson (1979) note, underscores a shift from physics to biology as the model for scientific analysis. Gibson (1979) states, "The size-levels of the world emphasized by modern physics, the atomic and cosmic, are inappropriate for the psychologist. We are concerned with things at the ecological level, with the habitat of animals and [human beings]" (p. 9). The ecological psychologist studies human experiences, not isolated bits that are not longer recognizable.

The relation between the stimulus or input of perception and the perceiver also changes dramatically in this new "ecological" approach to perception. Gibson (1979) is the best known advocate of this movement in America. (For an overview of Gibson's and Johansson's collaboration, see Reed, 1988; for a brief comparison and contrast of their views, see Johansson, et al., 1980.) Gibson looked afresh at the stimulus/perceiver relationship (although, as we will see, much in his views was anticipated by Dewey's essay on the reflex arc decades earlier). Contained in the patterns of movements and their interrelations as they flow over time, the stimulus information is "picked up," to use Gibson's term, by the perceiver directly. In lived experience, the goal of perception is hardly ever the apprehension of static, permanent objects; rather the goal is one of ecological relationship, in that the organism apprehends or perceives meaning while acting. Gibson argues that perception occurs in a changing flow of stimulation, which has ecological meaning for the organism. Gibson reinforces Johansson's (1973) view: there is a richness of stimulus information available to the perceiver prior to any "processing."

The traditional mechanistic model assumed that stimuli were registered passively and that association from past experience had to embellish them before perceptual recognition could occur. This traditional account of perceptual processing has been referred to as "indirect" perception because the perceiver only "sees" the stimulus internally (i.e., through memorial representation). The ecological theorists suggest that something other than a successive remembering and adding of positions of elements occurs in perception. Individual researchers investigating event perception explain the alternative to the traditional processing model somewhat differently. As I later argue, within the contextualistic framework, the role of the organism in event perception literature has remained theoretically problematic. (See Johansson, 1979, for an account of what is abstracted in perception; Varela, et al., 1991, for a summary of what they term an "enactive" approach; Winograd & Flores, 1986, pp. 38–53, for a summary of Maturana's biologically based theory of perception.) The ecological theorists unite, however, in arguing that the information for perceptual recognition exists not inside the perceiver's head but in the flow of stimulus information and in the irreducible transactions between the organism and its environment. Hence their theory of perception is commonly referred to as more "direct." The information is contained in the event, which includes the actions of the perceiver in the situation. In addition, the world already has meaning for the perceiver, meaning that the empiricist obliterates.

As Johansson's experiment confronts mechanism from a contextualistic perspective, it also expands and refines the contextualistic view of perception. Basically, the experiment illustrates much of Pepper's description of contextualism. For example, the organization and instantaneous recognition of a walking person from a series of movements of small spots indicates that the quality of the event is noticed rather than elements or details. The textures of the event are the patterns of movement and their interrelations, and these spread over time. Further, as Pepper (1961) notes: "[Contextualism] denies that a whole is nothing but the sum of its parts. It even denies that a whole is a sort of added part like a clamp that holds together a number of blocks. A whole is something immanent in an event and is so intuited, intuited as the quality of that very event" (p. 238). The experimental work of ecological psychologists has demonstrated the importance of the environmental context of perception and has opened up a new way of analyzing the world that realistically describes ordinary perception. As I urge at the end of this chapter, other contextualists also remind us that ecological habitat is not the only given in perception; culture and language participate in perception as well. For example, a contextualist might point to the "eventfulness" of the person walking in terms of its suggestiveness or ripeness for narrative description and elaboration (readings of the event) (Bruner, 1986; Sarbin, 1986a). That is, situated in culture, we also apprehend that the walking is "to" or "from" someone or someplace, or that it is dejected, or saucy. To explore more thoroughly the recent research on event perception and its elaboration of a contextualistic worldview, I turn to Gibson's (1979) theory of ecological optics.

A Contextualistic Reading of Gibson's Theory of Perception

In his book *The Ecological Approach to Visual Perception* (1979), Gibson emphatically abandons mechanism and lays out a new approach to perception (see Lombardo, 1987; Reed, 1988, for accounts of the development of Gibson's thought and the historical, social, and political influences that shaped his theory of perception). In questioning the appropriateness of the traditional physical sciences model as a basis for investigating perception and arguing for an ecological model, Gibson states, "The mutuality of animal and environment is not implied by physics and the physical sciences. The basic concepts of space, time, matter, and energy do not lead naturally to the organism-environment concept or to the concept of a species and its habitat" (p. 8). In adopting an ecological model as the basis for investigating and understanding perception, Gibson develops a set of categories and assumptions that extends contextualism.

Gibson protested the mechanistic account because it decontextualized perception and stripped it of its biological significance. The role of the environment in its fullness and totality is central to the contextualistic worldview. Noting the falsely elevated status of the perceptual object in psychological theory, for example, Dewey (1938) states, "In actual experience, there is never any such isolated singular object or event; *an* object or event is always a special part, phase, or aspect, of an environing experienced world—a situation" (p. 67). Contextualists such as Dewey stress the complexity of any situation. Cognition is seat`d in the already ongoing, complex interactions between the world and living creatures; we are, to use Geertz's (1973) phrase, "suspended in webs of significance," both ecologically and culturally.

In Gibson's theory the environment "refers to the surroundings of those organisms that perceive and behave, that is to say, animals" (p. 7). The environment consists of structured units embedded or imbricated in other units. In a definitively contextualistic description, Gibson states: "There are forms within forms both up and down the scale of size. Units are nested within larger units. Things are components of other things. They would constitute a hierarchy except that this hierarchy is not categorical but full of transitions and overlaps. Hence, for the terrestrial environment, there is no special proper unit in terms of which it can be analyzed once and for all" (p. 9). The organism's perceptual system has evolved to experience collaboratively this environment with its overlapping and nested units. "The words *animal* and *environment* make an inseparable pair. Each term implies the other" (Gibson, p. 8). Indeed, Gibson argues that senses should be defined as perceptual systems; that is, as active perceivers we do not simply receive information into our senses, but with our bodies explore our environment in ways that allow us to detect information skillfully. Perceptual systems respond not to static objects but to natural events occurring in the environment. Gibson states, "We perceive . . . processes, changes, sequences" (p. 12). The world we perceive is bathed in light. Gibson stresses how much information (about textures and edges, for example) is available in the light, specifically in what he terms the "ambient optic array" (p. 51).

As opposed to radiant light, which causes illumination, ambient light results from illumination and comes to a particular point of observation from all directions; it "makes available information about reflecting surfaces" (p. 64). As organisms sensitive to patterns of energy, we delineate relative persistences in our environments: medium (e.g., air or water), substance (e.g., the ground), and surface (e.g, of a given substance such as a cliff). Ambient light can be structured by the surfaces in an optic array which changes as the observer moves through the environment. But "one arrangement does not become a wholly different arrangement by a displacement of viewpoint," according to Gibson (p. 73), because certain features remain "invariant," that is, they persist over relatively longer periods of time. The horizon, for example, an invariant, is almost always present in any pattern, no matter how the observer moves. Perspective structure (e.g., information the perceiver has about locomotion) and invariant structure (e.g., what the perceived brings in terms of layout) provide different kinds of information. Gibson defines perceiving as a registering of certain definite dimensions of invariance in the stimulus flux together with definite parameters of disturbance. The invariants are invariants of structure, and the disturbances are disturbances of structure. The structure, for vision, is that of the ambient optic array" (p. 249).

Gibson also stresses that animate creatures change while maintaining their integral features. Often this change comes through in lived experience as a disturbance in the environment, as in my example of seeing changes in my daughter as she gets sick. In this situation I detect changes in her that evoke exploratory perceptual action, and such exploration leads to an awareness of my own bodily movements as the caretaker-of-a-getting-sick daughter. Perception is thus always part of a transactional event and involves skills developed over time. The contextualist argues that the situatedness of one's perception (being at a breakfast table on a busy school day) contributes to its particular meaningfulness and immediacy; in other contexts, the qualitative perceptual experience would be different.

The ambient optic array, which specifies information in the environment, affords information for perception. The concept of affordances reveals Gibson's view of the mutuality of an animal and its environment. Stated simply, affordances are those relative invariants in the environment that suggest action, "offerings that can be perceived and used by observers" (Reed, 1988, p. 280). Thus, for example, Gibson describes flat surfaces as "walk-on-able," "climb-on-able," or "fall-off-able" relative to the perceiving animal (p. 128). Certain objects afford grasping while others are too large, too hot, too slick; a cave may afford shelter but not a food supply. What the environment affords one species, it may not afford to another species. Gibson intends the concept of affordance to capture the transactional nature of perceptual experience by refusing to make affordances either subjective or objective. Because he does not have a contextualist theory of language, however, his explanations of the meaning of affordance have led to misunderstandings and to serious criticisms of his theory as a whole. His critics assume Gibson is a naive realist, a view easily discounted by simple examples often cited in the history of philosophy. Any adequate contextualist theory must interrelate biological and cultural influences in perception.

In identifying some compatibilities of Gibson's theory with contextualism, I have summarized only part of his complex and detailed ecological approach to perception (e.g., I have left out concepts such as gradient and effectivity). Its contrast to mechanism is dramatic. In bifurcating the perceiver from the world, the mechanist places control (in information processing, "central control") in some region of the mind of the perceiver, who, standing alone in the physical world, is "buffeted" by meaningless stimuli. This is the mind's I which, distanced from its own embodiment and environment, enjoys such improverished relations with the world that "*ad hoc* hypotheses [are] required to explain or reconstitute meaningful human involvement" (Wertz, 1987, p. 116). Here perception is a process of rational, often formal "reconstruction."

In contrast to more formal reconstructions, Dennett's (1991) mechanist revisions go a long way toward a looser conception of the evidence a science of the mind can consider. He adopts a method he calls heterophenomenology, which permits what he calls subjective reports about consciousness. He sees his challenge as "construct[ing] a theory of mental events, using the data that scientific method permits. Such a theory will have to be constructed from the third-person point of view, since *all* science is constructed from that perspective" (p. 71). Thus, he can give his subjects supportive sympathy for their convictions about their engagements in the world while the heterophenomenologist, with "the discreet charm of a [neutral] anthropologist," can collect the stories about mental events (such as perception). But this third person neutrality has a peculiar twist that makes him jumpy; for example, he recognizes that he "risks offending the subjects" (p. 96). And he is right to be skittish. Who would accept such a "report" in place of real world deliberations other than a presumptively neutral anthropologist? When we are in problematic situations, we want people to engage with us in mutual exploration of the situation and give it different cognitive renderings. Giving up the third-person method, however, does not mean giving up on objectivity. "It means only that we need to use objective standards that combine the first- and third-person points of view, as they are in fact combined in the ordinary concepts for attribution of conscious states that we all employ without difficulty, and that we use to correct experiential descriptions by ourselves and others" (Nagel, 1991, p. A14). Dennett's mind is still the mechanist I, thinking about his past perceptual experiences in third person (pp. 406–10).

In contrast to such accounts of perceptual experiences, contextualists stress the embodied, transactional nature of perception. In many ways Gibson attempts to reunite the perceiver with the perceived in mutual relationship. With his concept of affordances, he endows the environment with meaning and information, "the inexhaustible reservoir that lies open to further scrutiny" (p. 243). Reed (1988) extends Gibson's concept even further by noting that Gibson portrayed a single environment of and for all observers (not the lone individual observer in mechanistic perception theories). He states, "Gibson could conceive of affordances not as relations between things, but *as facts of the environment of all observers that can be used by particular observers*" (p. 294). Even though we cannot be physically in the same place at the same time, we can come close to perceiving from the same point of view because the environment affords meaning reliably and consistently. Unlike the isolated perceiver in the mechanistic account who builds an internal, disembodied world, in Gibson's theory, perceivers can form a community actively engaged in investigation. As Shaw and Pittenger (1977) suggest, "An ecologically based theoretical language would be in the first person plural mode of discourse" (p. 109)—what I call the mind's we of contextualism.

In Gibson's theory, as in all contextualistic theories, the organism interacts with its environment in mutually reciprocal exchanges, including perception of other people. The organism's perceptual systems "explore," "hunt," "scan," "detect," "pick-up," and "sweep the visual field" (Gibson, 1979). The total organism, not just its eyes, perceive. According to Gibson, in traditional theories, "the eye is considered to be an instrument of the mind, or an organ of the brain. But the truth is that each eye is positioned on a trunk that is positioned on legs that maintain the posture of the trunk, head, and eyes relative to the surface of support. Vision is a whole perceptual system" (p. 205). All the components involved in this visual system actively explore the environment (p. 218). Thus, Gibson states, "Perceiving is a keeping-in-touch with the world, an experiencing of things rather than a having of experiences" (p. 239). This view of perception echoes the naturalistic view central in contextualist thought. For example, Dewey (1951) states, "Every experience in its direct occurrence is an interaction of environing conditions and an organism. As such it contains in a fused union some*what* experienc*ed* and some processes of experienc*ing*" (p. 544). In contrast to the traditional account of perception which claimed that sensations are sequentially registered and then processed or filtered, Gibson claims "the perceptual system simply extracts the invariants from the flowing array; it *resonates* to the invariant structure or is *attuned* to it" (p. 249). Although identified as a theory of direct perception, it stresses perceiver activity and environmental context.

A number of interesting commentaries on Gibson's theory of direct perception summarize the philosophical derivation of the term *direct* (e.g., Lombardo, 1987; Michaels & Carello, 1981; Shaw & Bransford, 1977). In passing I note that Gibson's argument for direct perception does not imply simple perception. Rather he claims that the perceptual system can directly detect the rich, complex information in the environment and that the psychologist does not have to evoke some type of mentalistic processing (such as deduction or inference) to account for perception. The information is contained, not inside the perceiver's head, but in the light, in the ambient array. The perceiver picks this up directly; "information does not have to be stored in memory because it is always available" (Gibson, 1979, p. 250). In that Gibson rejects "the assumption that perception is the processing of inputs [sensory or afferent nerve impulses to the brain]," his theory "implies a redefinition of the so-called higher mental processes" (p. 255).

Not surprisingly, Gibson's theory of perception provoked strong critical responses from mechanists, and Gibson's followers have been engaged in several heated debates about perception. The issues at stake are clearly evidenced in the debate between Jerry Fodor and Zenon Pylyshyn (1981) and Gibson followers Michael Turvey, Robert Shaw, Edward Reed, and William Mace (1981) (see also the debate between Heil, 1979 and Reed & Jones, 1981; Heil, 1981 and Wilcox & Katz, 1981b).

The Gibsonians Versus the Mechanists: Blinded by the Light or Groping in the Dark?

Strong proponents of the establishment view of perception, Fodor and Pylyshyn (1981) find Gibson's constructs—especially invariant and pickup—highly questionable and objectionable. They argue that these terms fail to constrain his use of the term *direct* in direct perception. For example, they state that "Gibson's account of perception is empty *unless* the notions of 'direct pickup' and of 'invariant' are suitably constrained. For patently, if *any* property can count as an invariant, and if any psychological process can count as the pickup of an invariant, then the identification of perception with the pickup of invariants excludes nothing" (p. 142). After analyzing possible ways of defining these notions to avoid trivialization, Fodor and Pylyshyn conclude that, within Gibson's theoretical framework, there is no satisfactory way. "It looks as though whatever is perceived is *ipso facto* the proper object of a perceptual system, and whatever is the proper object of a perceptual system is *ipso facto* perceived directly; we have, in particular, no independent constraints on the individuation of perceptual systems that will permit us to break into this chain of interdefinition" (p. 152). They argue that only the information-processing account which depends on inferential mediation can suitably constrain Gibson's use of the term *direct* (p. 141). Perception, then, involves representation and matching through some kind of computational processes.

Fodor and Pylyshyn's arguments about the nature of perception depend on a restricted class of properties and mechanisms called transducers. "Transducers are technically defined as mechanisms which convert information from one physical form to another" (1981, p. 157). Establishment theories (e.g., information-processing theories) contend that we directly perceive properties to which given transducers respond, such as the retina for vision (p. 150). The retina, in visual perception, detects properties of the light, and then properties of the layout are perceived through an inference based on "(usually implicit) knowledge of the correlations that connect them" (p. 165). Properties of the light and properties of the layout are, according to Fodor and Pylyshyn, different states of mind: "Some process *must* be postulated to account for the transition from one of these states of mind to the other, and it certainly looks as though the appropriate mechanism is inference" (p. 166). Dewey (1938) would identify such a view as "representative realism." In Fodor's (1983) more modern representative view of perception, as opposed to, say, von Helmholtz's, the class of properties that perceptual organs respond to can be more than sensations; they can be *any* individual particular, perceptually discriminated. The red patch on my daughter's face can be, for example, my daughter's cheek, if it is converted into a proposition.

Fodor and Pylyshyn, then, advocate an indirect theory of perception, an account that relies intrinsically on memory. What is stored in memory constitutes, through a computational transformation of stimuli, the meaningfulness in our perceptual experiences. As Fodor and Pylyshyn summarize their main position, "Since the Establishment holds that the psychological mechanism of inference is the transformation of mental representations, it follows that perception is in relevant respects a computational process" (1981, p. 140).

In early accounts such as Neisser's (1967), theorists had to admit that a someone or something, commonly called a homunculus (or the ghost in the machine), had to "see" the representation, or the final product of processing. In information-processing models, the perceiver starts with meaningless units. The question, then, is, who sees the result of the processing? Of course, this leads to an infinite regress, since someone else has to see what the last homunculus saw. Fodor (1983) tries to exorcise the traditional homunculus by making lower level input analysis a matter of quick, unconscious inferential processing. In his view modules are computational subsystems that come hard-wired in the system. Encapsulated, they are unaffected by meaning and context. But Dennett (1991) argues that in artificial intelligence research "every theory, from the most rigorously neuroanatomical to the most abstractly artificial, posits some such units [homunculi, demons, or agents] and then theorizes about how larger functions can be accomplished by organizations of units performing smaller functions" (p. 262). Fodor's (1983) theory assumes that in perception inference links the stimulus with the resulting, centrally processed representation (even though Fodor believes central processing cannot be formally explained). "It is here that the notion of inference as *computation*, and the metaphor of the mind as computer, is so crucial. Since inferences can be carried out computationally and computations can be carried out by what is an entirely physical entity (as computers are), an inferential theory of language perception remains within a physicalist ontology. No ghosts are left in the machine to explain its inference-making behavior" (K. Smith, 1987, p. 171). Yet Fodor (1983) admits, "The ghost has been chased further back into the machine, but it has not been exorcised" (p. 261). (Dennett, 1991, believes his type of materialistic reduction exorcises it.) Fodor severely limits his claims to the forms of linguistic phenomena; he does not make claims for all thought and action. Given the limitations of Fodor's theory, "cognitive psychology is not now and is not ever likely to be a psychology of behavior (or experience) in context" (K. Smith, 1987, p. 179).

The contextualist feels such limitations are fatal. Gibson's theory may have limitations, but his theory invites discussions about the role of embodied action and lived experience in perception. As I show, Gibson's theory is vulnerable to criticism because he excludes an adequate account of the role of cognition in the organism-environment transaction (see Cutting, 1982, 1986; W. Epstein, 1977; Haber, 1985; Rock, 1977, Varela, et al., 1991, for critical reviews along this line). Mechanists such as Fodor explain elements of knowledge that are most easily construed as formal, objective, disembodied, and detached from experiential and pragmatic roots. (Thus, for example, Fodor and Pylyshyn would want to frame my example with my getting-sick daughter propositionally and inferentially.) How do Gibson's defenders respond to Fodor and Pylyshyn's attack?

Turvey, Shaw, Reed, and Mace (1981) respond to Fodor and Pylyshyn (1981) by reframing the theoretical issues. For example, Fodor and Pylyshyn state that they wish to read Gibson in a conciliatory fashion; and Turvey and his colleagues make clear that no such reconciliation is likely. They write, for example, "It is *not* obvious that Fodor and Pylyshyn are addressing the same *subject matter* [italics added] as Gibson and the proponents of his ecological approach. To the extent that they are not their arguments against Gibson miss the mark" (p. 238). Their statement contrasts with Fodor and Pylyshyn's conclusion about Gibson's theory: "Missing the point about inference, missing the point about mental representations, and missing the point about intentionality are thus all aspects of missing the same point" (p. 194). Gibson and Fodor and Pylyshyn address different types of perception: Fodor and Pylyshyn's kind of perception (in *percepts*) is whatever eventuates in a perceptual judgment of belief. Gibson's kind of perception, in contrast, is that which eventuates in the 'proper' adjustment of oriented (to various levels of the environment) activity" (Turvey, et al., p. 241). Linguistic and cognitive, perception becomes a matter of judgment and assertion. Fodor and Pylyshyn's canonical example is Bernard Berenson, who "managed to be so good at perceiving (i.e., telling just by looking) that some painting was an authentic Da Vinci" (1981, p. 142). In contrast, in an effort to better understand perception in the total organism-environment ecosystem, Turvey and his colleagues (1981) take their examples from animal behavior, which they portray as finely attuned to its surroundings. This disagreement persists—at the level of worldviews—between advocates of contextualism and mechanism.

Both sets of authors agree that the central problem for a theory of perception is to explain how past knowledge enters into perceptual experience. In the information-processing view, past knowledge (stored in memory) operates on the incoming sensory data through inferential reasoning. As Fodor and Pylyshyn state, "This is where the mental representation construct does its main theoretical work. . . . It thus comes to grips with the fact that the cognitive consequences of perception depend not just on whether the world is seen, but also on how it is seen" (p. 190). But how does one accumulate conceptual knowledge, propositionally formulated? Past knowledge enters experience in representational form: "the mind is a mechanism for the manipulation of representations, and how what you see affects what you know is primarily a matter of how you represent what you know and see" (Fodor & Pylyshyn, 1981, p. 195).

In the ecological view, the adaptation of the organism to its environment over time actually alters perceptual and cognitive processes, which are defined not as mechanical but as skillful. As Turvey, Shaw, Reed, and Mace argue, "In the Establishment's terms, the doctrine of meaningless 'inputs' . . . requires that 'inputs' be associated with meaningful concepts" (1981, p. 285). But how do the concepts get formed if input is meaningless? The only type of developmental explanation the mechanist has is associationism, but, as we have seen, this becomes very limited when dealing with complex perceptual experiences. Reasoning processes (needed in inference), for example, do not evolve over time or with use (see Ben-Zeev, 1988; Markova, 1982, for further discussions of this problem). The ecological view holds that organisms become more aware of information in the environment; they become more skillful detectors through action, which makes more information available. Contextualists such as Merleau-Ponty (1964b) argue that perception can be linguistic, but can also be "precognitive," that is, precategorial, preobjective, and nonlinguistic. As perceivers, we have available in perception a noninferential awareness of the world.

The crux of this debate, then, concerns the nature and role of representation and inference in mental life. Its disputes carry over into conflicting theories of memory, as we will see in the next chapter. Contextualists, of course, believe that one can have and use representations; they simply wish to avoid any such necessary mediation in ordinary perception. Dewey (1938), for example, argues that the fallacy of representative realism lies in the hypostatization of a representation: "[Representative realism] views representative power as an inherent property of sensations and ideas as such, treating them as 'representations' in and of themselves. Dualism, or bifurcation of mental and physical existence, is a necessary result, presented, however, not as a result but as a given fact" (p. 524). Those who now advance Gibson's view (e.g., Reed, 1988; Turvey, et al., 1981) no longer posit Gibson's (1979) phrase, "information in the light," as critical to developing an ecological theory of perception. (As Fodor and Pylyshyn argue, that concept suggests a simpleminded empiricism.) Turvey, Shaw, Reed, and Mace expand Gibson's theory through an account of the natural laws governing organism-environment interactions. (These are not the laws of the physical machine but of biological adaptation.) Contextualists agree that examples from animal behavior can illustrate the transactive relationship inherent in organism-environment interactions. But a theory of perception must also include human experience, namely, language and culture. Contextualists work to enhance ecological potential to situate perception in the natural world while simultaneously avoiding the reduction of perception to biological functioning alone.

A Contextualistic Transformation of Gibson's Theory

Gibson's criticisms of traditional image-cue theories (theories which, I have argued, assume a mechanistic stance) directly parallel those of a contextualist. Even before the publication of his last book in 1979, his earlier work challenged a mechanism that had overgrown its boundaries through increasing reliance on technical and abstract explanations of higher mental processes. Gibson shares with contextualists a realism in which, to cite Dewey (1938), "there is a natural world that exists independently of the organism, but this world is *environment* only as it enters directly and indirectly into life-functions" (p. 33). Additionally, his naturalistic description of the environment as an ecologically rich source for perceptual information; his concept of a perceptual system which encompasses the organism's total functioning; his recognition of perception as an active, exploratory process; and his identification of the affordances of the environment—these theoretical insights are central to contextualistic thought.

However, despite such similarities as these, Gibson's theory poses a central dilemma for contextualists—the way in which he postulates the environment's contributions seems to truncate the role of the organism in perception. That is, his theory seems to ignore the culturally given world and its public symbolic structures. Contextualism describes perception as "a first opening on things without which there would be no objective knowledge" (Merleau-Ponty, 1962, p. 62), but the contextualist must also give an account of the relation between perception and cognition. For example, in Gibson's theory, what is the relation between imagination and perception? The lacunae in Gibson's thought allow for readings of his work as an argument that culture is merely a smokescreen for the biological world.

In presenting his theory, Gibson continually stresses the importance of the environment in perception, in part because his goal is to rid psychology of theories in which the perceiver constructs the environment from insufficient stimuli; that is, he wished to reject all appeals to subjective representation. What emerges from his description, however, is an image of perceiving organisms sanguinely moving about their environment picking up—without much difficulty—the rich information completely specified in the array of ambient light. He (1979) states, for example, "Perceiving gets wider and finer and longer and richer and fuller as the observer explores the environment" (p. 255). As his supporters point out:

> The long-overdue attention that Gibson and his followers have paid to the role of the environment has been misconstrued by some critics to indicate that the animal plays no role in the theory. Some have even gone so far as to say that Gibson's is no more than a "black box" account of perceiving. . . . Such an interpretation is puzzling in light of the emphasis which ecological psychologists place on mutuality, compatibility, and reciprocity that characterize the animal-environment system. (Michaels & Carello, 1981, p. 165)

Although Gibson does stress mutuality, he only hints at how social, historical, political, and cultural influences contribute to perception. As Neisser (1976) asks of Gibson's theory, "What kinds of cognitive structure does perception require" (p. 19)? Even though they are committed to novelty and change, contextualists recognize that knowledge can be structured and represented. "How does contextualism justify its use of particular representations" (Hoffman & Nead, 1983, p. 550)?

Gibson does not attribute much activity to the organism outside the biological or organic realm. Even at the biological level, contextualists note, actions can be shaped by culture: worms afford edibility in some cultures and not in others. Reed (1988) defends Gibson's theory by suggesting that Gibson (1980) was beginning to refine this side of the perceptual story. To illustrate Gibson's recognition of subjective factors in perception, Reed quotes: "In humans the social and individual processes are thoroughly mixed" (p. 307). To make this insight concrete, however, ecological psychologists must be able to explain how, for example, a paper cup might be seen as *crushable* in an affluent culture that tolerates disposability but as *permanent* in a culture that values preservation. Working out non-dualistic, nonobjectivist alternatives will require community effort (see, for example, Shaw & Hazelett, 1986, for a recent Gibsonian account of the role of action and perception in knowledge; see M. Johnson, 1987; Winograd & Flores, 1986, for accounts of the difficulties in working against the rationalist, objectivist tradition). But it is because of Gibson's work that contextualist psychologists studying perception can bring their ideas and differences to a home.

A number of contextually oriented thinkers from many different disciplines are investigating the organism's contribution to the transactional cycle (see, especially, Hoffman and Nead, 1983). Many of them honor the work of Dewey, who as early as 1896 recognized that psychology was heading for trouble in its treatment of perception. His concerns are strikingly parallel to Gibson's (see Johnston & Turvey, 1980; Lombardo, 1987; Neisser, 1976, 1987a, for explicit connections between Dewey and Gibson; Dallet, 1974, for a relevant historical analysis of the relation between the transactionists and recent researchers such as Gibson; Noble, 1981, for a comparison of Gibson to Dewey and Mead). Like Gibson, Dewey rejects representational realism and stresses the reciprocal modification of the organism and the environment, but Dewey underscores perhaps more than Gibson the consequences of active inquiry in a world that raises simultaneously possibility and uncertainty.

More specifically, possibility and uncertainty evolve out of organism-environment interactions. An interaction produces what Dewey terms "disequilibrations." "Indeed, living may be regarded as a continual rhythm of disequilibrations and recoveries of equilibrium. . . . The state of disturbed equilibration constitutes *need*. The movement towards its restoration is search and exploration" (Dewey, 1938, p. 27). From the imbalance, "indeterminate situations" arise (see p. 105). The indeterminacy of the situation is characterized by the quality that pervades the particular way that existential materials arrange themselves. For example, I would perceive my daughter Gemma's slightly red cheek and drooping eye differently if she had been roughhousing with her older brother in the middle of the afternoon. The overall quality of the situation belongs both to the subject and to the existential situation. Because interactions with the environment include uncertainty, perception is interrogative, active, and eventful (see Bruner, 1986, pp. 46–49).

Like Gibson, Dewey wants perception to be taken as skillful activity in a broadly defined sense. Events have meanings which enter right into the experience. He (1928) distinguishes between meanings that function referentially and immanently. For instance, if I were Gemma's new, inexperienced babysitter, perceiving her red cheek would signify something else; that is, I "would have to *infer*—use the [color] as a symbol—and do something to find out what it signified" (Dewey, 1928, p. 351). On the other hand, because I am a mother who has cared for her sick Gemma before, her reddened cheek will *be* my getting-sick daughter. Meaning is immanent in that "the consequences of [my] prior-tested and verified inferences enter directly into the object of perception" (p. 351). Ordinary perception funds experience with meaning, according to Dewey. I thus see her across the breakfast table, both precategorially, as a disturbance in my field of vision, and socially, as my daughter for whom I care. I can intellectualize this perceptual experience as if it were only a proposition, disembodied from my experience of her as my child, but this would extract me from my relational context. Rather I am interested in corroboration of my seeing as active knowing.

For Dewey (1912), perception is best defined as "a process of determining the indeterminate" (p. 654) and "a process of choosing" (p. 663). Dewey (1938) argues that the indeterminate situation is "precognitive" (p. 107). Determining and choosing involve both the perceiver and the situation (context) in a mutual relationship. Out of frustration with the term *interaction*, which "assumes the organism and its environmental objects to be present as substantially separate existences or forms of existence, prior to their entry into joint investigation" (p. 123), Dewey and Arthur Bentley (1949) describe the exchange between organism and environment as *transactional*. In describing the ecosystem as transactional, Dewey and Bentley point to the irreducibility of perception either to cognition or to the environment. Rather, it lies in the exchange or in the cycle of exchanges. Although Gibson uses the term mutuality, he "hesitates" when he discusses the contribution of the organism, especially its symbolizing capabilities. For example, he asks, "What are the kinds of culturally transmitted knowledge?" and answers, "I am uncertain" (Gibson, 1979, p. 258). Gibson seems most comfortable when he defines the meaning that resides in dynamic geometric patterns or geometric summaries of information as it flows in the event. Dewey is, perhaps, less interested than Gibson in pushing for the directness of perception; he wants to avoid dichotomies.

Dewey's explanation of perception and his focus on the organism suggest ways in which researchers might develop Gibson's theory into a fuller transactional account. The contextualist holds that "the organism is involved in the occurrence of the perception in the same sort of way that hydrogen is involved in the happening — producing — of water" (Dewey, 1911, p. 105). Working out the theoretical and practical implications of this view is monumental, especially in light of the dominance of the mechanistic worldview that has set down the categories for discourse. As we have seen, Fodor, as a conscientious mechanist, backs away from trivial explanations of embodiment and context in perception; as a conscientious contextualist, Gibson backs away from trivial explanations of culture. Rarely admitted so honestly, these are the metatheoretical brier patches for the mechanist and contextualist respectively.

Recent psychologists sympathetic to Gibson's theory have revised it. How can a constructive subject enter into the perceiving process? Persuaded by Gibson, Neisser shifted from a mechanistic information-processing view of perception (1967) to an ecological stance (1976). I will summarize Neisser's (1976) theory of perception, a revision of Gibson's theory, and then summarize Frederick Wertz's (1987) phenomenological critique of Neisser's revision. In addition to the works of Gibson's followers, other contextualistic thinkers such as M. Johnson (1987) are working on the integrative role of imagination in cognition.

Neisser (1976) assesses Gibson's theory as offering more advantages than a traditional view. "The most important thrust of the theory is to suggest that students of perception should develop new and richer descriptions of the stimulus-information, rather than ever-subtler hypotheses about mental mechanisms" (p. 19). The drawback lies not in Gibson's challenges to the associationistically based theories of perception but in his challenges to constructivistic theories such as Gregory's (1973) and the early Bruner's (1957). According to Neisser's analysis, Gibson goes too far in claiming that perception is direct; as a result, he argues, his theory truncates the role of the perceiver in experience. Neisser's project, then, is to expand Gibson's theory by assigning a more active role to the organism in perception.

Neisser argues that the perceiver brings into the perceptual experience information that determines what information is ultimately picked up, and the information that is picked up modifies the perceiver's previous information. Perception is an ongoing process, cyclical in nature. The perceiver interacts with the information available in the light through what Neisser terms "anticipatory schemata" (singular, schema). "At each moment the perceiver is constructing anticipations of certain kinds of information, that enable him [or her] to accept it as it becomes available" (p. 20). For example, when walking alone through a park in a big American city, a woman perceives a man who follows her as dangerous. The perceiver's anticipatory schemata direct the exploration of the information available to her and are subsequently and continually modified by what she picks up.

Echoing Bartlett's (1932, p. 20) use of the term, Neisser defines *schema* as "that portion of the entire perceptual cycle which is internal to the perceiver, modified by experience, and somehow specific to what is being perceived" (p. 54). As a contextualist, Neisser tries to avoid any formalization or objectification of schemata that would separate them from action. He locates them in the nervous system, but not stationed in the brain apart from biological functioning. "[It is] an entire system that includes receptors and afferents and feed-forward units and efferents" (p. 54). Schemata do not operate sequentially or unidirectionally; rather, "organisms have many schemata, related to each other in complex ways" (p. 56). Neisser claims that in perception cognition and reality meet: schemata cannot operate apart from the existential contingencies of the situation (the context). Thus, they explain anticipations by connecting past experience with the information available to be picked up. The perceiver continues to be aware of the flow of information in the total event, but anticipations guide and direct the search. "The interplay between schema and situation means that neither determines the course of perception alone" (p. 44).

Neisser tries to address a critical problem in Gibson's theory, which in relying on information contained in the environment tends to homogenize its effects. If information is always available, how do particular contextual effects become salient in the event? How does the organism's perceptual history affect its pickup of information? While much of the organism's perceptual interaction with the environment is habitual, the contextualist assumes that perceptual action is initiated frequently by a disturbance in the perceptual field and that in the disturbance particular contextual features (i.e., strands) emerge. These contextual effects become the basis for action. Neisser wants to be able to stipulate how the perceptual system is directed toward particular contextual features in the event, especially those that are culturally and linguistically specified.

Neisser supplements Gibson's theory of direct perception with the concept of a schema which provides a basis for explaining perceptual differences. Differences in what perceivers pick up can be partly attributed to perceptual learning (i.e., their past experiences in detecting the information specified in the layout), but different features of the layout may also emerge given the activities or purposes of the perceivers. Exhausted from a night of grading, I may not perceive my daughter's reddened cheek at the breakfast table. As this example also illustrates, anticipations and situations directly link perception to action. Existential conditions exist in the situation, but different contextual features may emerge given the quality of the situation and the action it calls forth.

Much in Neisser's theory corroborates a contextualist's view of the transaction between the perceiver and the perceived. Neither the existential conditions nor the perceiver comes first; no separate mental image stands between the two. For the contextualist the continuous transaction of organism-environment is irreducible. And for Neisser, the hypothetical construct, schema, constitutes an adequate way to represent the organism's part of the transaction. In many ways this contextualist concept has liberated cognitive psychology to study more meaningful phenomena, such as scripts for ordinary experience instead of isolated words on lists. It has invited new, fresh models for explaining how past knowledge informs present experience. Social and cultural patterns can be represented in terms of schemata (e.g., Bem's, 1983, gender schema theory). Even some mechanists welcome it. What prevents schemata from being formalized and mechanized in simulations? While liberating and promising as a direction for cognitive psychology, the concept also introduces theoretical troubles for contextualism (as it does for mechanism).

Since the mid-1970s the use of "schemata" in cognitive psychology has become quite common as a way to represent past knowledge in present experience. Its widespread appeal indicates the force of contextualistic thinking in the field (see Ben-Zeev, 1988; Brewer & Nakamura, 1984; Holland & Quinn, 1987; Schank & Abelson, 1977; Schmidt, 1982; Solso, 1989; Thorndyke, 1984, for thoughtful openings into this extensive literature). If Neisser's notion of schemata adequately described "the subject side" of the transactional account, then he would have offered a fully worked out contextualistic account of perception. As we will see, however, a closer look at what Neisser means by a schema reveals some inconsistencies typical of the literature generally. Like Gibson's, Neisser's (1967, 1976, 1987c) work is an invaluable contribution to contextualistic psychology because he openly reveals the evolution of his thinking.

Neisser's theory of schemata participates in a wider contextualist discussion, as Wertz's evaluation from a phenomenological perspective demonstrates. While influential and promising, Neisser's explanation of schemata, as it is developed in his 1976 work, contains troubling theoretical difficulties. First, in locating the schema in the nervous system "that includes receptors and afferents, feed forward units and efferents" that he notes are "excruciatingly difficult to understand" (p. 54), Neisser suggests schemata are mechanisms, but he is unclear about their nature and the kind of reduction they imply. What will prevent schemata from becoming reified as internal representations? The second difficulty lies in Neisser's description of a schema as a set of plans, goals, anticipations. As Wertz (1987) points out, when Neisser refers to schemata from this perspective, he seems to mean they are some kind of "intellectually constituted entities" (p. 114). In this sense, Neisser does not emphasize enough the way in which perception is embodied. His account could easily lead toward an over intellectualization of perception and a separation of the perceiver from the perceived.

One proponent of Gibson's ecological view, Viki McCabe, cites objections to the concept of schemata as mediating structures:

It is unclear how these mental mechanisms might deliver on their promises to (a) aggregate separate features into integral wholes (association theories and networks beg the question) (b) compare present aggregations to past ones (What features of these aggregations are compared?), (c) augment present perceptions with past knowledge (on what basis is past knowledge selected?), (d) specify when one aggregation ends and another begins (impute meaning), or (e) even select when the past ends and the present begins (Capek, 1971; Gibson, 1966) without taking leaps of faith. As long as we explain cognition as relying on internal schemas, we must cope with unsolved puzzles. (1986a, p. 13)

The contextualist does not oppose schemata, per se; McCabe (1986a, p. 18) is willing to entertain the possibility of perceptual schemata as long as they avoid turning into reified cognitive structures, but her description is limited to schemata for flow patterns in naturalistic events. Many of Gibson's followers stay closely within the natural organism-environment level of analysis. They want to emphasize certain recurring natural geometric patterns that organisms, through evolution, become specifically attuned to over time and with experience. A contextually oriented response to such an emphasis would point to the significance of contingency in organism and environment transactions. The fit between the environment and organism is not always optimal (see Varela, et al., 1991, chap. 9, for a discussion of the view of evolution held in cognitive science). Further we would want to know how past engagements in the world take on new life as they participate in our ongoing actions without, as John Kirkland and Ruth Anderson (1990) put it, "hijacking the future by *informing* it" (p. 37). Alternatively, Kirkland and Anderson suggest that the past emerges as patterns or constructs that can best be described as catalysts or temporary scaffolds that allow the organism to anticipate and recognize possibilities for future actions.

In a view they call "enactive cognitive science," Varela, Thompson, and Rosch (1991) offer new insights into a contextualist (and perhaps organicist) theory of perception. Like Gibson, they reject traditional appeals to abstract representation and especially the view that "perception is the information-processing problem of recovering pregiven properties of the world" (p. 173). They turn away from Gibson's theory, finally, because to them it seems to hold perception hostage to the environment. They fear that in separating out the environment at the outset, ecological psychologists will treat perception as an interactional rather than a transactional process. In the enactive or transactional approach, the researcher cannot stand back and apportion contributions from either the environment or organism side. I have argued that in order to consider environmental contributions at all, Gibson had to break camp. In a more sympathetic climate and from an interdisciplinary framework, Varela and his colleagues can now plausibly propose what "would have been mere heterodoxy only a few years ago" (p. 209). And they press the full contextualistic argument, namely, that psychologists cannot separate the perceiver from his or her embodied actions. "Perception and action . . . are fundamentally inseparable in lived cognition. Indeed, the two are not merely contingently linked in individuals; they have also evolved together" (p. 173). The emphasis here is on mutuality and reciprocity in the ways that situations guide perception and, in turn, perception is directed toward situations. When regularities in experience arise, perceiver and environment become coupled structurally. In illustrating how perception can be studied as enaction, their theory offers more specific details than Neisser's about organism and environment transactions.

Meanwhile, advocates of Gibson's approach have persisted in the face of criticisms by attempting to appropriate physical theories of complexity. For instance, one interesting attempt is to outline a research program that would aim at expressing Gibson's version of the mutuality of organism and environment, including intentionality and goal-directed behavior, through a "marriage of the dynamics of self-organization and ecological psychology" (Kugler, et al., 1991).

Neisser's revision of Gibson and his thinking about schemata opened new possibilities for contextualistic dialogues about the relationship between perception and cognition. One of the most exciting can be found in the work of philosopher Mark Johnson (1987) who, drawing from cognitive psychology and linguistics, outlines a nonobjectivist, nonreductionist theory of meaning and understanding which assumes a contextualist view of perception. Although Johnson is more sympathetic to a Kantian perspective than the pragmatic one I favor, his theory of meaning and imagination centralizes the role of embodiment in cognition. Using his own work on metaphor (Lakoff & Johnson, 1980) and the work of cognitive psychologists on schemata, Johnson explores the implications of concrete bodily experience in the life of the mind. In bridging the realist (here identified with the Gibsonian) and the formal (i.e., Kantian) view, he tells a contextualist story about meaning and understanding. It is one Varela, Thompson, and Rosch (1991) find "consonant" with their enactive view of cognition (p. 178).

Johnson argues that bodily experiences enter right into mental activity, a valuable development of contextualistic premises. Per-

ception and other cognitive processes are interconnected and situated but available for scrutiny through meanings which can be
publicly shared. Arguing hard against any dichotomy of body and
mind, his theory provides a way of constraining the information
available to the organism for use in intellectual processes. Contextualism has been vulnerable to criticisms by both formalists and
mechanists who argue it cannot constrain information sufficiently,
thus opening the floodgates to anything goes relativism. By connecting levels of context—from bodily experience to abstract understanding of the world through formal theories—Johnson situates
our understanding in the lived world, and he ties our imaginative
life to that experience. His theory thus constrains meaning, not
through appeals to preestablished formal structures and procedures
that lie outside experience, but rather through an analysis of
varieties of physical, bodily experiences themselves as the basis out
of which cognition originates.

> The environment is structured in ways that limit the possi-
> bilities for our categorizations of it. But the structure of the
> environment by no means strictly determines the structure of
> our experience, which is to say, of our *understanding* of our
> world. When we speak of "experience," therefore, we do not
> mean merely a flow of mental representations. We mean to
> include bodily experience in all of its richness, and all that goes
> to make it up—the organism and its nature, the environment
> and its nature, and our understanding (our way of grasping)
> their ongoing interaction. (p. 207)

Here, perception is fundamental to cognition (as Gibson wants to
claim), but perceptual information is ripe with possibilities for
imaginative renderings and meaningful exploration (as Neisser
wants to claim).

To illustrate the connection between perception, language, and
reasoning, let me use one of Johnson's examples: the container
metaphor. As a flexible cognitive structure which schematically
organizes our experience and understanding, the experience of
containment originates in our bodily interactions; in this case, of
being oriented in space. We physically experience our bodies as
containers into which food goes and out of which blood flows.
Further, we experience our bodies as contained in bounded spaces

(such as rooms), and we physically manipulate objects by placing (or sometimes pushing or pulling) them into other containers (and/ or taking them out). So common are these in-out orientations that we are largely unaware of their pervasiveness in our ordinary lives. Over time our experiences provide a flexibly organized structure that includes regularity and coherence, what Johnson calls a schema. Just as Neisser discusses the dynamic quality of schemata, so Johnson emphasizes their interactive and adaptable character, but he is much more specific and detailed about how basic level schemata generate or evolve into other cognitive processes such as language and categorization.

Essentially, we project these basic level schematic structures onto a wide range of phenomena. Take, for example, the out part of the in-out orientation. In language use, we put *out* with a myriad number of verbs (i.e, take out, get out, leave out). All of these uses suggest outward movement recognizable from our bodily experience of, for example, going out of a room. This recurrent form of experience appears in language, in clusters of verbs with *out*. We can also, for example, project this schema onto objects (e.g., he poured out sour milk), onto social situations (e.g., she left me out of her group), and onto epistemic discussions (e.g., I am fleshing out a contextualist worldview). These out projections are interrelated but ultimately linked to perception and bodily action in ways that constrain meaning but allow for imaginative exploration. Many of our bodily interactions with the environment are so structured, and these basic patterns (what Johnson also calls experiential gestalts) infuse our understanding of the world, even at the most complex levels.

Contextualism needed Johnson's integrative perspective. His revolutionary theory suggests that cognition generally and perception specifically are not only situated in bodily experience but that we spin out of our bodily engagements schematic structures and metaphorical projections that include but are not confined to propositional representations. Further, he argues that understanding is a matter of shared, public dialogue. If perception is a transactive exploration by the organism of its environment, then experiential events come to be shaped by their social context. Their meanings must be socially or publicly negotiated (see Sweetser, 1990, chap. 2, for a linguistic analysis of the mind-as-body metaphor and, especially, her discussion of sense-perception verbs).

Mechanists often hold an objectivist view of meaning. Such meanings are rational and laid down in advance of experience. Johnson claims that this objectivist account of cognition itself originates in the bodily experience of containment and boundedness. Certainly such metaphors do reveal some of our experience as, for example, when we are overwhelmed by information. But this is only one metaphor, one that has been dangerously overused in cognitive psychology. In predefining what-is-to-be-the-case, it loses connection to the present felt or lived situation. Objectivism distances the individual from her own potential experience and leads to a view of meaning that, prefabricated, comes to impose preconditions on understanding and intelligence itself. This silences those whose exploration of experience may not be "had" in categorical or propositional form. Those engaged in active caretaking of others, for example, almost always know more than they can formalize; their ability to care effectively comes out of an awareness of history and contingency. Contextualism refuses to lay down in advance rigid logical conditions for perception, and so, as Johnson's work makes clear, perception must also rely on shared dialogue and interchange.

Because events always contain novelty, contextualists argue that perception can open us up to the world and invite us to make sense of the unexpected and ambiguous. If the mind's "I" sees objects from a detached point of view, the mind's we "hears" in the voices of others what has been seen and asks what it means. Although much in our perception is culturally given and historically situated, the contextualist asserts that perception has nonlinguistic meaning in the very sense Gibson wants to maintain, and this meaning is the chief source of novelty. That is why the perspectives of others can arouse us to see anew, even as they can entrap us in seeing again, in the same old ways. Contextualists do not want to reduce perception to culture and language any more than they want to reduce it to physical processes alone. Perception must always contribute something of its own or it gets swallowed up (either in vague intuitions or rationalist rules). And here is the strength of the contextualist argument for direct perception—there is never a pure or static context. Perception can be creative; we perceive in a world characterized by change, novelty, and flux, a world full of events in which meanings are emergent in our own and others' voices.

Climbing into Our Vision

In this chapter, I have shown how the empiricist tradition, as represented historically in the theories of Berkeley and von Helmholtz, supported a mechanistic worldview which came to dominate psychological research on perception. There is a paradoxical twist in the application of empiricism to psychology; in reducing experience to its particulars in order to gain objectivity (the mind mirrors nature), empiricism concomitantly attributes constructive powers to the mind, albeit only through associations passively formed (the mind stores snapshots). Understandably skeptical about solving this paradox in the study of higher mental processes such as concept formation, radical behaviorists tried to eliminate the mind from explanations of behavior. The unsinkable paradox resurfaced in the information-processing model, which proposed an indirect theory of perception as a way around it. A decade later, these information-processing theories seem unable to add insight to the paradox, let alone to resolve it.

Gibson (1979) boldly claims that his theory of direct perception will solve the paradox and make "old puzzles disappear" (p. 304). Categorically rejecting mechanistic assumptions about perception, he explores a new way of thinking about perception (and psychology as a whole) that approximates the categories of contextualism. Although all the ecological psychologists I have discussed, including Neisser, stress that perception takes place from the experience of our bodies, the Gibsonian tradition tends to limit this to a naturalistic account of the body's role in perception while Neisser wants to underscore the perceiver's hypotheses, plans, and anticipations. And what if, like Johnson (1987), we take seriously this ecological claim that the body looks, touches, grasps, and hears? The mind-body dualism so characteristic of mechanism disappears.

Because of his emphasis on the bodily basis of perception, Merleau-Ponty's thought is also relevant to the evolution of contextualism in cognitive psychology. In his theory of perception, past knowledge enters right into the perceiver-perceived transaction, not as an add-on layer of intellectualized meaning but as a result of extended, ongoing bodily engagement in the world. As Wertz (1987) points out, for Merleau-Ponty perceptual structure is layered in the anonymous, the habitual, the personal, and the cultural-historical. From his view culture makes available patterns of meanings in experience: "The immediately perceived world is pervasively inscribed with the gestures of others who have *created, used,* and passionately confronted the family of things, a cultural world for our use and appreciation" (Wertz, p. 133).

As contextualist cognitive psychologists develop their views of perception, they may turn more and more to the thinking of European philosophers, such as Merleau-Ponty, who advocate a return to perception as primary for experience and who advance a method of study through more concrete descriptions of ordinary interactions in the world. Other European thinkers have gained prominence in contextualistic reconsideration (see Winograd & Flores, 1986, for the importance of Heidegger and Gadamer). The developments in recent psychology toward narrative understanding of cognition (e.g., Sarbin, 1986a; Bruner, 1986) participate in the eventfulness central to an ecological theory of perception. These explorations of narrative as a central mode of cognition dovetail with recent work in linguistics (e.g., Langacker, 1987; Sweetzer, 1990), philosophy (e.g., M. Johnson, 1987; Lakoff & Johnson, 1980), and anthropology (Holland & Quinn, 1987; Geertz, 1983). What if Gibson's theory of perception could be tied to a theory of language and culture that stipulated how cognition also originates in bodily movement, which itself enters into perception and cognition in a naturalistic way? From Pepper's metatheoretical perspective, we would have a fully developed contextualistic worldview of cognition. But before turning to the promises of these developments, let us examine mechanistic and contextualistic accounts of the role of memory in cognition.

4

Memory: From Storehouse to Dramatic Event

> I remember [my mother] standing with her arms folded, pushing at the dust with the toe of her pump while she waited for us to finish our sundaes. We sat at a hot green metal table, weather-dulled and sticky, and loud black flies with rainbows in their wings fed at the pools of drying ice cream and then scrubbed their maws meticulously with their forelegs, like house cats. She was so tall and quiet in her silvery gray dress, never looking toward us, and we were sweaty and sticky and cloyed and tired of each other. I remember her, grave with the peace of the destined, the summoned, and she seems almost an apparition.
>
> But if [without stopping for ice cream] she had simply brought us home again to the high frame apartment building with the scaffolding of stairs, I would not remember her that way. . . . She would have remained untransfigured.
>
> —Marilynne Robinson, *Housekeeping*

If perception keeps us connected to the concrete information available in our world, then memory allows us to reexperience and interpret this world and ourselves. "Perhaps," the narrator of *Housekeeping* thinks, "memory is the seat not only of prophecy but of miracle as well." M. Robinson's exploration of memory in this novel reminds us of the term's origin: from "Mnemosyne," Greek goddess, the mother of the muses, a source not only of knowledge but of inspiration to those who gather up the past in ways that give new meanings to the present. In most modern accounts of memory, her transformative power vanishes. Like painters without depth vision, many modern psychologists see memory as a series of passive functions and devices. Their accounts invoke images of "executors" who "direct the flow of information between process-ing units and storage units"; such managers are accompanied by rational technicians, such as a "comprehender," who "interprets raw stimulus information in terms of previously acquired semantic concepts" (Wyer & Srull, 1989, pp. 18–19). On memory's power to infuse the present with the past, to enthuse, enrapture, and trans-figure, on all of these, most modern cognitive psychological theo-ries fall silent. Imaginative and active aspects of memory remain outside the scope of the mechanistic metaphors that inform much contemporary research.

For contextualism, these imaginative and reconstructive acts are constitutive of memory. In a world full of complex events, thick and rich with everchanging details and relationships, contextualists reject lifeless, compartmentalized depictions of memory; they balk especially at the managerial imagery brought in to direct the flow. In contrast to memory models that often describe information as filtering up to higher and more powerful executives, contextualists want more grassroots models. Because they find eventfulness cen-tral to cognition, they conceive of memory as narrative, embodied, and flexibly situated, and, to describe memory, they often turn to images of spreading and layering, such as *horizons*, *landscapes*, *multiple mappings*, *textures*, or *sedimentation*. In the *Phenomenol-ogy of Perception*, Merleau-Ponty (1962) describes how conscious-ness can reopen the past in a direct act of recollection. Yet, he notes, even when not consciously recollected, the past "provides the perceived with a present atmosphere and significance" (p. 22). So common is this foregrounding that we know it mainly by experienc-ing its absence, as when we are in shock, in another country, for example. Memory sets the stage in a world of change, uncertainty, and action (see Bransford, McCorrell, et al., 1977, for a full contex-tualistic description of this metaphor).

Historically, psychological studies focused on retrieval of pas-sively stored material. Using meaningless, impersonal stimuli, such as lists of letters, experimenters examined conditions that fostered or hindered recall and recognition. Somewhat more theoretical than the verbal learning tradition, cognitive psychology emphasized more interactive processes and functions. But, in these mechanistic models of memory, past knowledge is simplified and compartmen-talized in predetermined, inflexible structures (Spiro, et al., 1987).

Mainstream psychology has tended to conceive of memory as inert and passive. Receiving information, memory stores copies or impressions of it, usually in the form of images or traces. Contextualists point not only to the dullness of this vast body of literature, but also to its lack of ecological validity and its theoretical aimlessness. To account for context and meaningfulness, we must return to the total event, to its particular strands, as well as to their integration and significance. Faced with naturally occurring complexity and irregularity, memory responds generatively, by playing a constitutive role in making meaning.

Today in my psychology class, a student asked me, in an irritated voice, how learning about sexism and racism would help him in his accounting major. I found myself remembering Carl, a student in one of my classes some years ago. As I interacted with Tom, the student in this morning's class, I felt Carl hovering on the outskirts of our interaction. Only now, after class and in the solace of my office, I explicitly recollect my experience with Carl. I cannot remember the day or really even the year, but I remember how his hand shot up from the back of the class where he often sat alone, away from the other African-American students who usually sat together. His sudden movement startled me. And as our eyes met, before I could even speak his name, he blurted out loudly, "All this socialization stuff is just not true—it's all bullshit." I remember those words exactly . . . and the way his smile covered the intensity of his feelings. The class fell silent. Usually Carl entertained the class—if he participated at all—by making funny remarks on the side, just beyond my range of hearing. I remember distinctly noticing his hair as he spoke out—he had just tinted the front of it orange. Momentarily locked in his gaze, I suspected that this was his first public commitment to ideas—this "socialization stuff" mattered to him deeply.

I recall putting on my "look." It's really more like a holding position, a gesture toward something. I want my students to read my face this way: "She's really thinking about what he said; this is important and interesting to her. We all need to take note." Usually I feel this way, but that day it hid impatience and irritation fed by my fatigue. I have always taught nontraditional students, many from ethnic minority groups. Until Carl, I had found teaching this unit easy. Most of them "got" socialization like the Pepsi can that drops down from the vending machine. I was behind in the syllabus and the subject of most interest to me lay just ahead in the next readings. I wanted to be there already, and so I had dropped the coins in the socialization slot. But there sat Carl with his newly tinted orange hair and defiant hand protesting all my tacit expectations and assumptions.

In recollecting Carl, I feel myself being pulled back even further in time, to myself as the young teacher who has easy access to the world of her students. When I started teaching as a graduate student in the late 1960s, my African-American students, most from south side Chicago and some from Menard State Penitentiary, knew firsthand about civil rights. Almost all had read parts, if not all, of Malcolm X's autobiography, for example, or had seen him on television. I had used their knowledge of politics and civil rights as a bridge into courses and syllabi that excluded their perspectives. And right on through the 1970s, I tacitly held a frame of reference, a perspective about my students and myself, based on the 1960s. Sitting in my class fifteen years later, Carl had little experience with or knowledge of the civil rights movement, and I, caught up in committee work and research, I had grown distanced from the daily experiences of my students.

I remember, perhaps most vividly, how Carl came up to me the day after I finished reteaching the socialization unit through a simulation. All the other students had left the classroom. He told me that all his brothers were in prison and that his father, an alcoholic, had left his family. He fought theories of socialization because, he said, "I thought it meant I would wind up like all the other men in my family. I've always seen myself as an individualist, but now I see that these ideas are more complex and that things aren't one way or the other. How do you think like this without getting mixed-up and scared?" I didn't apprehend then, but know now in this act of recollection, that I was scared too. His actions were essential to my development as a teacher. Looking back, I realize it was my first serious encounter with being a middle-aged teacher. I had lost contact with some of the lifeworld of my students, with the backstage of our classroom.

And memory not only spreads backward, it also spreads out into the future. The white student who questioned the relevance of studying racism and sexism in class today challenged me on somewhat different grounds. And again, I question my tacit knowledge about my students' frames of reference and wonder how I can remain connected to them as I grow older. In this act of remembering Carl, and now Tom, I am gathered with my students in a story about my teaching and their learning. So woven together in narrative, some strands of memory recede into our pasts, pulling us with them while others stretch forward into our possibilities for future actions. Such types of ordinary memorial experience point to the contingency of past details and events. Had his hand not shot up in the air quite the way it did, had I not been tired, had I not had time and solitude in my office today, Carl would have remained untransfigured. My understanding of Tom still remains a challenge.

But the traditional memory theorist immediately jumps in to say: this is not what we purport to study when we study memory experimentally or through computer simulation. And in fact, those framing problems from the mechanistic perspective would argue that their objective is to discover the mechanisms and processes of memory, what Darryl Bruce (1985) calls general principles memory research. In the laboratory experiment, subjects are asked, for example, to recall information they have learned in a controlled environment. And certainly, based on a long history of research, the experimentalist can explain some of my experiences, for example, why I have difficulty recalling Carl's last name or the names of the other students in his class. They would argue that I would have to search out these names through processes or strategies involving inference and representation. Others might point to a categorization system, in which Carl might be depicted as a collection of features, some of which were made distinctive at the time of our interaction. From these experiments, they have proposed hundreds of formal models for explaining memory. Certainly these models have pointed to a variety of very important phenomena that are involved in remembering. But in focusing on the mechanics of memory, the contextualist wonders, do the cognitivists ever hear the story?

Many memory researchers are doubtful. In a review of coding theories, Benton Underwood (1972) humorously warns, "Our models and theories are overloading the subjects' memory" (p. 21). In perhaps the most critical examination of memory research, Jenkins (1974a) points to the use of unrelated materials and nonmeaningful tasks in memory experiments: "We make [our subjects] assume the role of a highly-limited, special-purpose machine, and they accommodate us by doing so" (p. 5). Such judgments about the validity and meaningfulness of traditional experimental results jarred the entire field. For example, well-known experimentalist Endel Tulving (1979) asserts: "After a hundred years of laboratory-based study of memory, we still do not seem to possess any concepts that the majority of workers would consider important or necessary. . . . Most of our concepts tend to be esoteric: They are used by small groups of people and either ignored or found confusing by others" (p. 27). In the early 1970s Jenkins (1974b) anticipated that the field would not recover from theoretical disarray without major theoretical revisions. Contextualism, he argued, was "a real, viable, and optimistic alternative to mechanism and its associationist doctrines" (p. 795).

Building on my discussion of perception, this chapter takes up Jenkins's call and explores the disarray in thinking about memory. In arguing that contextualism has developed as a viable worldview in the field of memory, I draw together a number of converging theoretical tendencies, including the ecological psychologists' views of memory (e.g., Bransford, McCorrell, et al., 1977; Bruce, 1985; Hoffman & Nead, 1983; McCabe, 1986b; Neisser, 1982, 1988; Turvey & Shaw, 1979) and the new interest in symbolic activity (e.g., Bruner, 1986; Bruner & Feldman, 1990; M. Johnson, 1987). So extensive is current interest in the role of context in the general memory literature that in a recent volume (Davies & Thomsom, 1988) entitled *Memory in Context: Context in Memory* Donald Thomson and Graham Davies cite in their introduction well over a hundred research articles, most of which have been published since the early 1970s. Such proliferation of research has led to serious difficulties, however, including the sometimes confusing use of the term *context*. They note, "In the absence of any theory of context effects, context as a concept lacks explanatory power. Nevertheless, context is frequently invoked" (p. 2). No one doubts that context is important in memory, but if memory is to be studied through mental representations, the structures must somehow constrain context (Shanon, 1990).

Certainly contextualists laud the recent attention and acknowledgement given to context in studies of memory. Carving up context into its multiple varieties, however, is not the intent of the worldview that is, ultimately, integrative and synthetic. In analysis, the context always gets tied back into the event and its felt quality. Often the recognition of different context effects has led to the postulation of different memory systems (e.g., semantic/episodic and implicit/explicit memories). Without examining how we think and talk about memory—without taking a metatheoretical view—the field may remain locked in debates that lead to further fragmentation and disarray. Following the pattern of explication in the perception chapter, I trace the lines of mechanistic and contextualistic thinking in the field of memory.

As in the study of perception, memory research has been dominated by mechanism. Paralleling von Helmholtz's work in perception, Hermann Ebbinghaus (1913) applied mechanistic assumptions to his experiments on memory. His reliance on associationism and an experimental approach dominated psychological research on memory until the 1950s. Mechanism continued to influence psychological explanations of memory in the information-processing framework that arose in the early 1950s even though associationist principles continued to be modified (e.g., J. Anderson & Bower, 1973; Newell & Simon, 1963). In the early 1970s, however, a dramatic series of experiments by Bransford and Franks (1971) called into question these commonly accepted approaches to memory. As with the experiments by Johansson in event perception, these experiments support an alternative, contextualistic view. The remainder of this chapter explores the influence of contextualism on memory research and the growth of contextualism as a fruitful alternative in its own right.

My purpose is not to undertake a comprehensive history but to illustrate and suggest the various ways in which mechanism has informed and controlled theory and research on memory. I briefly describe certain experimental developments that typify the evolution of the mechanistic worldview. Contextualism develops in contrast to and often in conflict with this mechanistic tradition. By identifying and interpreting important contextualistic experiments and theories, I can more vividly describe contextualism as an alternative worldview and explain its empirical and theoretical contributions to the study of cognition.

The Mechanistic View of Associative Memory

In the traditional mechanistic view, the account of perception relies on a version of empiricism, which holds that all knowledge can be reduced to certain types of particulars said to make up all of experience. A proper account of memory must, in this view, rely on the theory of association—the belief that predefined, particular elements, delivered from perception, bond together in experience in relationships that can be described in laws. These connections between elements are not necessarily rational; in classical empiricism, they are usually limited to those of contiguity, resemblance, and cause and effect. Of all the laws proposed, the law of contiguity remained foremost in accounting for association, particularly in psychological studies of memory. Citing the influence of the British Empiricists, for example, J. Anderson and Gordon Bower (1973) identify vividness, frequency, duration, and recency of experience as determining the strength of a particular association. "This set of principles should sound very familiar to experimental psychologists, since they have generated a great many experiments on memory and verbal learning" (p. 23). These laws were assumed to be very general in their effects, applying to all organisms and all stimuli (see McCabe, 1986b, p. 186, for a discussion). Through cooccurrence and repetition, well-formed simple associations build into more complex ones. A particular sensory experience and any associations between particulars must be stored somewhere while others are registered and bound together; in the associationist view, that "somewhere" is memory.

Because memory cannot be observed directly and its contents and functions can only be inferred, most conceptualizations of memory are metaphorical (see Lakoff & Johnson, 1980; Leary, 1990a; Marshall & Fryer, 1978; Roediger, 1980; Watkins, 1978, for further discussions on the metaphors underlying work on memory). In a classic associationist account, for example, Locke conceived of memory as "the storehouse of our ideas," a "repository." He (1959) states, "But, our ideas being nothing but actual perceptions in the mind, which cease to be anything when there is no perception of them; this laying up of our ideas in the repository of the memory signifies no more but this, —that the mind has a power in many cases to revive perceptions which it once had, with this additional perception annexed to them, that *it has had them before*" (p. 194). Mechanists studying perception assumed memory to be a container (or, more figuratively, the picture album) for the snapshots taken by the eye (in the case of visual perception). Associationism has historically bound psychology to a mechanistic way of thinking

about memory. As Jerome Bruner and Carol Feldman (1990) suc-
cinctly put it, "[Association's] metonymic rendering is that the
experienced world, here and now, is as it is because the world there
and then was as it was. This proposition has engendered a language
of copies, mirrors, and faithful renderings" (p. 235). To explain
mechanistic views of memory, I will highlight four interrelated
associationist assumptions about memory.

First, early associationists classify perception and memory as
two separate types of activities, but in more modern associationist
accounts, this explicit classification has become an invisible prem-
ise. For example, in the index of a recent volume entitled *Current
Issues in Cognitive Processes* (Izawa, 1989), there is no main
heading for perception ("perceptual learning" appears as a sub-
heading). In information-processing models, vision, for example, is
described as "an input channel for stimulus-item information"
(Izawa & Hayden, 1989, p. 236). Separate from perception of
sensory data, memory becomes groups of storage boxes and strategies for stacking and accessing them.

Associationists keep memory and perception separate because
they want to make certain kinds of knowledge claims. Perception is
the laying down of the unit of experience — via the senses — from out
there, while knowledge is the buildup of perceptual experiences —
via memory — in the mind. In this analogy, objects stored in memory are discrete, and the process of remembering is a search for the
location of these stored objects that were once "out there." Associationists assume that what enters memory "is thought to stand in a
one-to-one correspondence with . . . past reality, as remembered"
(Malcolm, 1977, p. 126). In recent associationist theories, it is not
so much an image "but rather an insistence on the presence of a
'complex structure' [usually linguistic] which will provide a representation by virtue of having a one-to-one correlation with what is
remembered" (p. 127). A proposition or "propositional representation" is an example of such a complex structure. Whether simple or
complex, the separation of memory from perception guarantees, the
associationist claims, a one-to-one mapping of the internal and
external world.

This separation makes it convenient to study cognitive functioning by methods that reduce cognitive phenomena to simple
components, the second assumption of associationist theories of
memory. Complex ideas or behaviors can be sorted by identifying

their basic, constituent units. Early theories privileged sensory experience described as stimulus features or properties. Traditional psychologists felt that these units were impervious to context and change, and so they isolated and manipulated them in laboratory experiments. Invariant, pure, and simple, the units were rearranged or reorganized in mental space; the relations between the units could be strengthened or weakened (based on, for example, repetition in experience). Information-processing theories privilege hypothetical informational units (such as words) that fit into propositions. Most preserve the integrity of the units which are assumed to function independently and passively in processing—from the bottom-up. Information-processing theorists frequently argue that operations can be decomposed as in a flow diagram, for example, "to specify the nature of a single *complex* operation in terms of information flow among a number of *simpler* operations" (S. Palmer & Kimchi, 1986, pp. 51–52). Because of their epistemological claim that the parts constituted the whole, mechanistic accounts of memory become critical in any mechanistic explanation of complex behavior such as problem solving (see Jenkins, 1974b, for a brief description of this relationship in the history of psychology).

The commitment to reductionism follows from psychology's loyalty to the practice of laboratory science. In such memory research the experimenter attempts to control variables in an artificial environment so that any relationship established among them will be generalizable across contexts. The goal of such general principles memory research is, of course, to rid the experiment of natural context effects which confound interpretation. In memory research both in the verbal learning tradition and in information processing, experimenters frequently used small linguistic units (syllables or words) or information chunks as variables. In semantic representations of memory, the use of such units assumes an objectivist account of language, namely, that these simple units are the constituent parts of holistic language meanings. As we will see in this chapter, stripping language of its context resulted in serious problems with the validity of laboratory findings on memory and for semantic representations of memory (Shanon, 1988). (In the concluding chapter I discuss the controversy over generalizability and validity as it relates to worldviews.)

Third, mechanists argue that the contents of memory have a spatiotemporal spread. The law of contiguity states that associations occur together in a time span. Since the particulars of experience never lose their qualities, any association that takes place between them must retain their separateness. Such a temporal connection implies mental space. Sense data (or in more complex versions of associationism, symbolic units) are thus distributed over space. Based on the law of contiguity, stored associations will be strong (e.g., close together) or weak (e.g., far apart). The spread of associations in memory concomitantly explains retrieval of past associations as a search through the storehouse. The concept of a memory trace, which can decay or be interfered with by traces previously or newly laid down, also emphasizes that associations spread out in time and space. Any other kind of organization of these associations is not possible because they must cohere and then break apart again in new experience. This spatiotemporal spread allows the particulars of experience to remain integral, discrete. In this type of reductionism, the raw data of experience have been stripped from the situation and its context, including emotion and bodily experiences, and mechanist theories must add these contextual factors back into their accounts.

The final assumption of this associative view of memory is the passivity of the organism in remembering. The British Empiricists thought that an individual could deliberately reflect on prior associations and so discover new ones, but the basic elements of such reflection simply produced new bonding among old elements. In the classic associationist view, what gets stored in memory has no capacity to organize or to make meaning; the organism makes no active contribution to memory. More recent associationist theories, such as those in information processing (e.g., J. Anderson & Bower, 1973), have tended to argue that their models portray the organism as more rational and, hence, more active; their adjectives suggest motion. Incoming stimulus information, for example, is processed in working memory. Yet, this activity remains theoretically problematic; as I noted in Chapter 3, who or what processes the image (or symbol) remains unclear and leads to postulations of homunculi who direct the flow of traffic. And in hierarchical models of memory involving word recognition, each storage center or processing stage makes decisions about what goes to the next higher center in the structure. If the basis of the sorting is comparison, how does new information enter the system? (See Rosenfield, 1988, pp. 63–64, for further discussion of the circularity of the mechanist account of recognition.) Over time, J. Anderson (1980b), like Hayes-Roth (1977), has postulated larger and more complex cognitive units such as schemata and scripts which are not as easily decomposable as the units in their earlier models. In this sense associationist models have become more intricately structured and holistic.

These four interrelated associationist assumptions contribute to a worldview: the output of memory is an objective, singular perspective. This conclusion follows, first, from the associationist's belief that contiguity, for example, occurs generally and mechanically regardless of the significance of the association for the organism. Second, the associationist assumes that the brain has a center, a central location. (See Rosenfield, 1988, for a history of the doctrine of localization of function and the belief in permanent memories.) Out of this center emerge the results of inferences or processes into a stream (an output flow) that is often called explicit or conscious memory. Older associationist theories suggest a serial processing more like factory piece work on an assembly line; modern information-processing theories suggest the processing is more like bureaucratic decision making, especially in bottom-up models, where a linear chain of operations through space and time leads up to a particular experience. In either case, the resulting outputs can be publicly defended by an account of procedures and by appeals to general laws. Mechanistic theories frequently exclude emotion and bodily movement (motor activity) from their account of perception and memory. In reading word recognition studies, for instance, one encounters filing systems of fixed memory stores full of safe, neutral terminology (usually animals and plants)—no blood, sweat, and tears in these fixed storehouses.

This view of memory as knowledge production isolates the individual who, alone with his memory, represents experience as a series of objective statements from a single point of view. Then this experience is put out for public scrutiny. The increasing use of terms imported from bureaucratic management (e.g., executors, procedural and substantive rationality) underscores the power of this mechanistic worldview for psychology; it is the canonical or official story one gets, for example, in many introductory courses and textbooks. (See Sampson, 1981, pp. 739–41, for an analysis of how "building block" cognitivists legitimize certain technical social practices.) These models of central-processing mechanisms offer explanations for routine and repeated (often artificial) functioning; in this sense, they are technically rational (see, for example, Simon, 1990, for a description of the principle of bounded rationality). Perception and memory lead to an objective, rational, and thus defensible account of experience — this description underlies many of our widely shared metaphors for characterizing the life of the mind (see Lakoff & Johnson, 1980, for a thorough account).

In sum, then, associationism assumes that memory functions autonomously from perception, that its contents can be reduced to units (however defined), and that these units spread out in spatiotemporal sequence based on laws of contiguity. In experience, context does not affect the discrete unit stored in memory; memory passively produces an internal representation that corresponds to the outside world. As a result, in many associationist theories, knowledge stored in memory tends to be depicted as assembled packages that are not free to interconnect and interact flexibly; rather these discrete data are linked through clear, neat, and often logical pathways connecting one segmented, fragmented aspect of a given domain to another in sequential order (Spiro, et al., 1987). Such an approach to memory handles regularities and consistencies in experience, as, for instance, variables that affect acquisition of words or concepts. In his account of mechanism, Pepper (1961) explains the appeal of the view that perception, memory, and ultimately thought consist of discrete mental elements, all of which correspond to the physical world: "This psychology of discrete mental elements is the neatest and, in that respect, the most intellectually satisfying psychology that has been developed. It almost works, and has been very widely accepted" (p. 219).

So dominant was this associationist view of memory in psychology that in the same year Edward Robinson's (1932) book on associationism was published, Bartlett's work critical of association theory was scarcely noticed. His alternative approach to the study of memory, with its strong contextualistic overtones, did not gain attention until the late 1970s, when contextualism began to emerge as an alternative worldview. Contextualists such as Bartlett challenge the mechanist's insistence on basic units isolated from experience. But mechanists hold tightly to this assumption. Recently, for example, Simon (1990) argued from a computational perspective that as scientist, the cognitive psychologist is searching for symbolic invariants. Like an elusive butterfly, however, the invariant flutters just beyond the mechanistic net. Historically, the search started in the laboratory with Ebbinghaus (1913), who thought that he could rid his laboratory experiments of the background of presuppositions subjects brought with them to the laboratory. His invariant was the nonsense syllable.

In order to study memory in the laboratory, Ebbinghaus recognized the need for a basic unit to serve as the independent variable in the laboratory setting. Such a basic unit had to be meaningless in and of itself, but bondable through a process of association. Unlike their counterparts in the field of visual perception, who could use objects or their parts, memory experimenters needed more abstract representations for their basic units in order to study language. Bartlett (1932) explains Ebbinghaus's choice of the nonsense syllable as the basic unit for memory experiments:

> [Ebbinghaus] realized that if we use continuous passages of prose or verse as our material to be remembered, we cannot be certain that any two subjects will begin on a level. Such material sets up endless streams of cross-association which may differ significantly from person to person. It is an experiment with handicaps in which the weighting is unknown. Provided the burden of explanation has to be borne by the stimulus, this is obviously a real difficulty; for the stimuli have every appearance of varying from one person to another in ways incalculable and uncontrollable. There appears an easy way of overcoming this obstacle. Arrange material so that its significance is the same for everybody, and all that follows can be explained within the limits of the experiment itself. Since the experimental conditions are both known and readily analyzable, the explanations can be expressed definitely and with the greatest possible certainty. (p. 3)

Indeed, the associationist psychologists at the turn of the nineteenth century investigated simple, elementary entities and how they combined to form more complex ideas. These researchers wanted to discover how elementary units become associated in memory, as a first approach to studying and explaining how more complex and meaningful materials could be remembered.

Ebbinghaus's experiments typify the application of early associationist assumptions to laboratory practice. He repeated aloud, for example, a list of nonsense syllables (to the beat of a metronome) and then tried to repeat from memory what he had read. His classic forgetting curve charts the number of nonsense syllables retained in relation to the number of trials required to relearn the initial material over various time intervals. The results of Ebbinghaus's experiments — that, for example, cramming is less effective than the spacing out of repetitions — were by and large less important than his experimental methods. These methods opened new possibilities for measuring different variables, such as distribution of practice, and how they affected the acquisition of material. (See Marshall & Fryer, 1978; Murray, 1976, for more extensive accounts of Ebbinghaus's influence on research.)

During the course of his research, Ebbinghaus modified assumptions about associative memory. He experimentally determined that it was very difficult to get subjects to suppress numerous associations that the supposedly meaningless stimuli elicited. He (1913) notes, "It even appears from this point of view as if the differences between sense and nonsense material were not nearly so great as one would be inclined *a priori* to imagine" (p. 3). Although his proposals for a general account of memory did not stand up, memory researchers enthusiastically endorsed his methodology. In recognizing that nonsense syllables are not meaningless, most researchers gave up trying to study the formation of simple associations and instead attempted to "describe the conditions that modify the strength of [already formed] associations" (Deese, 1965, p. 7).

Ebbinghaus's stimulus (e.g., a small linguistic item) and his methodological techniques led to new possibilities for experiments. As Marshall & Fryer (1978) note, "The precise, numerical parameters of [his findings] are . . . of paramount importance in the construction of finely detailed, fully explicit models" (p. 7). The concept of a span of memory provided unlimited opportunities to measure associations, variously manipulated in the laboratory. Ebbinghaus's methods were later adapted and revised by behaviorists. His serial reproduction became the basis for the verbal learning tradition, which focused solely on small verbal elements and their association. In serial learning, for example, subjects are presented one word at a time from a list. On subsequent presentations, they try to anticipate the next word that will be shown. During the next few decades, however, the paired-associate learning task, an outgrowth of serial learning, dominated experimental studies of memory. In this experimental procedure, subjects are presented pairs of items and then required to recall one (usually the second) by being shown the other. The paired-associate learning task, which evolved from Ebbinghaus's experiments, fit congruently not only with the associationist tradition but also with the behaviorists' emphasis on stimulus-response.

Under the influence of behaviorism, however, traditional associationist doctrines began to shift, especially any emphasis on the mentalistic or unobservable behaviors. Defining associations as connections, behaviorists instead viewed the stimulus and response unit as a unit of association. In his book *Association Theory Today*, E. Robinson (1932) revises associationism along behavioral lines by loosening the interpretation of the law of contiguity: "It would seem as though we ought to get varying degrees of association with varying degrees of contiguity" (p. 74). He emphasizes the secondary factors of association, such as frequency, intensity, and duration as sufficient conditions for learning, rather than contiguity alone. (Such attributes, of course, become potential variables in laboratory settings.) With the introduction of mediation into the behaviorist framework, the conception of memory as a storehouse of associations reappeared explicitly. That is, hierarchies of associative chains, organized from simple to complex, intervened between stimulus and response (see Maltzman, 1955, for an example of such mediation in an account of problem solving). As a consequence of this behavioral revision, associations took on a unidirectional character because the first unit of the association came to be equated with the stimulus and its properties and the second with the response (Deese, 1965, p. 7).

In the study of functional relationships in verbal learning experiments, researchers often presented to subjects single words as stimuli. The use of such variables implied an objectivist view of language, namely, that language can be studied as a system of independent units, associatively chained. Lakoff and Johnson (1980) describe the objectivist view of language: "Linguistic expressions are objects that have properties in and of themselves and stand in fixed relationships to one another, independently of any person who speaks them or understands them. As objects, they have parts—they are made up of building blocks" (p. 204). Actively involved in word association research in the 1950s, Jenkins (1974b) admits to just this view of language as sacrosanct in his earlier experimental investigations: "I believed that complex behaviors were built of simple subassemblies and that things got more complicated but not different 'in kind.' (This belief justified concern with simple units and relations and sanctioned experiments on such units in the faith that they would eventually add up to the complex behaviors of language)" (p. 786). But as Jenkins argues in his article, the faithful did not harvest the fruits of their early objectivist hopes. Like an early frost, Chomsky's (1959) assault on Skinner's *Verbal Behavior* killed the crop. Looking at organization and structure, linguists and information-processing theorists turned away from stricter versions of associationism and behaviorism. As in perception, associative accounts of memory had difficulty accounting for organization. Robinson's extension of associationism notwithstanding, "almost all of the experimental study of association was based upon contiguity in presentation and stimulus-response relations in analysis" (Deese, 1965, p. 29). In such contiguously formed associations, relations among units were a priori random and arbitrary. As in the study of perception, this lack of order available in the stimulus material produced awkward accounts of structure, especially at more complex and interactive levels (e.g., face recognition and problem solving). Persuaded by Chomsky's arguments about the nature of language acquisition (e.g., deep structure), a growing number of memory researchers turned away from associationist assumptions and toward organizational theory.

Information-Processing in Theories of Memory: Mechanism in Drag

Over two decades, newly emerging experimental findings from organizational memory research, work in computer simulation, new theoretical frameworks for cognition, and methodological developments all converged under a new framework called information processing (e.g., Attneave, 1959; Bousfield, 1953; Broadbent, 1958; Miller, et al., 1960; Murdock, 1961; Newell & Simon, 1961, 1963; Sternberg, 1966; Tulving, 1962, 1964). Focusing on the concept of memory structures, the organizational approach incorporated all of these new developments (see Mandler, 1962, 1967). With the introduction of information-processing approaches, a host of new technical concepts flooded the field, and memory research became increasingly specialized. Typically, information-processing theorists distinguished three memory stores: sensory, short-term, and long-term. This new approach to cognition raised serious questions about the viability of classical associationism as a theoretical basis for memory, even as it confronted radical behaviorism on its assumption that behavioral responses could be explained without an understanding of cognitive mediation. As we will see, however, it retained many associationist assumptions.

W. A. Bousfield's (1953) experiment on category clustering in free recall challenged the view that associations arise contiguously. Bousfield presented subjects with a list of words belonging to different conceptual categories; he presented the words randomly, without regard to class membership. When he asked the subjects to recall the list in any order they chose, he found that, in recall, they reorganized the randomly presented list into groups or clusters of words that fit the categories. The law of contiguity cannot easily explain such clustering. Clearly, Bousfield argues, categories mediate recall; subjects act upon the input and restructure it according to some higher order unit. This study initiated interest in how knowledge comes to be organized in long-term memory. It strongly suggested (as we will see in the categorization chapter) that relationships among parts affect cognitive functioning.

Not long after Bousfield's study, George Miller (1956) introduced his theory of chunking in short term memory. He argued that short-term memory could retain seven plus or minus two items, but that the items did not necessarily consist of single units (such as letters or numbers). Items could instead consist of larger, more subjective units (such as groups of words or numbers) depending on the subject's past experience. Both clustering and chunking defied the law of contiguity (and its subprinciples): first, they suggested the importance of the subject's ability to organize material meaningfully; second, they emphasized the structural properties of the stimulus material. This work supported processing as an extension of the mind-as-computer metaphor.

Tulving's (1962, 1964) experiments on subjective organization in free recall participated in this growing movement against traditional associationism and radical behaviorism. Unlike Bousfield, who used a categorized word list, Tulving asked subjects to recall as many words as possible from a list of 16 unrelated words, which he presented one at a time. He then had the subjects study and recall the list again over several trials (a procedure called multitrial free recall). As expected, subjects' recall improved with trials, but more important, they tended to recall words in the same order over successive trials—and not in the order in which they were presented. Tulving hypothesized that subjects were using a strategy that he called "subjective organization" to enhance their recall. Moreover, as Mandler (1967) and Tulving (1967) later found, use of subjective organization increased recall. "Tulving's analysis of output protocols convinced psychologists that active processes organized unrelated lists" (Mandler, 1979, p. 312). Studies by Underwood and his colleagues found that the stimulus took on different meanings for individual subjects (e.g., Underwood, et al., 1962; Underwood, 1963). Because these individual differences affected the processing of stimulus variables, researchers distinguished between nominal stimulus (e.g., what the experimenter presents) and the functional stimulus (e.g., what the subject represents the stimulus to be). Taken together, these experiments shattered the old assumptions about memory and made possible new conceptualizations of memory and perception.

A number of psychologists began to reassess the nature of the stimulus and to doubt that the experimenter could isolate in a laboratory a basic element that would remain invariant and irreducible across contexts and individuals. The stimulus of psychological research became more problematic; for example, R. B. Joynson in 1970 wrote a now famous critique of the experimental tradition that started with Ebbinghaus's stimuli. As one researcher puts it, "A simple response, such as a single word, does not necessarily have the properties of a functional unit simply by virtue of its extreme simplicity and comparative lack of internal structure: a functional unit of behavioral analysis may change during the course of an experiment" (Shimp, 1976, p. 117). Throughout the verbal learning tradition, the nature of the task, the effect of instructions, the setting of the experiment, even the verbal context provided by the stimulus materials themselves had drawn little attention. But the free recall memory experiments of the 1960s turned researchers toward the role of meaning and context in memory.

Like the Gestalt psychologists, organizational memory theorists criticized associationism for its failure to recognize structural properties of stimulus material. But, again like the Gestaltists, these theorists did not venture far from a mechanistic viewpoint, in part because without being aware of it, they were completely locked within a commitment to interpretation of all psychological phenomena in terms of physical entities. Mandler (1979) indicates the limitation clearly:

> As a belief, as a point of view, organizational approaches are not testable in any conventional sense of the term. The organization of mental contexts is assumed to be axiomatic—it guides the kind of theoretical endeavor its adherents propound; it does not itself lead to any testable or falsifiable consequences. Thus any kind of observation about human memory is grist for the organization theorists' mill. Even the remaining strongholds of association theorists, pairwise and serial "associations," are viewed as nothing but challenges. (p. 306)

Such theoretical elasticity does not, ultimately, contribute to the development of alternative metatheories; rather the organizational approach merged with and adopted the going program—information-processing views.

Although it changed the terms of discussion, information processing took the mind as machine analogy quite literally. By introducing formalism (i.e., rule-driven descriptions) into conceptions of memory and its functioning, this new approach operated within the confines of a very suggestive, albeit hybrid, worldview. Programmed on digital computers, information from experience is contained in knowledge structures in which isolated elements are connected through passive and automatic operations. In the computer program Human Associative Memory (HAM) (J. Anderson & Bower, 1973), for example, the memory component "does passively accept whatever is sent to it by the parsers and does indiscriminately proceed to encode links in that input. During decoding it generates output trees in response to probe trees in a similarly automatic manner" (p. 186). Such programs take from ordinary experience information that can be disciplined by formal logic and managed by prescribed organizational arrangements.

Machine programmers write out their theories, as diagrams or models, in advance (Hoffman & Nead, 1983). Using basic units and rules for relating them, programmers assume that their descriptions not only limn the world but represent it in the mind. These represented knowledge structures become mental representations.

The next step is often "reification" of the structure; that is, programmers take their particular attempt at a model to be actually efficacious. Hoffman and Nead describe this process: "We take that description of the mental event of re-presentation as *both* a theoretical description and a re-presentation (to the theorist) of the mental event of representation. The theoretical representation of perceptual and conceptual qualities get stuffed back into people's heads. The theory not only describes what heads do, it is believed to be what heads do" (1983, p. 543). Marvin Minsky (1969) states metaphorically that "mental processes resemble . . . the kinds of processes found in computer programs: arbitrary symbol associations, treelike storage schemes, conditional transfers, and the like" (p. 429). Over time the metaphorical status of the explanation can become invisible, and machine processes are seen to be mental processes. As an articulation of a reality principle, such a stance may dismiss or even fail to notice aspects of our experience with which it is not readily compatible—as in the rich possibilities my memory of Carl affords.

As I noted in the perception chapter, according to most information-processing accounts, information from the senses goes into what are called sensory stores (iconic or echoic, for example). Through some type of recognition process, such as feature detection, information gets transferred from the sensory stores to a short-term store. From there, if it is elaboratively rehearsed (and connected to hierarchically organized semantic representations), it enters a long-term store. Once the information reaches long-term memory, it must then be stored in a way that facilitates retrieval. In the information-processing framework, most attention has been given to the contents and structure of long-term semantic memory because, to cite Geoffrey Loftus and Elizabeth Loftus (1976), "in order to theorize about a *retrieval* process, we need to know something about the *structure* from which we are retrieving" (p. 124). Some kind of mechanism must operate on the elemental units to reconstitute them in integrated patterns of recognition.

Although such treatments of memory deviate significantly from the word association tradition, they did not totally alter traditional conceptions of associations themselves (Estes, 1979). Information-processing accounts generally rely, for example, on a store that holds "raw, sensory information, as yet unanalyzed for meaning" (Loftus & Loftus, 1976, p. 21). As noted in my chapter on perception, such an assumption implies that perception is indirect; that is, the information received is somehow impoverished and must be reconstructed (or processed). "In this way perception and memory are separated in accordance with the traditional definitions: The information is *obtained* in a series of unchangeable percepts and *stored* and combined by memory acts" (Johansson, 1979, p. 96). The nature of the information that undergoes processing varies from model to model, but most models posit some basic, elemental units from a sensory array. Whether features or nodes in an associative network, these combine into subsets through a process of formal abstraction.

Consider, for example, the work of Alan Collins and Ross Quillian (Quillian, 1969; Collins & Quillian, 1969). Unlike earlier formulations of association which stressed contiguity, their theory uses activation and network analogies that emphasize relations or connections between stored words. "It seems reasonable," Quillian (1968) explains, "to suppose that people must necessarily understand new sentences by retrieving *stored* information about the meaning of isolated words and phrases, and then combining and perhaps altering these retrieved word meanings to build up the meanings of sentences" (p. 236). In a hierarchically organized network, a more specific object such as canary is nested under a more general category such as bird, which is nested under the more abstract concept animal. Pointers or links connect individual units to other units in the total network structure. Memory activities are assumed to involve a spread of activation in a parallel process. The participation in the relationship determines the association, not contiguity (Woods, 1975). Other neoassociationist models that developed subsequently conceive of knowledge stored in memory as even more abstract and hierarchically structured (e.g., J. Anderson & Bower, 1973; Kintsch, 1974; Rumelhart, et al., 1972).

The emphasis on hierarchical relations and abstract knowledge resulted, in part, from the impact of Chomsky's linguistic theory, which pointed to grammatical relations not apparent in surface structure. Several researchers however, were frustrated by the formal architectural features of Newell and Simon's information-processing model, especially its serial processing, and they turned from representing memory as determined by fixed rules and operations to representing it as determined probablistically and as spreading activation. Many of these semantic network theories had radical potential. In fact, according to Allman (1989), Rumelhart became interested in "cooperative computation" (part of connectionism) through the work of Quillian's knowledge webs. But these early networks were confined to objectivist views of language and linguistics (e.g., that words are discrete units with clear meanings). Recently developed by linguists such as Ronald Langacker (1987) and Eva Sweetser (1990), a contextualist view of language emphasizes meaning as encyclopedic, context-dependent, and emergent in linguistic events. To reach their more radical potential, these network theories needed a natural grammar to avoid overly rigid, formal notions of association.

Such interest in nonsequential architecture also led to more formal neoassociationist theories of memory, the most influential of which is J. Anderson and Bower's (1973) HAM. Their work illustrates the influence of associationism and logical positivism on their "neoassociationist" information-processing account of memory:

> Unlike past associative theories, we will not focus on associations among single items such as letters, nonsense syllables, or words. Rather, we will introduce propositions about the world as the fundamental unit. A proposition is a configuration of elements which (a) is structured according to *rules of formation*, and (b) has a *truth value*. . . . We will suppose that all information enters memory in propositional packets. On this view, it is not even possible to have simple word-to-word associations. Words can become inter-associated only as their corresponding concepts participate in propositions that are encoded into memory. However, propositions will not be treated here as unitary objects of Gestalt wholes in memory having novel, emergent properties. Rather, propositions will be conceived as structured bundles of associations between elementary ideas or concepts. (p. 3)

This "quite mechanistic interpretation of sentence learning" (p. 332) illustrates a commitment to an objectivist view of language (as described by Lakoff and Johnson, 1980).

Most of J. Anderson and Bower's experiments involve the presentation of simple sentences (propositions) isolated from any context (much like experimenters isolated individual words in word studies). Such decontextualization proves troublesome, however,

and other network models, such as Hayes-Roth's (1977) discussed in
my chapter on perception, depart from Anderson and Bower's
model. In an attempt to be more sensitive to context, for example,
Hayes-Roth argues against the independent associate links and for
higher order units. These higher order units (now adapted by
J. Anderson, 1980b) are more compatible with the notion of gestalts,
which change in the learning process and under the influence of any
given structure imposed upon them. The emergence of such associationist revisions to take account of context came from the increasing
recognition of what happens at the time of encoding (taking in the
stimulus) and how it determines the way that the stimulus material
is stored and retrieved (Tulving, 1972; Tulving & Thomson, 1973;
Tulving & Wiseman, 1975; Watkins & Tulving, 1975).

Remembering Context

Because of its focus on eventfulness (breadth, uniqueness, and
meaningfulness), context challenges the boundedness and rigidity
of both mechanistic and formal memory accounts. Contextualists
argue that associationist theories of context in memory tend to be
dismissive or awkward. In a typical neoassociationist move, for
example, Bower (1972) describes all the possible contextual features in an experiment as "contextual drift," which simply en-
hances recall. Bower's drift ignores the this-ness of concrete details.
Or the associationist sometimes claims that the more situational
information the subject encodes, the more cues will be available for
retrieval. Context thus increases the probability for successful
recall of the item. But the system gets impossibly awkward: "If the
number of senses a word has depends on the number of possible
contexts of the word, the number of nodes for a single word in the
system may become unmanageably large" (Watkins & Tulving,
1975, p. 28). Associationists must put information in "tags" or
nodes, which are stored with each memory trace; thus, as Bransford, McCarrell, Franks, & Nitsch (1977, p. 440) state in their
analysis of HAM, there are "list tags," "time tags," and "experiment tags." J. R. Anderson and Bower (1973) convert all context,
even autobiographical information, into propositions.

The contextualist argues, further, that neoassociationists cannot continue to reduce the overall context to just another set of
propositions (Shanon, 1988). Propositions constructed out of stim-

ulus material ("I was presented with X") must be seen through the total context of the experimental situation. Context is essential to recognition. Since context is constantly changing within a dynamic event, memory is never fixed and static. Moreover, as representations of the external world, stored propositions freeze the flow of time in the dynamic event. J. Anderson and Bower (1973) honestly admit the problem with context: "HAM does not provide any magical truths about encoding strategies" (p. 419).

To deal with context, some information-processing theorists have leaned more heavily on formalisms. Recently, for example, J. Anderson (1989) endorsed "*the principle of rationality*: Human memory behaves as an optimal solution to the information-retrieval problems facing humans" (p. 195). Here the problem becomes not mechanisms so much but identification of "how to frame human [memory] so that *it will be rational* [italics added]" (p. 196). In the face of the declining power of mechanism to address context, such a move toward formal rationality is not surprising. Such formalism assumes we know the world only as it is already known (by the programmer), only as it already conforms to a predefined rationality. From within the mechanist camp there is skepticism—"the underlying medium of production systems is *still* too idealized and oversimplified in its constraints" (Dennett, 1991, p. 267). The contextualist warns that such a movement may dangerously detach memory from the ambiguity and contingency always embedded in lived experience.

From a contextualistic vantage point, such adjustments have led memory researchers into theoretical quagmires. Recent debates center around an apparently endless series of postulations of forms of memory. Tulving (1985) highlights this theme in current memory research when he asks in the title of his now famous article, "How many memory systems are there?" Those still rallying around information processing defend the now fragmented versions of memory. Max Coltheart (1989) argues that the movement toward what he calls "fractionation of [memory] systems into subsystems" is a result of more precision in accounting for experimental findings (p. 285). "There are a number of advantages in taking seriously the idea that any interesting information-processing system is made up of separable processing components, each of which itself may consist of a set of separable subcomponents, and then even more specific fractionations should be contemplated with equanimity"

(p. 286). But many students of memory do not contemplate such a theoretical possibility with equanimity. A proliferation of different classes of memory tasks, processes, and systems has dissipated the hope that the "essence" of memory will be discovered. In the same volume, for example, Robert Lockhart (1989), states that current memory theory suffers "from a taxonomic crisis, if not a full-blown case of terminological chaos" (p. 3). Most troubling to Lockhart is the dichotomous nature of memory investigation: implicit and explicit memory (e.g., Schacter, 1987; Schacter & Graf, 1986), episodic and semantic memory (Tulving, 1984), procedural and declarative memory (Squire, 1986). Although a review of these dichotomies and the research surrounding them is beyond the scope of this chapter, it is clear what a more contextually oriented view might suggest—information processing has spent its theoretical usefulness. It can probably not address fundamental questions raised by research that reveals dissociations, for example, in memory functions. We need new metaphors and approaches that encourage observation of memory in its fullest possible context.

Schemata and Frames

During the later 1970s and early 1980s, researchers in artificial intelligence tried to develop more context sensitive data structures such as scripts, goals, and plans (e.g., Schank & Abelson, 1977; Schank, 1981); frames (Minsky, 1975; 1981); and schemata (Bobrow & Norman, 1975; Rumelhart & Ortony, 1977). Replacing associationistic views of knowledge representations in memory, these more holistic structures attempted to represent the background knowledge of everyday situations and ordinary language. As I noted in previous chapters, researchers such as Rumelhart and Ortony (1977) and Neisser (1976) called for schemata to represent the organization units of memory in more flexible, less brittle, interactive data structures. In these conceptualizations of memory, situational context became an important focus for the study of memory, not an irritating limitation (see Winograd & Flores, 1986, pp. 111–24, for a discussion of frame-based computational systems approaches to recognition).

Daniel Bobrow and Donald Norman (1975), for example, even suggest that schemata are event driven. They explain, "By this, we mean that all input data invoke processing" (p. 142). In earlier, more associationist models, processing was primarily data driven; that is, dependent on feature analysis of sensory data which then passed upward to higher level units. New processing strategies of the mid-seventies included top down conceptually driven analysis, which is "guided by the contextual information" available in situations (Norman, 1979, p. 135). In another fairly dramatic departure from traditional associationist approaches to memory, researchers such as Roger Schank (1981) classify human memories as "event memory," "generalized event memory," "situation memory," or "intentional memory" (pp. 121–23). Describing familiar situations, this research scripted such events as eating in a restaurant, going to a birthday party, and watching a football game. The programmer assumes that in typical situations, information can be represented less formally, in defaults; that is, certain details may be typical or likely but not always present. From the perspective of Ebbinghaus's memory research with nonsense syllables, such a shift to more holistic phenomena seems striking. This shift attempted to recognize the importance of situatedness for the study of memory, but, in addressing complexity, it highlighted problems in the formalist/mechanist approach itself.

Essentially, scripts contain stereotypical, routinized social activities. These knowledge representations in memory are prepackaged. What is represented in memory can be formalized in a structured description of a sequence of actions in a familiar situation. Knowledge of situations is simplified in advance of the experience. As the most outspoken contextualist critic of this type of information-processing depiction of memory, Dreyfus (1979) points to the circularity in this approach to understanding recognition. The central question is how someone can explain the original recognition if the structure is already in the head. For example, how do I come to recognize "this" event as a birthday party? Dreyfus concludes, "The holist thus faces a vicious circle: relevance presupposes similarity and similarity presupposes relevance" (pp. 54–55).

The appeal to broader contexts that can be activated from the top down does not solve the problem either (e.g., Norman, 1979, on "nested" hierarchies). Dreyfus notes that "the programmer must either claim that some features are intrinsically relevant and have a fixed meaning regardless of context—a possibility already excluded in the original appeal to context—or the programmer will be faced with an infinite regress of contexts" (p. 221). In addition to pointing out the circularity in this way of accounting for recognition, contextualists such as Dreyfus oppose the split between the organism and the contextual situation as these scripts become reified as representations in heads. For example, Bobrow and Norman (1975) bring into cognitive processing "a multilayered assemblage of experts. Each expert is a process that knows how to handle the data and suggestions provided by it" (p. 145). To handle variations in the script, however, the assemblages proliferate and quickly become complex. Such problems have led some researchers to abandon conceptions of the mind as a unitary system. "One could say little about 'mental states' if one imagined the Mind to be a single, unitary thing. Instead, we shall envision the mind (or brain) as composed of many partially autonomous 'agents'—as a 'Society' of smaller minds. . . . To give this idea substance, we must propose some structure for that Mental Society. In fact, we'll suppose that it works much like any human administrative organization" (Minsky, 1981, p. 88).

This line of thinking led to Minsky's *The Society of Mind* (1986), a theory that does not rely on representations but on distributed processes and networks. In this view agents can form networks or self-organizing agencies that can be connected to other agencies to produce larger networks. Varela and his colleagues (1991) note that Minsky's "disunified, heterogenous collection of networks of processes seems not only attractive but strongly resonant with the experience accumulated in all the fields of cognitive science"; further it does not "lose sight for too long of the personal and experiential" (p. 107). With Minsky (1986) the mind's I is now fragmented into self-enclosed series of managerial functions. But do we want such bureaucratic accounts of everyday reasoning even if they are in principle possible to compute (see Boden, 1988)? Such a model of the mind is still hobbled by an official formality and impersonal social relations.

In going to great lengths to preserve regularity and consistency in formulations of memory processes, mechanists swing from reduction of experience to formal, logical systems to neurological reduction. Given the technical and formal climate in artificial intelligence, it was no wonder connectionism and parallel distributed processing (PDP) struck such a responsive chord (or caused synapses to fire off) in cognitive psychologists, especially in those whose work on schemata recognized the importance of situated

cognition (Rumelhart, et al., 1986). In formal computer simulations, such as Newell and Simon's (1972), the mind is a serial
system. Each specific unit retains its integrity and represents a
particular information item. Thus, long-term memory is conceived
as a fixed storehouse. In contrast, in PDP devices, the collection of
interconnected neurons contain memories which are distributed
throughout the network structure and are meaningless without
activation and connection. Memory is more dependent on the
circuitry and complexity of the interactions in the system than on an
individual unit. Contextualism embraces many of the connectionist's assumptions about memory such as distribution, activity,
interconnection, and learning from experience. In addition, when
the network is activated, it is integrative and holistic, as opposed to
analytic and formally rational. Finally, connectionists evoke images
of the mind as a community—from bureaucratic agency to friendly
neighborhood. Is this the mind's we of contextualism?

Contextualism remains open. It recognizes that local mechanisms exist and become functional in behavior, but these mechanisms must be able to adapt to novelty and change in the evolving
context. As I mentioned in the introduction, some contextualists
(e.g., Dreyfus & Dreyfus, 1986, 1991) seem to be optimistic about
neural networking research. Others are very skeptical. In his book
on memory, Rosenfield (1988) is disturbed by the "prefabrication"
of the generalizations produced by parallel distributed processing.
The distribution of neurons and the information that initiates
excitation are specified in advance by the programmer, who also
determines the type of interactions that go on between them (i.e., he
weights the strengths of the connections in the distribution). Arguing the limitations of PDP, Rosenfield states, "In fact, PDP stimulations are really based on the nineteenth-century principles of
localization and the matching of stimuli to fixed memory stores.
The 'generalizations' of these devices are nothing more than overlapping patterns in *predetermined* codes. Real generalization creates *new* categories of information; and from an organism's point of
view, such new categorizations are the consequences of unforeseen
elements in the environment" (p. 149). Most recent attempts have
been focused, however, not on programming, but on getting systems
to learn; that is, the programmer does not set the weights but sets the
conditions for the network to set its own weights (e.g., see Allman,
1989, for a discussion of NETalk). Such unsupervised learning is

not tailored in advance. Of course, mechanists such as G. Johnson (1991) want to claim neural networking research as evidence for the view "that intelligence is mechanistic" (p. 3). Hence, at present, some interpretations of the extrapolations of connectionism seem compatible with contextual assumptions, while other interpretations seem to insist again that all such models confirm mechanistic assumptions. Such debates exemplify how worldviews shape the interpretation of research.

Memory for Events

The view that memory is contextual in nature, however, is not wholly dependent on connectionist alternatives to information processing. In the early 1970s a number of experiments by Tulving and his associates (e.g., Tulving, 1972; Tulving & Thomson, 1973; Tulving & Wiseman, 1975; Watkins & Tulving, 1975) demonstrated the importance of context—what happened in the experiment during the encoding of information determined how information was stored and retrieved. At the same time, John Bransford, Jeffrey Franks, and their associates found in a series of experiments that both the context of an experiment and what the subject brings to the context powerfully influences what the subject remembers (e.g., Bransford & Franks, 1971, 1972; Bransford & McCarrell, 1974). This line of research on how the subjects' knowledge of relations and events influenced memory was a pivotal turning point in the reformation of perception and memory. Bransford and Franks's (1971) findings not only parallel those of Johansson (1973) on event perception, but, as I show in the next chapter, they also corroborate the contextualistic work in categorization undertaken during this same period by Rosch and her colleagues.

The entire experimental research program of Bransford, Franks, and their colleagues challenged the objectivist view of language assumed in much past memory research. Words had been taken to be basic objects not only of linguistic analysis but also of the world itself (Bransford & McCarrell, 1974). In the objectivist view, a sentence's meaning is the sum of its parts. Meanings lie in words or propositions that become combined in sentences or networks of propositions. Contrary to this analytic view of linguistics, Bransford and Franks's experiments revealed that subjects construct meanings 1) based on their knowledge of the total event or situation (including nonlinguistic factors) and their background knowledge and 2) by finding relationships among parts that change the whole. Subjects often used more than what was directly available in the sentences presented to them. Not passive encoders of information, subjects integrated and assimilated the information in ways that produced a considerable degree of semantic precision.

Let me illustrate with one of their experiments (Bransford & Franks, 1971). To carry out their study, they constructed four complex sentences which could be broken down into four simple, declarative sentences. For example:

> COMPLEX: The ants in the kitchen ate the sweet jelly which was on the table.
> SIMPLE: The ants were in the kitchen. The jelly was on the table. The table was in the kitchen. The jelly was sweet. The ants ate the jelly.

The complex sentences represented a minievent. Like Johansson questioning part-whole relationships in event perception (recall the walking person experiment), these researchers were interested in part-whole relationships in memory for events. Would the subjects remember the pattern of input by reconstructing each part (i.e., simple sentence), or would the parts fuse in an experience of the whole event (complex sentence)?

Bransford and Franks took the simple sentences (which they termed one-component ideas) and recombined them to form sentences containing two of the component ideas (e.g., The ants in the kitchen ate the jelly) or three of the component ideas (e.g., The ants ate the sweet jelly which was on the table). For the experiment they developed a complete set of sentences for each complex sentence (or FOUR component ideas); each set contained one FOUR, three THREES, four TWOS, and four ONES. Using four different idea sets or complex sentences, they constructed an acquistion list that contained twenty-four sentences, six from each of the four different idea sets (i.e., two ONES, two TWOS, and four ONES); the subjects, however, were never presented with the FOUR component sentence. The sentences were randomly arranged so that no two sentences from the same idea set occurred consecutively. During acquisition, the experimenters read the twenty-four sentences; following acquisition, they again presented the subjects with the recognition set of sentences that contained new sentences in addition to the ones they had heard. The new sentences (which included ONES, TWOS, THREES, and FOURS) were taken from the four-idea sets originally constructed but not included on the acquisition list. The subjects were instructed to decide whether they had heard the sentence during acquisition. For each sentence, they were to assign a confidence rating to their judgment. In a second experiment, Bransford and Franks repeated the first experiment but added "noncase" sentences, sentences that were syntactically similar to those in the original acquisition set but that had different content.

Quite remarkably, subjects gave their highest confidence ratings to the complex sentences (FOURS), even though they had not heard them during the acquisition task. In addition, the recognition and rating increased with the complexity of the sentences. Bransford and Franks found an ordinal relationship between FOURS, THREES, TWOS, ONES, and NONCASES. The THREES and TWOS received positive mean ratings; the ONES slightly negative ratings; the NONCASES very low ratings.

These findings suggest that memory is more than the recollection of individual items presented during acquisition. Bransford and Franks conclude that the subjects "acquired something more general or abstract than simply a list of those sentences experienced during acquisition" (p. 348). Certainly, the subjects relied on the information presented since they readily recognized and confidently rejected noncase sentences; nonetheless, some type of integration of the individual items into holistic semantic ideas occurred. Subjects remembered the semantic information; they went beyond the parts of the stimulus materials. Bransford and Franks emphasize the integrative phenomena their experiment reveals as the abstraction of linguistic ideas. But more important than abstract construction, these experiments underscore the productive and generative nature of remembering. The subjects actively engaged with the materials to render them meaningful.

Like Johansson's (1973) study of motion perception, the Bransford and Franks study does not presuppose that memory can be reduced to a static collection of elements totally contained within the stimuli; rather the stimuli (moving dots in Johansson's experiment and sentences in Bransford and Franks's) consist of relational sets that interact and alter the characteristics of individual stimulus components (a dot or a simple sentence). Subjects thought they recognized both complex sentences that they had never seen and novel sentences that were consonant with the abstracted ideas. Because they did not hear the sentences consecutively, subjects actively integrated the information contained in individual sentences presented to them (in the same way that subjects integrated the dots of light). Contrary to associationists' claims — namely, that visual perception and remembering depend on the reconstitution of experience from particulars that accumulate over time — Johansson's and Bransford and Franks's findings indicate the total perceptual or memorial event, including the subjects' knowledge of the interrelationships of contextual features, determines what is perceived and remembered.

In sum, Bransford and Franks's findings cannot be easily accommodated by most associatively constructed information-processing storage theories. Different network models posit various kinds of elemental units (input) and different types of linkages between them. Individual input entities, however defined, must remain impervious to the integrative or abstraction phenomena identified by Bransford and Franks or else one loses access to any *control element* that functions as a gate in a network of associations (Estes, 1972). Moreover, the concept of activation in such theories usually assumes a spatiotemporal spread of nodes. In Bransford and Franks's study, the linguistic strings interacted in such a way that their individual identities were transformed, yet the meaning remained.

Bransford and Franks's study lent impetus to a movement among cognitive psychologists who were rethinking the basic premises of traditional memory research. Most dramatically, Jenkins (1974b) used the study as a paradigmatic example of what he calls "event recognition." Using Pepper's terminology, Jenkins offers the following contextualistic account of the experiment:

> The subjects have used the various strands repeatedly available in the texture of the experiment to construct four events that are completely described by the four long, complex sentences. The quality of each of the events is indeed the total meaning of the complex sentence. Once the fusion of the strands into events has occurred (particularly since the strands are heard over and over again in various combinations), the subject cannot perform an analysis to recover the exact pattern of input that furnished support for the construction that he made. (p. 190)

The contextualistic category of fusion states that different strands and textures in the event merge together without regard to consecutiveness in time and space. What is remembered is not the individual linguistic items but the quality of the subjects' interaction with the stimulus material: *"Remembering is a function of the total set of experiences to which an input belongs"* (Bransford, McCarrell, Franks, & Nitsch, 1977, p. 455).

Of course, associationists responded to Bransford and Franks's findings. J. Anderson and Bower (1973) argue that subjects encode "context tags," something on the order of, "In context C, I studied that the ants ate the jelly" (p. 348). Because the sentences overlap, each sentence has several context tags (in fact, an infinite number). Thus, a kind of interference effect explains why the subjects cannot discriminate between OLD and NEW sentences. In this ad hoc account, subjects are confused rather than constructive and agential. (J. Anderson and Bower do admit that there are problems with such an explanation; for example, the subjects must compute these complex interrelations between propositions.) Bransford, McCarrell, Franks, and Nitsch (1977) reply, however, that "the subjects are not confused about the global information derived from the total set of acquisition experiences. They know the overall events that were communicated" (p. 456).

Such factors as the nature of the experimental task and the activities of the subject (e.g., problem solving, inference, and effort to understand and construct meaningfully) determine what is remembered in an experiment; all combine to constitute the quality of the event.

A number of experiments explored and extended Bransford and Franks's findings (e.g., Barclay, 1973; Bransford, et al., 1972; Bransford & M. K. Johnson, 1972, 1973; Bransford & McCarrell, 1974; M. K. Johnson, et al., 1974). Coupled with the increasing dissatisfaction with the proliferation of information-processing models of memory, these experiments pointed to alternative explanations other than storage and retrieval as fruitful for memory research. As Fergus Craik (1979) notes, researchers such as Bransford and Franks treat memory as a skilled activity "rather than the matching of the products of perception against postulated memory traces from perceptual experiences" (p. 96). By the end of the 1970s, leading memory theorists such as Lars-Göran Nilsson (1979) argued that "we have to abandon the idea that memory is some kind of

object—a storehouse for holding information—or a process" (p. 7).
Context plays a crucial role. In fact, as Jenkins (1974b) radically
asserts, "*What memory is depends on context* (p. 786).

Toward a Contextualistic View of Memory

It is one thing to point to the shortcomings of the dominant
worldview and protest its hegemony; it is another to think one's way
out of the mechanist canon and construct an alternative worldview.
But as we have seen, contextualism has been, historically, a real
contender in the debates about the nature of both perception and
memory, and it has propelled empirical research toward concerns
about ecological validity. In this section I point to two crucial areas
in the development of contextualistic memory research: 1.) ecological psychologists' metaphor of event memory as an important
alternative to mechanism and 2.) cross-disciplinary development of
a new understanding of language, with important implications for
how we conceive of perception and memory. Let me begin this
discussion, however, with a brief account of the traditional contextualistic account of memory.

For the contextualist, the quality of an event determines what is
retained from experience as memory. This means that contextualism does not separate perception from memory, or at least not in the
prepackaged manner of information-processing models. It is not
easy to determine where perceiving ends (if indeed it does) and
memory begins. Nor is the contextualist particularly anxious about
cutoff points. In the lived event, the organism and environment
contribute meaning in a transaction that occurs over time. Dewey
(1934) writes, for example: "Whenever anything is undergone in
consequence of a doing, the self is modified. The modification
extends beyond acquisition of greater facility and skill. Attitudes
and interests are built up which embody in themselves some deposit
of meaning of things done and undergone. These funded and
retained meanings become a part of the self" (p. 264). This dynamic
relationship between the organism and environment demands a
flexibility and adaptability that orients the organism in the event
and its historical context. Recall that Bransford, McCarrell, Franks,
and Nitsch (1977) use the metaphor of memory as stage setting.
Dewey (1925) employs the analogy of watching a play in his
explanation of perception and memory. (The following summary is

taken from p. 306.) As viewers of a play, we understand each presented phase of the play by bringing into the present phase the accumulated meanings from the previous parts. But we do this, Dewey argues, without deliberately remembering the past parts; for if we remember the past actions or events, then we are cut off from the present action of the play. In the act of recollection, our attention would be divided so that we could "not be aware of what is now said and done." The meaning from the past "suffuses, interpenetrates, colors what is now and here uppermost." Somewhat ironically, Dewey states that words such as "context and background, fringe, etc." suggest "something too external to meet the facts of the case." Not only do the present actions contain past meaning, but they also anticipate future actions. "It is this double relationship of continuation, promotion, carrying forward, and of arrest, deviation, need of supplementation, which defines that focalization of meanings which is consciousness, awareness, perception. Every case of consciousness is dramatic; drama is an enhancement of the conditions of consciousness." Meanings do not result from discrete acts of recollection; rather meaning enters right into the textures and strands of the events in action over time. This is "the dynamic active event" of contextualism (Pepper, 1961, p. 232).

In the contextual view memory is a constant background and foreground, "a field of habitual meanings" (Kestenbaum, 1977). Meanings from the past penetrate our present situations. As another contextualistic philosopher Merleau-Ponty (1962) states, "We find, as a basic layer of experience, a whole already pregnant with an irreducible meaning" (pp. 20–21). This means that the past is "in" the present situation; perception "carries its meaning within itself" (p. 21). As I suggested in my chapter on perception, both Bartlett's (1932) earlier and M. Johnson's (1987) more recent use of the term *schema* "refers to an active organization of past reactions, or of past experiences" (Bartlett, p. 201); it functions as a dynamic, unitary whole in this situation. Remembering is an active process because the events in which organisms participate are characterized by novelty and change. Thus, remembering involves production, construction, and integration rather than reproduction; Dewey (1925) explains that past experiences leave remainders of meanings that we use in our ongoing activities (p. 328).

Contextualistic metaphors emphasize the transactional nature of exchange between the organism and the environment. For example, Bartlett (1932) uses the metaphor of playing tennis: "It is with remembering as it is with the stroke in a skilled game" (p. 204). Here the "momentary needs of the game" determine action, not repeating past movements. So adaptive and holistic is Bartlett's treatment of memory that Robert Belli (1986) makes the case that, in terms of Pepper's framework, Bartlett's theory exemplifies an organicist rather than a contextualist worldview. David Wechsler (1963) argues that "memories are not like filed letters stored in cabinets or unhung paintings in the basement of a museum. Rather, they are like melodies realized by striking the keys on a piano. Ideas are not any more stored in the brain than melodies in the keys of a piano" (p. 151). And finally, Bransford, McCarrell, Franks, & Nitsch (1977) propose that "a major role of past experience is to provide 'boundary constraints' that set the *stage* for articulating the uniqueness, as well as sameness of information" (p. 434). They compare their stage setting metaphor to Gibson's conception of attunement to invariant information. Eschewing permanent, immutable structures and the localized units demanded by generalized mechanistic processes, contextualists use metaphors that suggest cohesion, specificity, and spreading temporality.

Ecological Perspectives on Event Memory

"Toward Unexplaining Memory" by Bransford, McCarrell, Franks, and Nitsch (1977) has been the anchor for a growing literature on ecological perspectives on memory (for a broad sampling of this literature, see Bransford, 1979; Bruce, 1985; Hirst & Levine, 1985; Hoffman & Nead, 1983; Jenkins, et al, 1986; McCabe, 1986b; Neisser, 1982, 1988; Wilcox & Katz, 1981a). As I suggested in the last chapter, Gibson (1979) and his collaborators focused most of their attention on perception and its salience in cognition. In light of the experiments done by Bransford and Franks (1971), ecological psychologists continue to build a strong case that memory must be studied in natural contexts. Furthermore, they argue that memory for an event may contain more than the sum of its parts. For example, in a series of studies similar to the ones by Bransford and Franks (but using slides and photographs instead of sentences), James Jenkins, Jerry Wald, and John Pittenger (1986) conclude, "*We see events as natural wholes that are, so to speak, perceived through the slides, rather than built up from the slides. The slides are* windows through which the event is glimpsed, rather than Tinker Toys that are used to construct some kind of event-like edifice" (p. 129).

In explaining memory, some ecological psychologists focus primarily on Gibson's notion of affordance and invariant structure. In specifying information in the environment and in the types of structures available, these Gibsonians deemphasize the role of memory. Typical in their emphasis, Stephen Wilcox and Stuart Katz (1981a) argue that *"memory may be understood as the apprehension of an unfolding environment in which the past affects the present and the present affects the past"* (p. 235). In their focus on structure and invariance, these interpreters of Gibson lean more toward the worldview of formism; that is, the structures available in the environment determine learning. Those ecological psychologists who stress relationship lean more toward contextualism. Viki McCabe and Gerald Balzano (1986), for example, discuss the importance of finding relations among things as important determinants of what is learned. As they state, "Invariants are specifically interdefined with a set of transformations that preserve them; a different set of transformations would specify a new set of invariants" (p. 114; see also McCabe, 1986b, for further experiments from an ecological perspective). Contextualistic interpretations of Gibson stress memory as an activity and as an adaptive function, but as I argued in the last chapter, they must also include linguistic meaning in their metaphor of organism.

In 1982, Neisser published a book of readings called *Memory Observed: Remembering in Natural Contexts*. Encouraging memory researchers to broaden the nature of their experimental focus, he presented some forty examples of naturalistic or ecologically valid memory studies. In a more recent book entitled *Remembering Reconsidered: Ecological and Traditional Approaches to the Study of Memory* (Neisser & Winograd, 1988), researchers present findings on autobiographical memory, event memory, and ordinary memory. Nelson's (1988) article, which examines the memories of a young child named Emily from ages 21 to 36 months, exemplifies a paradigmatic contextualistic memory experiment, as does her entire ten-year research program (see her work on knowledge representation, 1986). In a brief account of her study of Emily, we can see how the metaphors of machine and organism become inadequate in the face of linguistic or textual understanding.

For example, her study of memory examined Emily's routine everyday experiences by recording, with the help of Emily's mother, her nightly, presleep monologues and dialogues; she found, by examining her language, that the everyday experiences were very evident and important to Emily. She argues that Emily's memory developed through the formation of general event schemata that were adaptive in her encounters with the world. Emily's talk primarily centered around those experiences that she needed to organize and resolve; they were not evoked by external cues. Nelson found that events that were too novel could not be so organized or integrated and appeared to drop out of the memory system. She concludes: "The claim here is that [Emily's] solitary memory talk was different from shared reminiscing as a social activity; she engaged in such talk in the service of organizing knowledge, not in the service of social bonding. As such, the memories talked about would be expected to disappear as specific episodes as they became integrated into her personal knowledge system. In contrast, socially shared memories are expected to be retained in specific narrativized form" (p. 268). It is only with the onset of language and dialogue and the increased ability to share her memories in social exchanges that she develops an autobiographical memory. Sociality is important, perhaps necessary, for reflection about the past. In Nelson's research, we see memory studied contextualistically, as an adaptive system, not as an essence or process in and of itself and not without language and other people.

The Storied Nature of Our Memories

The contextualist argues that there is no memory without context and history. Memories are not fixed in a storehouse but are part of a dynamically evolving system that attunes us to events and our experiences over time. With our memories we engage with others to give our experience continuity and meaning. This sense of memory as a dynamically evolving system can be seen in the Robinson epigraph at the beginning of this chapter where the narrator struggles to understand her mother's suicide. Her reflection leads to a transfiguration of the past, in the same way that my remembering Carl transformed fragments (the raised hand, the orange-tinted hair, the boldly uttered sentence) into a new event made coherent by my present situation. In these examples—one from fiction and one from real life—we see how context keeps cognition situated in the concrete experience of the actual event (and its thick description) and open to the multiple meanings these textures suggest for the rememberer.

Because diversity of meaning orientations and imaginative interpretations tend to be equated in many accounts of science with the irrational and emotional, psychology has had little to say about the storied nature of memory. Scientific practices in psychology were so divorced from reality that not even the laboratory experiment was seen as eventful. The experimenter hoped to strip context away so that mechanisms and processes of memory would be revealed. In trying to discover a set of basic principles about memory, traditional memory research pointedly ignored and distanced itself from ordinary experiences of memory. Rebuffing the movement toward ecological validity, Mahzarin Banaji and Robert Crowder (1989) make just this case for traditional laboratory research: "Our view is that the more complex a phenomenon, the greater the need to study it under controlled conditions, and the less it ought to be studied in its natural complexity" (p. 1192). (See my concluding chapter for a detailed discussion of their arguments.) In information-processing models researchers reconstructed experience in formal, analytic systems of thought. As a result, both laboratory experiments and simulations separate perception and memory, treating them as two separate mechanisms, and further both extricate the subject from ordinary experience. In their insistence on literal, logical language as "the" represented content of memory, mechanistic psychologists have derogated both ordinary memory experiences, and especially fiction, as invalid and unreliable sources for inquiry and insight.

Dennett's (1991) new mechanistic theory of consciousness attempts to revise and revive mechanism on just these grounds. Some streams of his thinking are contextualist in import if not in final interpretation. For example, perception and memory are not boxed up; there is no final product for presentation to a central processor or meaning maker. Through a multitrack process, visual stimulations "yield, over the course of time, something *rather like* a narrative stream or sequence, which can be thought of as subject to continual editing by many processes distributed around in the brain. . . . At any point in time there are multiple drafts of narrative fragments at various stages of editing in various places in the brain" (p. 135). Memory and perception interact freely, and the self becomes like a center of narrative gravity. It spins out a web of words which "are potent elements of our environment that we readily incorporate, ingesting and extruding them, weaving them like spiderwebs into self-protective strings of *narrative*" (p. 417). After making the physical reduction and adapting a third person point of view (his heterophenomenological method) for studying the mind, then he can admit anything from anyone's experience: "You're the novelist, and what you say goes. What more could you want" (p. 96)? One could want, among other things, problematic situations with real people engaged in socially shared projects — ones that matter and make a difference in ours and the lives of others.

Dennett's (1991) mechanistic development shows how necessary it is to understand worldviews and their divergent categories. His arguments reveal the sometimes hidden assumptions of mechanism — about science, the self, and experience. As a loyal mechanist, he starts from a materialistic reduction to the brain and then reconstructs a subject for science. From a contextualist orientation, we might ask, why start there? Why not start with problematic situations? Perception, memory, and consciousness arise in and through real situations. How can we examine the interwoven contributions of the world, the subject, and other people in such situations? Contextualism does not reject reduction as a method in an ongoing investigation, the findings of laboratory research efforts, or models that simulate cognition (see E. Winograd, 1988; Cohen, 1989, for illustrations of some important continuities between the traditional research approaches to memory and ecological ones). But these methods and findings must be used to understand something, namely, a full and rich account of human experience.

Among mechanists, the type of reduction one seeks is hotly disputed. For example, during a recent conference (1991) entitled "Perspectives on Mind," Fodor, disagreeing with Dennett's form of reduction, pointedly and dismissively called Dennett a metaphysician, not a scientist. This attack makes clear the stakes: mechanists "aspir[e] to a science of the mind" (Dennett, 1991, p. 458). But increasingly critics are pointing to faulty scientific assumptions that have resulted in erroneous conceptions of human cognition. In an analysis of scientific laws, Horgan and Tienson (1990) note that computer simulations of memory are essentially closed systems unlike human cognition which is "relevance-sensitive and open

ended" (p. 264). No isolated pieces of information can be reconstituted in such a way as to replace situated human understanding.
But traditional mechanists continue to assume that ordinary experience needs to be restrained and controlled through representations,
and so researchers preanalyze and predetermine objectively what
can count as memorial experience. Here, the story is told in
advance. (In contrast, Dennett's new mechanistic view overwhelms
us with multiple drafts of stories. The story itself does not seem to
matter.) In contextualism meanings can be publicly and socially
negotiated through refiguration or transformation of the context.
Here, the importance lies in telling the story.

Two movements in psychology especially resist objectivist
reductions of meaning in memory: increased interest and attention
to metaphor (e.g., Leary, 1990a, b) and narrative (e.g., Bruner,
1986; Sarbin, 1986a, b). (See Dennett, 1991; Rosenfield, 1988;
Sacks, 1990, for different theories that employ the narrative metaphor in neurological descriptions of the brain). When memory is
seen as social and participatory, it engages us in narrative. Our pasts
are called back to us as we find ourselves in situations, especially
those where we feel our circumstances changed. Such novelty in our
existential situation awakens the past for use in the present. Problematic situations are more often than not socially given in that we
construe them with and through the perspectives of others. But we
are not imprisoned by this sociality, although we can be. Through
imaginative reconstruction and critical reflection, we change our
situations, their meanings, and our relationships. This suggests that
cognition needs a "we" — including others who listen to our stories,
even when the "other" is another part of the same mind. In her
research, Nelson (1988) calls Emily forth to tell her day's events to a
mother who listens. In my teaching story, Carl calls forth my story
as a young teacher as I call forth his story about the men in his
family.

Because perception and memory are interactional events, many
differences are a matter of how long we want to choose to wait before
calling something a "memory" rather than a perception. The
separation is somewhat arbitrary, although at the extremes the
differences are clear. Contextualism does not oppose framing or
structuring information from a given event, nor does it oppose
descriptions of local mechanisms. Rather, it objects to the reification and rigidity of either the structure or the mechanism superim-

posed over experience itself. A contextualistic theory of memory thus works to integrate past experience, perception, and language in interpretations of ordinary situations. The current interest in metaphor and narrative helps uncover an interpretation of perception and memory as flexible structures that involve connectings and reconnectings (categorization or recategorization) in the organism's adaptive responses to the environment, especially in the face of novelty and change. Language enters right into perception and memory, not to overshadow them (although it can) but to enable interrogation and to help with our efforts to construct meaning.

I argued in my chapter on perception that Mark Johnson's theory of imagination interrelates bodily phenomena with conceptualization. In fact, his theory corroborates contextualistic research about memory (such as Nelson's), where language and sociality appear fundamental to the development of memory for ordinary events. Recall that in Johnson's theory perception originates in bodily experience and informs meaning structures through various abstract reconceptualizations of concrete experience. We saw in the example of the metaphor of the container how bodily experiences with spatial orientation (e.g., in-out, as in tears flowing out of our eyes) become structured or patterned over time, as organized activity. These dynamically structured patterns of activity, called schemata, can then be projected metaphorically onto other levels of experience (for instance, we bodily get out of a car and by extension get out of a social obligation).

Although schemata provide coherence, regularity, and consistency, as patterned gestalts, they are not formal structures in the sense of the rules and representations approach in information processing. They do not become pure concepts since they always retain something of the texture and complexity of the temporal events and historical circumstances out of which they arise. When our present situation and actions conform to the typical schema we have, we act, though without explicit awareness, as skillful perceivers in the sense that Gibson emphasizes. But when the situation and/or our actions deviate from a particular schema we have, say in the face of novelty or change, then memory and perception interact in what Dewey calls the drama of the problematic situation. We become more consciously aware of what we perceive, and we are likely to remember past problematic situations, actions we may have undertaken, and the process of our former inquiry itself. Problematic situations become memorable in this way, and we often tell them, to ourselves and others, as stories.

In remembering, we also have the opportunity to reflect on our experience; as Rosch (1988) recognizes: "Memory is the way in which we communicate with ourselves over time" (p. 379). For the view I am espousing here, shared dialogue is critical to perception, memory, conceptualization, and reasoned inquiry. Through dialogue with others whose perspectives may differ from ours, we come to understand situations anew. For example, it was after my experience with Tom that I began conscious reflection about Carl. As I remembered my experience with Carl, I recast that experience through the metaphor of losing touch with my students. The losing touch metaphor exemplifies, for me, what M. Johnson means by a schema that originates in bodily experience and is then projected onto, in this case, a social situation. I think, for example, of the physical and emotional touching that informs good parenting. I extend this metaphor to teaching as an intellectual touching of minds. But I can also shift my perspective on the problematic situation and entertain new metaphors that restructure, in this case, what cannot be easily touched: the iceberg—the huge, underlying structure of the students' conceptions and misconceptions about our subject matter, a structure we do not see as we teach (Norman, 1980). This way of thinking about the situation with my student leads to new possibilities for transforming my actions as a teacher. Such metaphorical ways of knowing need not be irrational or sentimental, though they may become so in the form of cliches. Informal linguistic meanings and reflective practice can be quite reasonable ways people make sense of their worlds (Bruner, 1986, 1987; Leary, 1990a). But the contextualist does not reduce the world to a text either. The external world participates in all its concreteness in shaping life prospects and possibilities. The contextual nature of memory is even more evident when complex mental processes are involved, as we will see in the next chapter on categorization.

Under the auspices of formalism and mechanism, information processing and traditional artificial intelligence reduced memory to inert space and its contents to symbols. In doing so, these cognitive programs employed an objectivist vocabulary. This view of memory is not objective and neutral, however; it participates in shared social and cultural practices and discourses about what counts as reason and information. As sociologist Richard Harvey Brown (1989) notes of all positivistic science:

> Because it can do certain things so well, [its discourse] easily expands to include more and more social life and experience. It thereby leads us to ignore history and tradition, to turn political and moral questions into technical or instrumental ones, and to treat every problem as though it had a "solution". . . . By constituting an official discourse of meaning and legitimacy, scientized politics imposes a preemptive, cognitive closure on the present even as it suppresses the lived experience of societal members. (pp. 13–14)

In calling for narrative and metaphor as central to memory and perception, the contextualist threatens the current practices and discourses of the dominant psychological model of cognition, laden as it is with technical jargon and hierarchically defined categorial relationships. In traditional memory research literature, the hierarchical structures and their categorial contents are bland and safe—plants, birds, animals. In looking outside established, allegedly context-free practices, contextualism gathers the ambiguous, the forbidden, and the troublesome. Our experience is more than we can articulate: "Hence, the unreflected, signified world is always larger than whatever version of it becomes canonized into formal knowledge" (Brown, 1989, p. 9). And it is to the world outside the neat storage boxes that I now turn—to the world of women, fire, and dangerous things.

5

Categories: From Static Structures to Dynamic Processes

The beauty of a good story is its openness—the way you or I or anyone reading it can take it in, and use it for ourselves.

—Robert Coles, *The Call of Stories*

It was a hot day in late June, 1960. I had just turned thirteen and was on my way to Susan's house—for the hundredth time. I went to her house every chance I got. As I sauntered along, I watched Susan's mother, golden brown from sunbathing, backing the new white Thunderbird convertible out of the driveway. From as far as two blocks away, I could see her sunglasses, makeup, and hot pink sundress; as usual, she was going to the country club. Convertible, makeup, a suntanned mother—these were simply unthinkable possibilities within my own family.

Walking down the street, I glanced toward the Fuller house. Ten years older than I, Ted often worked on his car outside. Over the last year we had exchanged silly remarks about his car, the weather, and how boring it was to live in Danville, Illinois. He liked to tease me, probably, I think, because I have always been able to giggle like a fool. He wasn't handsome like the movie stars whose pictures I collected and mooned over, but I had noticed how rhythmically his body moved; he was sensuous, solid, and confident. In contrast, my tall, lanky body stumbled awkwardly all over itself. Sometimes in midafternoon he would sit on his front porch with a beer in his hand. Because the curtains were always closed, I could only see a darkened, smoke-filled room through his front door; sometimes I could hear music and laughter, and I imagined the steamy interior.

On this hot day in June, however, I was preoccupied with my own thoughts and had not noticed Ted—or maybe he'd opened the front door after I had walked by—but suddenly I heard the slowly delivered and carefully pronounced words: "There goes my blonde bombshell." Maybe it was how he said the word *bomb*, like a cat pouncing on a chair cushion and then lighting down off it, but the words swirled around me, circling my legs and moving right up my backbone. I turned to see him standing relaxed against the door frame, his body leaning into it; a huge grin crossed his face. Giggling nervously, I tried to wave away the words, but when I turned back toward Susan's, my pace quickened and his "bomb" exploded inside me.

I turned this phrase over and over in my mind; I had never heard it before. Now, out of his sight, I could feel my body compose itself and rise up. And then I thought, Wait 'til I tell Susan and Jill. During the last months our curiosity about sex had bound us together in a tangle of colored threads. Bursting into Susan's house, I ran up to the room where she and Jill waited. Like a boy just back from his first successful hunt, I offered my prey: "Ted Fuller just called me a blonde bombshell." Rolling her eyes as if I had brought her a dead rat, Jill spat out, "Oh how disgusting." Shrugging this off, Susan smiled seductively as if I had brought her a fox pelt and said, "Oh, what a wonderful thing. I think he's a very handsome, sexy man." Her tongue rolled very slowly over the roof of her mouth. I was spellbound. "He's a creepy crawler," replied Jill.

Susan's worldliness won over Jill's revulsion and my confusion. Without speaking, we rushed to the closet where her mother kept the book on sex. Published in the 1930s, it contained only dry information and ink drawings of male and female anatomy. It was all we had, but it was enough. We pored over it like gardeners looking for the first cracks in the ground that signaled growth. When the dry facts could no longer evoke our imaginations, we agreed, with an attitude of insight and understanding, that, yes, Ted Fuller had a penis, one that probably looked something like this inked anatomical drawing. To Jill's horror, Susan pronounced emphatically as she closed the book, "And he probably knows what to do with it."

I walked out of Susan's house to the corner and stopped short as I looked down Ted Fuller's block. Without the tangled web of giggles and friendships to protect me, I felt alone, uncertain, and confused. Unable to frame my reaction, I tried to absorb this new knowledge about my identity. Although I could not have articulated it then, I sensed a shift, a dissipation. Even as he had given me the powerful sexual compliment, he had, in the same moment, taken something away, something I never had a chance to name for myself. All my life, I had had my wonderful yellow hair, integral and distinguishing. All of a sudden it wasn't quite mine anymore. It meant something else. And what did it mean next to *bombshell*? I had only seen pictures of effects of bombs already dropped. I had never seen a real bomb in its shell. I knew this description was not unique or for me. It was connected with all the "dumb blonde" myths that had seeped into my unconscious. This language was about somebody else's stuff. It took away my power to name and articulate my experience in my own words and with my own images.

Turning left, away from Ted's house, I walked home slowly down the other street. This street felt safe but different now. The walk home was uneventful, lackluster; no one even noticed as I walked by. This was part of an initiation into womanhood: to be sexual in terms outside our own experience or to be invisible—this is the double bind with which many women struggle.

My story is about how we come to know the way the world is organized, how concepts and categories can come to define our experiences in predetermined ways. We live in a world already loaded with meanings that we did not construct. For women and people of color, these concepts are often experienced as dangerous double binds. If we adapt ourselves to the limiting concepts by which we are defined, we lose our power to clarify and claim our own experience. If we do not conform to such concepts, we become invisible, often barely able to tell or hear our own stories. A full-fledged theory of cognition should provide access to understanding the debilitating functions of such concepts. This I argue contextualism does. As one reads the traditional literature in cognitive psychology, however, one sees a different world from that experienced by women and people of color, a world made safe by neutral words, propositions, and features. It is a controllable world, disembodied, circumscribed, and often preconceived. Classic experiments often use, for example, blue squares, dots on cards, or letters, all of which have logical relations, whether they be "symbolic" or "fuzzy." No blonde bombshells. No discrimination. No blues. No dialogue. No ambiguity. Until the mid-seventies, studies of concept formation in cognitive psychology did not consider ordinary experience; in using artificial materials to appear objective and scientific, researchers stripped experience from its social embeddedness and meaning. In this way it has historically predefined the discourse, the terms of the dialogue.

But what my ordinary experience tells me is that these boundary lines are very hard to draw and maintain. And Grumet (1988) reminds us of this in her discussion of the practice of reflective thought: when and where one draws the line is as much a matter of aesthetics as of science. The background context, the dialogues in which I engage, the novelty and contingency of my experience, and the struggle to give it meaning—all of these suggest that we should not pretend that cognition and concepts can be studied as though isolated in a separate mental realm. Rather, they should be regarded concretely, as always already situated in our complex, multilayered interactions with the world. One would not attempt to study the overall development of children by investigating only the chemistry of bone growth.

As in the study of perception and memory, the root metaphor of mechanism has strongly influenced the way in which concepts have been defined, discussed, and studied experimentally. Most psychologists have assumed that concepts and categories are essential in reasoning. The two terms are used very loosely in the literature, often interchangeably. Typically, a concept is defined more generally than a category; some concepts such as sleepiness may not include a category. But a concept often includes more than one category, sometimes hierarchically arranged. For example, we may have a concept of protective clothing that, in the midwest, includes categories such as coats or rain gear. A category is usually defined as a mental construct that somehow "picks out" a group of things or characteristics of things that are deemed to be similar. As Neisser (1987c) defines the process, "To categorize is to treat a set of things as somehow equivalent: to put them in the same pile, or call them by the same name, or respond to them in the same way" (p. 1). How fluid are the boundaries of our concepts and categories?

Working from a strictly mechanistic worldview, some psychologists have tried to establish objective definitions of categories based on necessary and sufficient conditions that, when met, constitute a given category. They have used artificial materials (e.g., letters, dots) to isolate the underlying mechanisms. They would be quick to point out that my example of "blonde bombshell" is not an analytic category (or they might call it a category mistake) and thus one

whose meanings cannot be sufficiently controlled to yield information about underlying mechanisms. Early psychological research on
categories followed from mechanistic assumptions about perception
and memory; features registered during perception become bundled
together in the storehouse of memory through association. The
result—a category—is an abstraction, detached from experience
and used to make objective, transituational knowledge claims.

In contrast to such traditional views, contextualism points to
the dynamic references within and between concepts which are
always embedded in the practices of a community. The title of
Lakoff's (1987b) book refers to the category *balan*, which, in the
Australian aboriginal language Dyirbal, includes all three elements: *Women, Fire, and Dangerous Things*. My story plays upon
the metaphorical extensions of these categories in American culture. In either case, for the contextualist, categorization cannot be
reduced to a matter of shared but discrete parts or units that result
from analysis and cut across context. Such objectivist descriptions
devalue (often by neglecting entirely) the role of the actual, felt
quality of the event in experience.

For the approach I am exploring here, a category occurs in a
particular context and is evoked almost always by indeterminacy in
the situation. In stories of this and earlier chapters, I used concepts
such as kindergartner, questioning students, and blonde bombshell;
these arise naturally out of my attempts to make meaning from my
experience. For example, in describing the event with Ted Fuller, I
work from within an experience that originally disrupted my sense
of identity. I wrote the story in interaction with my writing group,
and as I told them about my experience, new meanings emerged as
the context expanded. I become increasingly aware of the multilayered social and political structures involved in the use of this
category. In such reflection, the circumstances "become transpar-
ent or even luminous, and capable of clarifying not only the aspects
of the world which resemble them but the others too" (Merleau-
Ponty, 1964a, p. 64). The felt quality of the experience also shifts
from power and confusion (for the thirteen-year-old) to loss and
irritation (for the forty-three-year-old). As my community of middle-aged women writers investigates different possibilities for understanding the concept "blonde bombshell," we develop meanings
different from those that emerged from my earlier community of
adolescent girlfriends.

Given the different responses to even such a comparatively contained concept as "blonde bombshell," it is not surprising to find that mechanistic and contextualistic accounts of categorization sharply diverge. Such divergences, of course, result from differing assumptions about perception, memory, and their interrelatedness. Nowhere is contextualism currently more active in eroding the assumptions of traditional mainstream psychological research than in the area of categorization. As Lakoff (1987b) notes, "We have categories for everything we can think about. To change the concept of *category* itself is to change our understanding of the world" (p. 9). We have seen how American psychology grounded itself in a mechanistic worldview in part because, as Bartlett (1932) and Joynson (1970) have argued, psychologists "stood in awe of the stimulus" — some basic unit that could be isolated in the laboratory. In the study of concepts, mechanists argue that the pieces of a jigsaw are importantly constitutive by themselves while contextualists argue that they have comprehensible meaning only in relation to the whole, or at least that the meaning of an individual piece is quite different from its in relationship or participative meaning.

I emphasize again that it is the dominance of the mechanistic view that is at stake, not its integrity or insight. In its more tolerant manifestations, such psychology has simply claimed that it aims to reconstitute the process of categorization as a psychological experience; and discreteness does characterize some of our experiences with categories (e.g., Is this mushroom edible?) Such a stance isolates the particulars of a given category and studies the relations among their attributes so that we can reliably generalize. In its more dogmatic phases, however, it often bases its appeal on commitment to positivistic science. It then asserts that all categorial experience can be reduced to particulars and that meaningful psychological phenomena can only be explained by appeals to laws which combine the particulars into wholes. Many psychologists have privileged association as the most adequate way to describe how the mind works. I have suggested that psychology might not be best served by adhering to one view. That the mind works only by association is questionable at best; it is certainly not the only legitimate view. This becomes especially clear in explanations of more complex mental processes such as the ways we conceptualize our world.

Many researchers have grown frustrated with the limitations of a mechanistic account of conceptualization. Not surprisingly, since its root metaphor is similarity, formism appears as an active metatheoretical alternative in the concept formation literature (see the section on formism in Chapter 1). Although this worldview is not extensively evoked by researchers in perception and memory, the studies of Bruner and his colleagues in the 1950s interjected the hypotheses of this worldview into the study of concept formation. Formistic criticism seriously damaged traditional mechanistic, and especially stimulus-response, accounts of concept formation (e.g., Bruner, 1957; Bruner, et al., 1956). But formism did not have an opportunity to fully emerge as a viable alternative theoretical framework. From Pepper's point of view, it was displaced in cognitive psychology by interest in routine employment of propositional logic (or interest in formalism). As I noted in my earlier discussion of Penrose (1989), who defends a contemporary version of formism, such "formalisms" are expressions of dependency on fixed structures and algorithms. They do not generate new insights or strategies. Information processing treats categories in just this formalistic way, as elements in propositions on which operations can be performed.

After a brief review of the traditional accounts of categories, I turn my attention to current dimensions of contextualistic research which has grown increasingly influential in the study of categorization. Gardner (1985) identifies this shift when he notes, "Today it is no exaggeration to say that the *classical* view of concepts has been replaced by a *natural* view of concepts" (p. 341). In particular, the studies of Rosch and her colleagues (e.g., Rosch, 1973, 1978; Rosch & Mervis, 1975) called into question widely held claims about the nature and role of categorization in cognition. Published in the 1970s, the findings from her research program have been variously interpreted by psychologists advocating different approaches, and her own early characterizations of her work were often more formal than contextual. I argue, however, that the following assumptions typical of her research make it contextualistic: (1) She attacked the then popular Whorfian hypothesis that language determines perception; as we have seen, ecological psychologists strongly reject such a claim; (2) She and her colleagues focused attention not on artificial but on natural categories with boundaries that were fluidly conceived, not rigidly determined; (3) Rosch not only argued for a different organizational structure for natural categories, but she also shifted the focus in cognitive functioning. While previous research had emphasized defining properties, formal judgments, and abstraction, Rosch emphasized the power and salience of middle-sized objects, what she calls basic level categories (e.g., chair or dog). Concepts at this level make powerful claims on our knowledge; we often, for example, spin meanings out of these basic level categories.

Rosch (1978) has briefly discussed the importance of the basic level for event analysis in a suggestive contextualistic description, and we will see how the enactive approach to cognition that she now proposes (Varela, Thompson, & Rosch, 1991) takes the basic level of categorization as "the point at which cognition and environment become simultaneously enacted" (p. 177). Other researchers have actively advanced the implications of her findings along contextualistic lines. Like M. Johnson's, Lakoff's (1987b) work in linguistics points to ways people quite naturally start with basic level categories to make imaginative leaps through analogy and metaphor in our efforts to understand. This extension of Rosch's research has opened up an exciting contextualistic discussion about conceptual knowledge.

Traditional and Modern Mechanistic Views of Categorization

Early mechanists defined a concept as an abstraction derived from the association of objectively defined properties. A person moves from supposed perceptions of things and their properties to abstractions based on association. If perception registers parts of objects and memory stores these discrete units, then conceptualization results from association of similar features, abstractly reconstituted. Neil Bolton (1972) emphasizes the origin of this approach in British Empiricism:

> Substituting "concept" for "idea," [Locke's] view asserts that it is by a process of abstraction that concepts are formed; we observe a number of particular objects and abstract (literally, draw away) from them those features that are common to several of them. Concepts are formed when objects are classified. From Locke's account, it is evident that there are two aspects to this process. Not only must we notice similarities to

form a general idea, but we must also set aside particular differences, which are not relevant to the concept in question. The former corresponds to what we may call generalization, the latter to discrimination. (p. 100)

The early mechanists defined the relation between concept and percept as one of direct correspondence. According to Pepper (1961), if symbols in sentences can be taken to correspond to elements of objects and the relations among the symbols and objects can be specified, then one can determine a sentence "true" (p. 225). But this move, according to Pepper, still begs the question of the relation between the symbols and the attributes of the particular object (which are themselves only perceived indirectly). How could mechanistically oriented psychologists avoid this bifurcation?

Adapting the stimulus-response framework, behaviorists assume that category-relevant features become configured over time through conditioned responses. For example, through experience, we come to group sharp objects that cut. If we doubt a particular object's cutting ability, we can test it. In the behaviorist framework, responses of the organism in the presence of certain features become conditioned so that habit sequences develop. Pepper notes the reductionism of the stimulus-response explanation: "It is simply specificity of response in an organism carried to a higher degree of refinement. . . . [Learning concepts] is simply a complicated chain of physiological reactions, the whole sequence being explicable in physiological terms" (pp. 226–27). Concept formation is similar if not equal to discrimination learning, which is based on a kind of hypothesis testing. If this is the case, then the psychologist can isolate simple stimulus materials and try to investigate how elementary behavioral processes become compounded, usually in hierarchical, chained structures (e.g., Kendler & Kendler, 1962).

The influence of behavioral assumptions is particularly evident in the experiments of the 1950s and early 1960s. Consider the following description of stimulus materials for an experiment by Gordon Bower and Thomas Trabasso (1963) where subjects were asked "to classify a set of patterns into two classes" by using a simple principle:

For exp. 1, patterns were constructed by sampling a single letter from each of four pairs of letters, (V or W), (F or G), (X or Y),

(Q or R). Thus, VFYQ was a pattern, WVXR was not. The four
letters were printed in a diamond shape on a 3 x 5 in. card. The
letters appeared fixed in the order given above, but their locations
at the four diamond corners rotated randomly from trial to trial.
Location was an irrelevant cue. For Groups C and R, the letter
pair (V, W) was relevant; the classification depended on which
one of the letters was present on the card. One of the other letter
pairs was selected randomly to be initially relevant for each S in
Group NR, whereas (V,W) was irrelevant. (p. 411)

Here we find isolated stimuli presented to subjects who must
decide, trial by trial, whether a particular configuration is an
instance of a pattern. The researchers have constructed binary
concepts (i.e., by formulating a set of features that are *either*
positive *or* negative instances of the concept.) They assume that
concept learning is linear, progressing in a step-by-step fashion. The
authors state, "Our aim was to explore initially the most elementary
form of concept learning, in a situation similar to a conventional
discrimination learning procedure" (p. 418).

Although Bower and Trabasso used experimental conditions
similar to those in the stimulus-response tradition, the results of
their experiment are not predicted by the associationist model. They
found simple concept learning to be an all-or-nothing event, not a
gradual process (e.g., a linear chaining of associations). Their
experiment contributed to a growing anti-associationist literature
encouraged by the work of Bruner and his associates in the 1950s
(e.g., Bruner, et al., 1956). He and his colleagues investigated the
types of strategies that subjects used in forming concepts and the
role of hypothesis testing in problem solving generally. Comment-
ing on his early work in concept formation, Bruner (1966) writes, "I
was enormously impressed at the logic-like or 'rational' quality of
adult human conceptualizing. . . . One could discern systematic
strategies in behavior that had the quality and creases of well
practiced rule-governed routines" (p. 2). He and his colleagues not
only introduced coding or categorization into the description and
prediction of behavior but also stressed the active nature of cognition generally, albeit in fairly formal terms (see Levine, 1975, for an
account of hypothesis theory in concept formation from a formal
logic point of view; see Bruner, 1986, pp. 88–92, for an alternative
explanation of these early experiments).

The stimulus-response model continued to influence psychological investigation of concept formation, but many researchers
became interested in how subjects learned relationships among
features of a particular concept; in this move, researchers appealed
to mathematical formalism but still experimented with isolated,
meaningless materials. Concept formation is here equated with
rational behavior, in the sense of formal deductive logic. Lyle
Bourne (1970), for example, conceives of concept formation as rule
learning ("a relation or a connection between any set of attributes")
(p. 554). For example, he uses rules "derived from a simple logic
system, the calculus of propositions, which generates a total of 16
possibilities for partitioning a stimulus population using at most two
stimulus dimensions" (p. 547). Contesting the traditional behaviorist claim that behavior is "a linear, cause-effect mechanism," he
claims, controversially at the time, that "behavior is better represented as a hierarchical, rule-following system" (p. 556).

This development in the study of categories typifies what
Lakoff (1987b) and M. Johnson (1987) describe and criticize as the
objectivist approach to categorization. As I noted in earlier chapters, objectivism unsuccessfully welds mechanism and formism in
information processing. Lakoff (1987b) explains:

> Modern attempts to make [objectivism] work assume that
> rational thought consists of the manipulation of abstract sym-
> bols and that these symbols get their meaning via a correspon-
> dence with the world, *objectively construed*, that is, indepen-
> dent of the understanding of any organism. A collection of
> symbols placed in correspondence with an objectively struc-
> tured world is viewed as a *representation* of reality. On the
> objectivist view, *all* rational thought involves the manipulation
> of abstract symbols which are given meaning only via conven-
> tional correspondences with things in the external world. (p. xii)

An objectivist view of categories is the epistemological linchpin in
many modern theories of cognition that stress representation (see
E. Smith & Medin, 1981, for a well-known overview of theories of
category representation). Objective knowledge of the world can be
contained in categories that have certain necessary and sufficient properties for defining them (or have properties that probabilistically determine membership in a given category). In information-processing

models, these categories are structured, usually hierarchically, and are translated into symbolic form and then interpreted as mental representations.

Most information-processing models make objectivist assumptions about categories in their simulations (see, e.g., Winston, 1975, for a typical information-processing approach to concept formation; see Boden, 1988, pp. 187–90, for criticisms of its design and applicability). Using experimenter-defined rules, programmers manipulate these concepts in simulations of reasoning and problem solving. In the last chapter I argued that most psychological theories of semantic memory use static, clearly defined concepts to represent abstract knowledge. When we perceive a feature, say a feather, we pull out of long-term memory a conceptual structure, an internal representation, that allows us to recognize it through a matching process that takes place in working memory. As Lakoff (1987b) makes clear, in machine models, "concepts are internal representations of external reality. In other words, the symbols being manipulated are given meaning only via their capacity to correspond to aspects of reality"; a second, complementary belief is that "there is a completely general and neutral conceptual framework in terms of which all human knowledge can be represented" (p. 340). Thus, in information-processing theories, knowledge that gets represented as conceptual must be ultimately decomposable into defining properties. Stored in knowledge structures (i.e., propositions) in long-term memory, categories are blanks to be filled in—abstracted from bodily experience, the physical environment, and social context.

For example, in information-processing approaches, concept formation is equated with hypothesis testing in problem solving. The subject's response is not linked to an effective stimulus or a real situation, but rather to different sets of elements called symbols which are internally encoded. In representing concepts as symbols (which have relations), computer simulation programs do not define and isolate the stimulus unit; rather they emphasize the internal representation of symbols and their manipulation. Newell and Simon's (1972) work in problem solving focused on a wide range of task variables which influence problem-solving behavior (what they call the task environment). They simulated various problem-solving activities (what they term heuristics). In these simulations, the categorial criteria are set by the programmers in advance. First, in the simulation, they choose a data base to represent knowledge of the current state of affairs. Stored in long-term memory, these symbols integrate to produce concepts (which lead to problem solutions). Second, the programmers choose formal rules which govern the type of integration that can occur between symbols. Information processing thus introduced to the study of conceptualization not only mechanical operations but also an "essential formalism to describe and explain its phenomena" (Simon & Newell, 1971, p. 148).

In this version of the function of categories, all the previously noted assumptions merge. Concepts are reduced to their objective properties or smallest units; these properties build up through association to form a conceptual structure based on similarity; the resulting concepts are abstract and disembodied; they have no connection to affective experience; and because a given concept is abstracted from many particular experiences, nothing of the particular need remain—it is, thus, treated as acontextual knowledge. Detected in the initial act of perception, features are rejected or confirmed by analysis of what has already been laid down in memory. Like all mechanistic approaches to categorization, information processing is analytic, but in its reliance on the digital computer, it becomes especially committed to certain kinds of analytic units and their relations: "The most common kind of data base now in use happens to fit an objectivist metaphysics: It stores representations of entities, their properties, and the relations holding among them" (Lakoff, 1987b, p. 183).

But this all-or-nothing approach to category boundaries leads immediately to insurmountable problems for mechanistic psychology, especially when generalizing to ordinary conceptual experiences. For example, consider the following questions: Why do some members of a category seem so unnatural? Why, for example, is a tomato not a good example of a fruit? What are the necessary and sufficient conditions for *mother* that will cover all cases? (See Lakoff, 1987a, for the impossibility of such a task.) How many common features do *plums* and *lawnmowers* have in common? (See Murphy & Medin, 1985, for a substantial list.) What makes unlike properties in categories cohere (Medin & Wattenmaker, 1987)? These examples illustrate psychologists' troubles with establishing objectively defined attributes of concepts outside experiments with highly artificial and isolated stimuli. Their meanings leak out of the boxes and network nodes: "There may be more to birdness than is captured by adding up a bunch of birdlike properties" (Medin & Wattenmaker, 1987, p. 38). Further, we can subtract features and still have a bird.

A second major difficulty with an objectivist account of concept formation is that it presupposes what it attempts to explain. We saw this difficulty with the mechanist view of perception and memory. If concept formation is simply a more complicated version of perceptual feature detection, then how do the features get into the system in the first place? Or if conceptual learning is a matter of hypothesis testing and confirmation, then how do the original properties of the concept (against which the present one is matched) get into the system? And if one uses hypotheses to discard some features but not others, how do these hypotheses about the relevant/ irrelevant features originate in cognition, and where are they stored? Problems such as these are now widely considered intractable (see Balzano & McCabe, 1986; Lakoff, 1987b; Neisser, 1987b, c). Most critics point out that the objectivist view is not altogether wrong, but, as Lakoff (1987b) notes, it is only a very small part of a much more complex story. As a result, many researchers such as Michael Ghiselin (1987) have concluded that the process of categorization "is concrete, adaptive and contextual, not abstract, formal and intrinsic" (p. 84).

In an influential article that introduced contextual effects into the literature on categorization, Douglas Medin and Marguerite Schaffer (1978) address the effects of context in learning ill-defined concepts. They assume that not all categorization is rule governed and that people reason by analogy from examples stored in memory. For instance, when a new fruit appears in the grocery store, one is likely to classify it based on its similarity to other familiar fruits. This research points to the importance of the interaction among properties within a given category and to nonanalytic learning processes. Most important, their research calls into question the "independent" (acontextual) status given to categories by objectivistic accounts. Information within and between given categories interacts dynamically with a subject's other conceptual knowledge (see Murphy & Medin, 1985; Medin & Wattenmaker, 1987).

Prototypical Theories of Categorization

Perhaps no one has been more influential in the metatheoretical revolution taking place in the study of cognition generally and

categorization particularly than Rosch. Seldom making strong theoretical claims about her findings on categories, she (1978) is well
aware of the dominance of what she calls the standard concept-
identification framework which treats the perceived world as "an
unstructured total set of equiprobable co-occurring attributes"
(p. 29). In a telling description, she portrays the standard information-processing view typical in the 1950s and, more importantly,
identifies the consequences of abandoning it:

> The processor was assumed to be rational, and attention was
> directed to the logical nature of problem-solving strategies. The
> "mature western mind" was presumed to be one that, in
> abstracting knowledge from the idiosyncracies of particular
> everyday experience, employed Aristologian laws of logic.
> When applied to categories, this meant that to know a category
> was to have an abstracted clear-cut, necessary, and sufficient
> criterion for category membership. If other thought processes,
> such as imagery, ostensive definition, reasoning by analogy to
> particular instance, or the use of metaphors were considered at
> all, they were usually *relegated to lesser beings such as women,
> children, primitive people, or even to nonhumans* [italics add-
> ed]. (Rosch & Lloyd, 1978, p. 2)

In chapter 2, I noted that certain views of science dismiss alternative
norms of evidence, and many feminist psychologists and philosophers (Bordo, 1986; Hawkesworth, 1989) have described the pro-
clivity in Western thought to reduce all reason to a monolithic
conception of objective rationality and discard any remainder as
illegitimate. Although Rosch's research during the 1970s has been
widely recognized and appreciated within cognitive psychology,
the truly radical nature of her metatheoretical shift is just now
beginning to be recognized (Lakoff, 1987b). In this section I argue
that the research program and findings of Rosch and her colleagues
on categorization are best accounted for by contextualism; in fact,
to borrow her own term for my purposes, I suggest that her later
work (1978) is "prototypical" of contextualism in cognitive psychology. Further, her explanation of concepts encompasses and
corroborates the findings of ecological researchers in perception
(such as Johansson's, 1973) and in memory for events (such as
Bransford and Franks's, 1971).

In her latest work, a collaboration with Varela and Thompson (1991), Rosch connects her research on categories with the enactive approach to cognition. The overall aim of this approach is to build a genuine bridge between cognitive science and human experience, between the computational and phenomenological mind. In this effort they identify troublesome theoretical problems in traditional cognitive science such as the status of representation and the definition of the self. It is particularly interesting to note that these three scholars explore the end of the commitment to the Cartesian self through meditative mindfulness as practiced in Buddhism. They describe how new architectures in cognitive science lead to picture of the mind "as a disunified, heterogenous collection of networks of processes" (pp. 106–7). This view of the mind as fractured agencies with emergent properties can also be found, they argue, in an open-ended analysis of human experience through the mindfulness/awareness meditation tradition. An exploration of their integration of Buddhism in cognitive science is beyond the scope of this book, but their efforts to increase the dialogue between cognitive science and human experience parallels what is called for here. Further, they argue persuasively that cognitive science has avoided ordinary experience because cognitive scientists have taken it in its most degenerative form, as unreliable, murky, incoherent, and irrational and hence in need of reconstruction and replacement. Like other contextualists, they start with the generative potential of ordinary experience and find pathways from embodied experience to science.

Rosch's experimental research results on basic level categories and prototype effects have been widely summarized (e.g., Lakoff, 1987b; Neisser, 1987b & c; Rosch, 1978). I highlight here the findings most central to a contextualistic reading of her work. Rosch (1978) insists that basic level categories provide the cornerstone of a categorial taxonomy; that is, a system for arranging categories from specific or least inclusive to general or most inclusive levels (e.g., from river birch to birch to tree). The basic level corresponds to those phenomena in the middle of the taxonomy, the mid-sized facts of our experience. They frequently include the concrete objects of world (such as chairs and horses) with which we interact at a bodily level. Earlier research had simply not focused very much on this level as important in categorization. For example, in traditional laboratory experiments researchers used isolated stimuli which they took to be very particular and discrete (e.g., a dot or letter). In information-processing simulations, symbols are abstract units. In contrast to these mechanistic and formal approaches, Rosch uses perceptually apprehendable, naturally occurring categories "in the most common taxonomies of biological and man-made objects in our own culture" (p. 32).

For example, in one series of experiments, Rosch, Carolyn Mervis, Wayne Gray, David Johnson, and Penny Boyes-Braem (1976) presented subjects with sets of words taken from nine different taxonomies, all of which were understandable to English speakers and had simple class inclusion relations that would be familiar to subjects.

Table 1

Examples of Taxonomies Used in Basic Object Research

SUPERORDINATE	BASIC LEVEL	SUBORDINATE
Furniture	Chair	Kitchen chair
		Living room chair
	Table	Kitchen table
		Dining room table
	Lamp	Floor lamp
		Desk lamp

In Table 1, furniture is an example of a superordinate level, the most abstract level of her taxonomic system (Rosch, 1978, p. 32). Chair, table, and lamp are examples of what she calls the basic level categories. And finally, kitchen chair and living room chair are examples of the subordinate, the most specific, level of categorization.

Rosch found that her subjects did not list many attributes for superordinate categories (e.g., furniture) but gave many more for the basic level categories (e.g., chair). There were not many more attributes for subordinate level categories (e.g., kitchen chair) than for the basic level, and many of these attributes overlapped. In addition to the clustering of attributes that occurs at this level, the basic level includes references to objects with which people interact bodily. For example, one might speak of a recliner in recognition of possible bodily action in a chair, but one would not use such a term with *furniture*. Furthermore, the basic level has objects with a large degree of similarity in shape among its varied members. Instances of chairs can be superimposed and still retain some standard shape, but this is not at all true with superordinates such as furniture. A car, for example, is easier to imagine than a vehicle. Such evidence for the prominence of basic level categories in cognitive functioning led Rosch to describe the basic level as cognition's anchor.

Rosch's claims about mid-sized facts in cognition challenged the role of (superordinate) abstraction in categorization, the level revered in the objectivist tradition, and the emphasis on judging as the most important cognitive action. Although mechanistic accounts seem to honor the particulars of experience, it is, paradoxically, the abstraction—the supposedly culturally independent category—that becomes sacrosanct in Western intellectual traditions. As an objective product of the mind's I, such thought is supposedly theory independent and thus detached from the experiential realm of the knower. But Rosch's research indicates that the superordinate level, the most abstract level in a taxonomy, may not be as central to human cognition as mechanism supposes. It may be important for formal, rational thinking but not as relevant to everyday thinking. In Rosch's theory, however, attributes of basic level objects are defined very formally by a probablistic concept called cue validity, which can be computed. Here the researcher measures (in set theoretical representations of similarity) which cues are more frequently associated with one category and less so with others. The contextually oriented approach to psychology that I am developing here appreciates and supports formal accounts that recognize continuity and avoid dichotomy. The danger of an exclusive focus on formal accounts is that other dimensions of basic level categories are neglected, such as the opportunity for mutual social explorations afforded by them.

The basic level is accessible and equally available to members of a given community; it is the soil for dialogue about the meaning of the situation—the mind's we. In interactions with the environment, we do not easily shed this level for the sake of abstraction alone, but go upward to abstractions and downward to particulars given certain purposes or undertaken actions. As Lakoff (1987b) notes, "Basic-level categories have an integrity of their own. They are our earliest and most natural form of categorization. Classical taxonomic categories are later 'achievements of the imagination,' in Roger Brown's words" (p. 49). In contextualism, the abstractions are temporary integrations or scaffoldings.

The basic level category takes priority epistemologically in contextualism because that is the level of our bodily interaction with the world; as such it is an important source for the analysis of events. This emphasis on perceptible objects that invite interaction is strikingly parallel to Gibson's concept of affordance. Theories such as Rosch's and Gibson's tend to exhibit the textures, strands, and references available for meaningful interaction between people and their environment. Thus, Rosch notes with her colleagues, "The basic level of categorization . . . appears to be the point at which cognition and environment become simultaneously enacted. The object appears to the perceiver as affording certain kinds of interactions, and the perceiver uses the objects with his [or her] body and mind in the afforded manner" (Varela, et al., 1991, p. 177). Novelty and ambiguity in the ongoing event are often experienced at the basic level of categorization. For example, when the mother said she was going to hold her four-year-old back from kindergarten, I did not so much feel this as a disruption of my concept of public school grade level as I became aware that I could explore different ways of interrelating with my daughter as four years old. Our experience of disequilibrium commonly occurs at this level of interaction with the world.

In addition to her findings on basic level abstraction in categorization, Rosch's theory of prototypicality offers important evidence for the role of context, as her own recent analysis demonstrates (Rosch, 1988). This evidence confronted the acontextual nature of both formistic and mechanistic accounts. As analytic worldviews, they emphasize clear, well-defined boundaries for categories and insist on strict similarity for category membership; categories transcend time and space. In formism, for example, the norm for the category exists somewhere in nature, never fully present in experience, but apprehendable through inductive evidence. Alternatively, mechanism usually proposes a correspondence between concrete particulars and reality and assumes that the organism engages in verification of hypotheses through controlled, analytic investigation.

Prototypicality challenges both these accounts by questioning the existence of discrete boundaries for categorial membership.

Rosch (1978) argues that categories are not rigidly bounded but fluid; we use them as flexible structures as we make sense of events and situations. Rather than using a list of properties, Rosch claims that categories are organized through our judgments about clearest cases. Prototypes of categories are "the clearest cases of category membership defined operationally by people's judgments of goodness of membership in the category" (p. 36). For example, subjects list a robin as the prototypical bird, not a penguin or an ostrich. One can arrange instances of a category in a graded fashion so that the instances go from most to least typical of the category. This lack of emphasis on boundaries is very characteristic of contextualism; its root metaphor theory is synthetic, with fusion fundamental to cognitive interaction in situations. In contrast, the worldviews of mechanism and formism isolate certain particulars that, unconstrained, would overwhelm efforts at precise categorial description. Contextualism spreads out categories to gain the fullest possible scope or perspective. The concept of a prototype suggests variability is at least as important in categorization as similarity. Rosch (1978) states, "If categories form to maximize the information-rich cluster of attributes in the environment . . . prototypes of categories appear to form in such a manner as to maximize such clusters . . . within categories" (p. 37). We have not only information about the prototypical bird, robin, and its attributes, but we also have information about its nests and eggs, for example. And, as Lakoff (1987b) points out, symbolic meanings cluster with the prototype. (For instance, when we call someone "flighty," we are thinking of a robin or a sparrow, not of an ostrich or a homing pigeon).

The existence of prototypes in and of themselves does not lead to a theory of context, however. And information-processing psychologists have tried to capture Rosch's phenomena in their theories and simulations. For example, in these theories, prototypes become the product of formal rationality. As Rosch (1978) herself claims, the information-processing appropriation misuses prototypicality as she means it because prototypicality is a judgment, not an instantiation of a configuration of particulars, a form or a product, formally derived. "Prototypes do not constitute a theory of representation of categories" (p. 40). They may be representative, but it does not follow that they are representations in the mind. How does the contextualist represent conceptual knowledge if not in formal, usually propositionally based models?

In a very important development and extension of Rosch's research, Lakoff (1987b) argues that concepts and their properties are not objectively given in the real world but evolve out of our interactions with our social and physical environment: "Such interactional properties form *clusters* in our experience, and prototype and basic-level structures can reflect such clusterings" (p. 51). Such clusterings form what Lakoff calls cognitive models in which the properties or features of a given category can be rationally related, but the types of relationships are not confined only to the formal rationality characteristic of the propositional structures embedded in information-processing and computational approaches. If a prototype becomes normative and powerful as a model, then it becomes idealized in the sense that it does not neatly fit real situations.

Consider the concept of spinster (see Lakoff, 1987a, for a similar analysis of bachelor). One can define a spinster as an unmarried woman who is beyond the age women normally marry. But this definition makes sense only through a larger understanding of certain social, cultural, and historical practices and conditions. For example, at what age does one become a spinster? A lesbian, a woman cohabiting with a man, and a nun are all poor examples or fuzzy cases of the spinster prototype, but not in ways that are easily formalizable, even on a continuum. The definition of spinster is what Lakoff terms an idealized cognitive model; it idealizes a certain type of family structure—one based on, for example, legal contracts and heterosexual orientation. Even a nonworking, never-married woman of independent means is a poor example since a spinster spins or weaves in order to support herself economically. (Part of the background of this concept is also its contrast with the concept of bachelor. That concept conveys, connotatively, a freedom and buoyancy not conveyed with a spinster burdened, supposedly, with the task of struggling to support herself.) Idealized cognitive models treat prototypical categories as if they had clear boundaries, but such models also mask complex social circumstances that nevertheless are evoked even though we may be unconscious of them (see Bem, 1983, for a related discussion of gender schema).

In more complex category cases, concepts such as spinster become clustered with other concepts to form cognitive models which take on an internal structure, but not necessarily in the form of a linear representation. Such clustered categories are even more complex in terms of their prototype effects and thus further defy classical theorists' insistence that only necessary and sufficient conditions can function in determining category membership. To exemplify the power of clustered cognitive models and the dynamic interaction of their internal properties, Lakoff (1987a) analyzes the stereotype *housewife*.

Stereotypes are the result of metonymy. In metonymy, we take a part of a category or member and use it to understand (and stand for) the category as a whole. He argues that through metonymy *housewife* has come to stand for the whole category *mother*. The stereotype is then supported with contrasting categories (such as *working mother*) and linguistic markers (such as the word *but* in the following sentence: *She is a mother, but she doesn't have a job*). The upshot, Lakoff explains, is that "[the model of *mother* and its subcategory *housewife*] form a structure with a composite prototype: the best example of a mother is a biological mother who is a housewife, principally concerned with nurturance, not working at a paid position, and married to the child's father" (1987a, pp. 73–74). In cascades of engaging examples such as these, Lakoff illustrates how powerful, flexible, and interactive categories are in ordinary experience. Like M. Johnson's analysis of the metaphorical projection of schema, Lakoff's analysis of cognitive models illustrates how cognition functions to integrate experience into meaningful configurations; such processing does not lead to rigid formal constructions— or to cognitive chaos.

Rosch's research on basic categories and prototypes and Lakoff's (1987b) and Johnson's (1987) description of imaginative cognitive processes call into question the tendency of traditional approaches to confine thought to static structures, formulas, and bounded knowledge. Formal representational structures "concern nothing but closeness to the prototypical case, and thus they hide most of the richness of structure that exists in the cognitive models that characterize the category" (Lakoff, 1987a, p. 74). These new theories emphasize experience, context, integration, and imagination. Such models also give accounts of what comes to be visibly and invisibly given in experience. Because of the bodily basis of these cognitive models, we can always reexperience and interrogate the world and learn to see it anew. Our concepts are rooted in ordinary experience. As Rosch (1978) states:

Actually, both basic levels and prototypes are, in a sense, theories about context itself. The basic level of abstraction is that level of abstraction that is appropriate for using, thinking about, or naming an object in most situations in which the object occurs (Rosch et al., 1976). And when a context is not specified in an experiment, people must contribute their own context. Presumably, they do not do so randomly. Indeed, it seems likely that, in the absence of a specified context, subjects assume what they consider the normal context or situation for occurrence of that object. To make such claims about categories appears to demand an analysis of the actual events in daily life in which objects occur. (p. 43)

Within the field of cognitive psychology, to consider ordinary experience worthy of study is very radical, epistemologically and politically. Let me briefly speculate about a connection to women's studies.

Rosch disrupted the usual research practices and ways of thinking about categories. In focusing on ordinary experience, she broke with traditional assumptions in psychology. Within the physical and social sciences, feminist theorists have documented the association of masculinity with the objective, the ordered, the unified, and the rational in contrast to the association of femininity with the concrete, the multiple, the temporal, and the disorderly (e.g., Gilligan, 1982; Harding, 1986; Keller, 1985). These associations have created double binds for women researchers who fear that they will entrench stereotypes about femininity if they study women's own experience at a concrete level (as, say, Gilligan does in her 1982 work on women's moral development) or that they will obfuscate gender issues by participating in the traditional, objectivistic research, which falsely claims to be gender neutral. In my conclusion, I will urge that Pepper's theory of worldviews—and particularly the availability of alternative views—can help women rethink their intellectual commitments. Rosch's research on the primacy of basic level abstraction will, I believe, develop both contextualism and the study of women's experience in psychology. "Basic-level objects are part of the cultural, consensually validated forms of life of the community in which the human and the object are situated—they are basic-level activities" (Varela, et al., 1991, p. 177). As such, they are open to thoughtful reflection and criticism and ultimately to social change.

In a turn that clearly links her to a contextualistic position, Rosch (1978) applies her findings on basic level abstraction to the study of events. Although she studied events informally, she found that subject identified events were also structured by basic level abstraction. That is, people do not recount events in terms of the most general or most specific levels of abstraction. They do not report, for example, that "they got themselves out of the house" or that "they squeezed toothpaste out of a tube" (p. 44). Rather they choose the middle ground—they recount brushing their teeth, getting dressed, or driving to work. In short, subjects remembered the events and determined how the events were organized at the basic level. This extension of her theory to events has implications for interpreting the experiments on perception and memory that were discussed earlier.

Both perception and memory may be most active at the basic level of abstraction—where the body and the environment intersect. In the Johansson (1973) experiment, for example, subjects recognized otherwise meaningless dots as a person walking or skipping. These context cues were basic level action events. (They did not say, "I see the movement of a homo sapien" or "I see a hand swinging"; instead they said, "I see a person walking.") Rosch uses as an example Bransford and M. K. Johnson's (1973) experiment. In this experiment, subjects read paragraphs not easily comprehended without a context cue. For example, "The procedure is actually quite simple. First you arrange things into different groups. Of course, one pile may be sufficient" (p. 400). Only when subjects hear the cue "washing clothes," does comprehension click in. Rosch explains that the context cues used in the experiment are basic level events. A similar interpretation would hold for the Bransford and Franks's (1971) experiment: subjects remember the complex sentences, each of which contain information about a basic level event. Subjects forget information from the subordinate level once they understand the whole action.

Problems and Possibilities: Relativism, Environment, and Narrative

In the contextualistic view, categories evolve and enter into events in ordinary experience in a process of dynamic interaction.

The relationships among and between features and levels of abstraction in *this* situation become important for knowledge. Further, as we have noted, acknowledgment of disorder is fundamental to contextualism. A creative process, categorizing helps us define and resolve problematic situations and so is always tied to action and interpretation of the ongoing event. This is why contextualists look to narrative to find the tracings of these creative processes. It is the richest source for seeing the process of understanding as it is taking place. A given category can never be separated from thinking, the quality of the event, or purposeful action. It is always situated. If mechanistic formalism freezes concepts in tightly confined analytic relations, then contextualism loosens and nudges thought toward investigation that can be publicly shared and negotiated. If mechanists and formists labor to define precise criteria, then contextualists labor to release and make visible the accidental and unexpected (from biology, see, for example, Gould, 1989, on the Burgess Shale).

Just as I have raised the question of how far to go with formalizations of prototypes and basic level categories in my contextualist reading of Rosch's work, let me now turn to other similiar questions about contextualism's problems and possibilities. Especially from the perspectives of other worldviews, relativism, environment, and narrative appear as problems, but these same areas are fields of possibility for a contextually oriented psychology. Rosch recognizes concrete experience and eventfulness but finds strong evidence of categorial structure in basic level abstraction; Lawrence Barsalou's research (1987), however, pushes the contextualist view of categorization even further—into extreme relativism.

Relativism

Rosch's research clearly loosened the boundaries of traditionally conceived categories. No longer focusing on equivalence, membership in a category becomes dependent on typicality, on how close or related a given member is to the exemplar of the category. Barsalou (1987) terms this theme in the categorization literature "graded structure," by which he means the "continuum of category representativeness, beginning with the most typical members of a category and continuing through its atypical members to those nonmembers least similar to category members" (p. 102). Because of its current ubiquitous status in the literature, Barsalou examines what determines the structure and holds it together. After reviewing a number of claims that explain the determination of such structure, he argues that contextual effects are so pervasive and disruptive to categorial structures that these structures are highly unstable. "The graded structure within categories does not remain stable across situations. Instead a category's graded structures can shift substantially with changes in context. This suggests that graded structures do not reflect invariant properties of categories but instead are highly dependent on constraints inherent in specific situations" (p. 107). For example, in studies determining how subjects judge the typicality of a given category, he (1987) found both within-subject and between-subject agreement to be much lower than other research had suggested. To the extent that graded structure is a meaningful phenomenon for discussing categorial organization, he concludes, first, that any structure must be viewed as highly flexible and dynamic and, second, that "invariant representations of categories are analytic fictions created by those who study them" (p. 114).

Barsalou extends contextualism by claiming that category boundaries are so fluid that categorization may not be as important in cognition as has been traditionally supposed. In spelling out implications of his research for the study of memory, we see the dynamic nature of categories Barsalou defends. Conceptual structures vary so dramatically—given the immediate situation and the person's purpose—that it is not likely that memory is a storehouse filled with a collection of invariant conceptual structures (bundles of features) that represent themselves in experience. This account simply cannot explain the variability his research reveals:

> The fact that many of the properties generated for categories cannot be neatly assigned to a single knowledge domain suggests that the knowledge in long-term memory from which concepts are constructed is relatively undifferentiated or continuous—it does not appear to be divided into packets of knowledge associated with particular categories. In general, it may be extremely difficult, if not impossible, to identify where the knowledge for a particular category in long-term memory begins and ends. To the extent this is true, it is hard to imagine how there could be invariant representations for categories stored in long-term memory. (p. 121)

Barsalou proposes that concepts are temporarily and productively used and actively constructed in working memory. It is important to remember in the midst of these claims that contextualism is an integrative, not dispersive, worldview. How far to go in an exploration of some particular context before integration (or fusion) is a creative tension within the worldview.

A contextualist would place Barsalou's explanations of categorization in a discussion of its role in interrogation. Categories are part of cognitive processes and participate in investigations of the indeterminate situation where action is ongoing and already meaningful. They regulate interpretation at the same time that they imbue it with possibilities. Like a cloth weaving itself, we bring textures and threads from the event into integrations and structures that can be taken up for other weavings or be unwoven and begun again, though the established fabrics can hamper us like a burnoose. As in my opening blonde bombshell story, established meanings are not always so easy to untangle and reweave.

Nonetheless, this felt quality and indeterminacy invites public investigation and shared interaction about experience (its reliability, coherence, validity). Social psychologist Derek Edwards (1991) pushes Lakoff's cognitive theory of categories in just this direction—toward the pragmatics of social interaction. He explores "the *relationship* between [linguistic] 'resources' [such as Lakoff's idealized cognitive models] and situated talk. . . . Categorization is *something we do* in talk in order to accomplish social actions" (p. 517). Contextualism recognizes our efforts after meaning in indeterminacy—the hearing of what there is to say or the seeing of what is available. In our bodily experiences with the world, we use basic level categories to construct or weave what a Gibsonian might call "social" affordances. Affordances are the multiple (but not infinite) possibilities the environment offers the organism for action (e.g., the chair affords sitting); an affordance always stipulates reciprocity between organism and environment. Social affordances would be our shared conceptual renderings of the problematic situation, those made available, for example, by my writing group as I explored my experience with the stereotype "blonde bombshell."

The Ecological Basis for Categorization

Ecological psychologists might ask of psychologists, such as Rosch and Barsalou: How seriously should we take the environment "as places within which, among other things, 'mental life,' 'behavior,' and 'symbol use' occur" (Balzano & McCabe, 1986, p. 103)? Like Rosch and Barsalou, ecological psychologists working on categorization and concept formation deal lethal blows to objectivist explanations. Neisser (1987b, c) laments the lack of ecological validity in traditional studies; Gerald Balzano and Viki McCabe (1986) attack information processing as a closed system where "all the potential predicates must be there in advance" (p. 104). Because in their system concepts are dynamic and change over time and situation, they prefer viewing the organism as an open system which "exhibit[s] a large number of qualitatively different behaviors that correspond in complex ways to states of their environment" (p. 105). Linking the organism and environment in reciprocity, they state, "The hallmark of the concept is not the uniformity of its instances, as the prototype theory chided the 'classical' definitional theory. But, we hasten to chide the prototype theory, nor is it the unprincipled variability of instances about some (arbitrary) conjunction of feature values" (p. 107). The ecologists seek the middle ground. Information from our experience in the environment must be naturally integrated in our conceptual processes. Concepts are coordinated with the environment but in ways that are constrained; not surprisingly, ecological psychologists turn to Gibson's notion of affordance to supply the constraint.

Ecological psychologists join Rosch's findings about basic level categories with Gibson's theory of affordances. Because of the richness of their features, their overlapping shapes, and their availability for physical interaction, basic level categories function like affordances and, like affordances, can be directly perceived (Neisser, 1987b, p. 14). Balzano and McCabe (1986) suggest that affordances are "the earliest proto-concepts," and not the words that designate them (p. 107). In the act of perception, the environment contributes directly to cognition. But as we saw in the chapter on perception, at some point cognition, and especially language, enters into perception and can even overwhelm it. Neisser (1987c) recognizes this and does *not* define category solely in terms of the environment or as another form of perceiving. "Perceptual systems are tuned to certain definite forms of information, which in turn specify relatively definite, local, and ecologically relevant state[s] of affairs. Those states are complex, but perhaps they are not complex without limit; some day we may really understand how they are specified to perceivers. But our conceptual systems have a far wider scope; for all we know, there may be no limit to what forms they can take and what domains they encompass" (p. 5). In using Rosch's model, Neisser argues that similarity cannot be a reliable basis for categorization, even in natural categories, but he underscores the importance of experience with the environment and its affordances at the basic level of abstraction.

Though it is only briefly suggested by Balzano and McCabe (1986), concepts become meaningful in problematic situations. Dewey (1938) always stresses how the indeterminate situation "not only evokes the particular inquiry engaged in but . . . exercises control over its special procedures" (p. 105). Such indeterminacy exists in the situation and not in the person alone. Indeterminate situations are precognitive, but once they are taken as the subject for inquiry, they become instituted in cognition and relevant for action. Both perception and conception functionally correlate "in such a manner that the former locates and describes the problem while the latter represents a possible method of solution" (p. 111). As perception and conception evolve, a person's past experiences fund the present situation. "There are conceptual objects, and objects of perceptual experience, which have been so instituted and confirmed in the course of different inquiries, that it would be a waste of time and energy in further inquiries to make them objects of investigation before proceeding to take and use them" (Dewey, 1938, p. 140). Experts, for example, immediately apprehend situations and thus see them differently from novices. Such refinement of perceptual skills and conceptual knowledge is highly situated in terms of the history, theories, and aims of sciences. Experts see more meaning in relations and interconnections; the textures and strands of the situation become richer sources for interpretation. For example, skillful practitioners often recontextualize knowledge via metaphorical implication to a more appropriate context within the more generic one. (Some ecological psychologists have termed this process a "decontextualization" [Bransford, Nitsch, & Franks, 1977, p. 49], but conceptual knowledge never moves beyond some situated context and its history.)

In contextualism, then, no matter what the level of abstraction, categorization will always be open for testing, as no category will be evoked in quite the same way across situations, and certainly the ways in which the strands and textures interrelate are open for investigation. As Barsalou (1987) concludes, "It may generally be more useful and more accurate to view concepts as temporary constructs in working memory" (p. 135); but, as Lakoff's work on idealized cognitive models indicates, the more crusted, sedimented layers of background experience and culture are not so easy to dislodge. Habit blinds us to the richness of information available in the environment. Basic level categories may indeed come to be perceived directly; these perceptual and conceptual habits can build up in such a way that the perceiver can no longer see subtle discontinuities in the situation, as I will illustrate through my experience with Ted Fuller and my student.

Contextualism raises tensions between change and stability. Weighted by its history, thinking becomes routine, stereotypical, mechanical, as the story of Ted Fuller's sexist compliment ("blonde bombshell") so clearly exemplifies. These habitual threads of thought are powerful because they are closely interwoven with other concepts in our culture (Lakoff's clustered cognitive models). Contextualism warns us that when habit overlays the present situation, thought becomes degenerative. Ted's sexism failed to honor the specificity of the event; it prevented me from authoring my own experience. In circumstances like this one, then, where we come to see situations in the same way, through the same fixed concepts, we are not fully open to the present and its possibilities. When we cover over the felt quality of a situation, we tend to lose touch with the possibility for generative responses.

My story about my student Carl (Chapter 4) reveals how categories can more subtly overtake perception in this way. I had, for example, developed habitual patterns of thinking about my students' background knowledge. I assumed they remembered important events in the civil rights movement. I had not seen or noticed new textures that had probably been emerging in my classroom before Carl challenged me. Such thought cannot even see itself turn back on the situation because it does not see new details and anomalies in the situation. In this way, categorization removes live options from the situation; gradually, habitually used categories become reifications or intellectualizations. They trick us into thinking we have a present, concrete explanation of this event when we only have abstractions. We become cut off from ourselves (and our bodies) because the felt quality arising from new discontinuities in the situation cannot be fully recognized and experienced. I needed

Carl's assertiveness—the perspective of the other—to disorient me in the situation; as a result, the situation became problematic. I could then allow a fuller context to emerge before taking new actions as a teacher. Often others prompt us to see situations differently by pointing to new aspects. In contrast, the mind's "I" of mechanism cannot regenerate itself in this way because patterns of cognitive change are not linked to particular situations.

Narrative and Generative Conceptual Systems

The mechanistic-objectivist tradition in cognitive psychology tries to correct ordinary reasoning. It disconnects variables and arranges them algorithmically into decision procedures and thus provides structures for the content of thought. In this process inquiry proceeds by what Bartlett (1932) called the "assumption of simplification by isolation." It reconstitutes thought from its isolated components. As Bruner (1986) writes, "It employs categorization or conceptualization and the operations by which categories are established, instantiated, idealized, and related one to the other to form a system" (p. 12). Leaving out the irregular, the ambiguous, and the aesthetic, it rests its case on one type of knowledge— abstraction to objective categories. Skeptical about what gets left out in this process of simplification, contextualism accents the potential of ordinary thinking; it cultivates, for example, the qualities of thought that carry us forward in the flow of events: its interconnections, imaginative renderings, meaningful integrations, and contextual explorations. All of these drop out of mechanistic reconstructions of thinking.

In current psychology, those concerned with the meaningfulness and significance of ordinary thinking frequently dichotomize modes of thought: objective/subjective, paradigmatic/narrative, scientific/interpretive, expert/folk models of the mind. Usually contrasted with the first adjectives, which describe the objectivist tradition, discussions of the second set (the remainders of the first) attempt to reclaim these ways of knowing. Noting this imbalance in psychology, for example, Bruner (1986) states, "In contrast to our vast knowledge of how science and logical reasoning proceed [the 'paradigmatic' mode of thought], we know precious little in any formal sense about how to make good stories [the 'narrative' mode of thought]" (p. 14). Especially significant in this new discussion is the role of language in cognition and the type of vocabulary each mode of thought produces, commonly called its discourse.

The stories we tell to ourselves and each other disclose the ways we conceptualize the world and in turn reveal how others have prepackaged the world for us. Constantly negotiating the contingencies of experience, storytellers strain toward coherence as they integrate the interrelationships among the features in given events. No one has made a stronger case that contextualism corresponds to narrative than Sarbin (1986b), who states, "I propose the narratory principle: that human beings think, perceive, imagine, and make moral choices according to narrative structures" (p. 8). In narrative, we use categories and concepts to help us tell stories about the world, to make our experiences meaningful. Bruner (1986), for example, defines the narrative mode of thinking as leading "to good stories, gripping drama, believable (though not necessarily 'true') historical accounts. It deals in human or human-like intention and action and the vicissitudes and consequences that mark their course. It strives to put its timeless miracles into the particulars of experience, and to locate the experience in time and place" (p. 13). Narrative fleshes out the historical event and uncovers actors' purposes and intentions. We often cast the problematic in situations as stories. The telling helps us to reconstruct, organize, and investigate the multiple sources of information available as we move to resolution and action. It opens up our conceptual experiences to discussions of meaning; it welcomes interpretation and community interaction. Clearly, narrative analysis is a central methodology for students of contextualism (see, for example, Mishler, 1986). Can we, then, equate contextualism with narrative in the way Sarbin does? Can we say cognitive psychology itself is narrative? Is that the fullest development of the contextualist worldview?

Contextualists have no difficulty accepting the assertion that when and where we draw the categorial line is as much an aesthetic and social as scientific consideration. But the view I want to advance is suspicious of dichotomies, because equating narrative with contextualism might preclude access to procedures of science. Pepper's framework argues that all relatively adequate worldviews have scientific value. In using stories throughout this book, I hoped to illustrate how narrative, as a contextualist tool, leaves traces of cognition at work in a world full of complexity and diversity. I do not present these stories in opposition to a particular method of doing

science. The strength of Pepper's analysis is that it eschews dichotomies, and contextualism is a particularly synthetic worldview.
That is why the works of M. Johnson (1987) and Lakoff (1987b) are
so important in its development; they actively advance integrative
approaches to the study of language and cognition.

To remain committed to ordinary experience, contextualism
resists any one formal theory of language or narrative structure, just
as it resists reducing experience to mechanisms. Psychology has
been influenced by other disciplines such as linguistics, structural
anthropology, and philosophy, where formal language models have
been popular. But in the view I am laying out, perceptual experience
lies below and prior to language; it is interrelated with conceptualization, of course, but it is not linguistic. Situations always include
more than can be captured in formal systems, even stories or their
texts. David Olson (1990) states the danger inherent in identifying a
particular version of a story with the originating experience:

> A final legacy of texts is that texts, including narrative ones,
> come to be seen as existing in nature quite separate from the
> storytelling practices of the culture. The world comes to be seen
> as being composed of texts. . . . The historian is seen as
> simply telling the story rather than inventing the story. . . . the
> historian invents the story; narrative provides a form for inter-
> preting and reinterpreting the past. Yet the notion that there is
> an untold story present in the events themselves comes from the
> assumption that the world has the properties of a fixed text,
> written once and for all time. (p. 104)

We saw interest in this kind of formal approach to narrative memory
among researchers studying schemata for memory of events. Frequently, these stories, called scripts, described a common sequence
of actions within an event, such as eating at a restaurant. The
danger, however, lies in the tendency to reify these scripts into
mental representations; these representations then become curi-
ously detached from ordinary experience.

An important contextualistic tool for getting at situations,
narrative helps to construct meanings that can be shared. A story is
a prototype for the given situation (see Olson, 1990, p. 105). It is
evocative, an open invitation: "it dwells and makes us dwell in a
world we do not have the key to" (Merleau-Ponty, 1964a, p. 77). A

story engages us in what Bruner (1986) terms the landscape of action and consciousness. I am, for example, a mother who must decide whether to send her daughter to kindergarten; that is the level of action in one story. The other level, of consciousness, is "what those involved in the action know, think, or feel, or do not know, think, or feel" (Bruner, p. 14). Among much else that might come to light in the telling, I know that entering kindergarten will be easier if Gemma has a friend with whom she can go. In interactions, these levels create tension or drama while engaging us to think about presuppositions and possible actions in situations. Because stories are openings on the world, they are interpretable.

Acts of interpretation can evoke from others different perspectives on the situation; in this way, others' stories or viewpoints help us to see more and to inquire differently. For the view I am advancing, social exploration of problematic situations is optimally one of mutual engagement. When thought becomes mechanical, it overlays on our present experience an already formulated interpretation or solution. Terry Winograd and Fernando Flores (1986) point to the need to recognize sociality in traditional psychological accounts of cognition. "Knowledge and understanding (in both the cognitive and linguistic senses) do not result from formal operations on mental representations of an objectively existing world. Rather, they arise from the individual's committed participation in mutually oriented patterns of behavior that are embedded in a socially shared background of concerns, actions, and beliefs" (p. 78). Indeed, traditional psychological accounts of categorization failed to construct objectively defined boundaries for categories, and so many psychologists turned to formal systems and models, based on representational structures. These theories derive their explanatory power from logic or computability. In the move away from the situation and toward the nature of the machine or the computation, dialogue emerging from the situation is often replaced by technical descriptions that ignore significant parts of the original situation. Against this, a contextually oriented approach to psychology becomes corrective. It reintroduces the regenerative possibilities for understanding our situations through shared public dialogue, including the views of those who might not have been included in the original situations. If the dialogue is mutual, then the self and other engage in an effort to see and know the situation as fully as possible. When dialogue is not mutual—when only one kind of evidence is admitted, a perspective is silenced, a situation is closed off from further investigation.

But mutual dialogue—the move from I to we and back again— is difficult and tense. In telling the blonde bombshell story to my writing group, for example, I find the members both an internal and external audience. Like interpretive lenses, they suggest meanings for the categories of my experience. Unlike Ted's stereotype, they do not lay interpretations over my experience but offer me more opportunities to author it. Their interest and responses lead me to more fully reconstruct the event and to see my experience from different viewpoints. As the dialogue evokes my memory and imagination, the context gets richer and thicker; as the present dialogue calls forth memories from the past, so the past funds the present dialogue. In this process, where do I begin and where does the community end? Whose story is it? Contextualism points not to fixed boundaries but to positionality as central to revealing context; when I know that I have been heard and understood through a community in dialogue, I not only gain the courage to tell the story but also to take personal responsibility for telling it in public. It is a multivocal story because it contains the voices of others, but it is also my own story told in my own voice.

In contrast to this approach, most major trends in cognitive psychology describe cognition through constructions of experience closed in formal systems, in advance. Until recently, it was thought that without formal constructions, researchers would be unable to constrain mental phenomena. Contextualism looked to them like wild abandonment of reasonable standards. The research of Rosch, Lakoff, and M. Johnson suggests, however, that ordinary experience can be mindless, unreasonable, or unreflective but it can also be mindful, reflective, and imaginative. The study of imaginative projections in categorization, Lakoff (1987b) suggests,

> opens up the study of human reason to areas that were previously closed off because reason was viewed as being limited to objectivist logic. . . . The study of categorization is a key to the study of reason . . . which is embodied and imaginative. Reason is embodied in the sense that the very structures on which reason is based emerge from our bodily experiences. Reason is imaginative in the sense that it makes use of metonymies, metaphors, and a wide variety of image schemas. (p. 367–68)

Like Johnson's theory of the imagination, Lakoff's theory of categorization links context with thought, experience with understanding, imagination with structure, the body with the mind, and the self with others. Such thinking undercuts the old dualisms. Contextualism is not a metatheoretical panacea for understanding complex processes such as categorization; it does not solve all metatheoretical problems. But of all the worldviews, it encourages a cognitive psychology in which reasoning can be self-reflective and publicly negotiated. It allows us to tell our stories to someone who can hear them.

6

Worldviews, Science, and Personal Knowledge

Approaches to cognition as a human practice emphasize the expansiveness of rationality and the irreducible plurality of its manifestations within diverse traditions. Perception, intuition, conceptualization, inference, representation, reflection, imagination, remembrance, conjecture, rationalization, argumentation, justification, contemplation, ratiocination, speculation, meditation, validation, deliberation—even a partial listing of the many dimensions of knowing suggests that it is a grave error to attempt to reduce this multiplicity to a unitary model. The resources of intellection are more profitably considered in their complexity, for what is involved in knowing is heavily dependent on what questions are asked, what kind of knowledge is sought, and the context in which cognition is undertaken.

—Mary E. Hawkesworth, "Knowers, Knowing, Known:
Feminist Theory and Claims of Truth"

In gathering contextualistic theories and research in cognitive psychology, I have, no doubt, overlooked certain kinds of fabric, torn some of the edges, cut the cloth along peculiar lines, or misarranged sections in the pattern. But since this is a contextualist quilt, it will always be, by its own definition, rearranging and mending itself. Its metatheoretical backing welcomes the additions over time that come with multiple perspectives and various subject materials. (The formist can dazzle you with possibilities for a permanent arrangement; the mechanist can build in the electrical mechanism for artificial warmth; the organicist can overwhelm you with the interconnection of this pattern with all others in the universe). I have argued that contextualism frames the possibilities and problems of cognition along very

188

different lines from the dominant mechanistic tradition. Thus, this is not only a book about pulling together but also about cutting apart. Acts of breaking away have a rich history in contextualism; among others, Dewey's split from the reflex arc, Gibson's from the eye as camera, Wittgenstein's from younger version of himself as logical atomist. I want to tell yet another story about breaking away, one from a different perspective and in a different voice.

Raised a Missouri Synod Lutheran, I attended the church's parochial school from third through eighth grade. Talk about educators who wished the mind were a simple cranking machine. Through indoctrination, I learned, for example, that Catholics were members of a bizarre cult, that if I were ever to think about sex outside of marriage I would go to hell, that Mary was an irritating necessity in bringing forth God's son into this world, that I should feel relieved and grateful to be saved by grace alone. Obedient and well-trained, I took in this "wisdom" without questioning. I was not encouraged to reflect; rather I was rewarded for memorizing Bible verses, which I regurgitated every day on demand. The church was run by men whose views and procedures I never saw questioned. Strangely neutered, the two women teachers pulled their brown hair back in buns and wore plain, drab clothes; humorless, dutiful, they led the church choir and planned social activities. Without power and voice themselves, they never had a chance to act as sponsors in my intellectual development. In fact, I had to learn their social manners and morals like the Bible verses: whatever you do, Diane, don't cause trouble, please other people, and be a good girl.

In all these, I was indefatigable—until the end of my eighth grade confirmation class, led by the Reverend Wallace himself. Dictatorial, desperate to save our souls, in love with his position as a man of the cloth, he prepared us for our first communion. Now, I can look back and smile at the paradox: to commune, to be one in relationship, to be joined together in body and mind—a definition simply crossed out of this minister's dictionary. For him, communion was a matter of being the right kind of Lutheran. Afraid we would take this ritual too lightly, he drilled us daily in Luther's catechism to prepare our minds. Our ritual was to be a matter of mental and spiritual suffering, not of communion.

Luckily, I was in the midst of pleasure: a new relationship with a bouncy, spontaneous, red-headed friend, Sandy. Life-giving to each other, we sat together and, on threat of separation, tried not to disrupt the litany. Under Reverend Wallace's daily onslaught of God-given truths, we gradually emerged as one mind unmoved by the holy current. Taking courage in each other's intuitions and insights, we became more daring in our religious thought. We still believed the minister's words were powerful, but when he told us, point blank, that we should die before we let ourselves be raped, we flinched: looking into each other's eyes in disbelief, we silently said, "No way" and were gone like lightning from the class, from the church, from organized religion. Two eighth graders, we didn't even know the word *hymen*, but we understood intuitively that our lives were worth more than any mucous membrane, more even than any one attack or violation. Delighting naively in our new self-assertion, we read each other's thoughts in our own subjectivistic communion.

Like many young women who must hide their thinking, we kept our rebellion concealed. Sitting in the balcony as far from minister and parents as we could get, we tried to stuff down the gunny sacks of giggles as we revised hymn titles into profanities. Together, insulated in a web of subjective reactions and feelings, we tried to think our way out of the Lutheran church. Our laughter, rebellion, and shared intuitions protected and nourished our growing sense of ourselves as knowers and learners. Although we could never have admitted it then, we held too tightly to our own ideas because there were no alternatives; they became too private. Our isolation kept others at a distance and limited our access to different ideas. Had we been afforded a broader context, our minds would have assimilated new possibilities. Affectionately dubbing ourselves doubting Thomases, we could be "intellectuals" only with each other and even in private had only the masculine mode of dissent available.

Our intellectual development occurred in opposition to an inherited system; paradoxically, we were complicit in the very system from which we sought liberation. There was no one to cut the either-or, to show us the grey, the ambiguous. Jubilant in our rebellion and cognitive prowess, we could not have imagined a world in which the minister valued our minds rather than our virginity. What if he could have taught us to think more openly? What if he could have nurtured and encouraged our growing female voices? And what if we had had access to other women whose voices and perspectives were valued equally with his?

My story is about breaking away from traditional authority and cognitive claims to certainty. Any of Pepper's four worldviews—mechanism, formism, organicism or contextualism—offers respite from such dogmatism, which always blocks cognitive progress. Without knowing it, to escape such dogmatic claims on my thought, I adopted components of the mechanistic worldview as my education advanced. Then I welcomed the detached and more objective position it offered me. I needed clear cognitive procedures and criteria to evaluate for myself the validity of knowledge claims. But I could never fully embrace mechanism because I always sensed that something was missing: Sandy, our communion, our relationship to knowledge and to each other. Intermittently, but only in my private life, I longed for an intellectual system that would interweave the many strands of my social world and leave me still at the center as mediator. To use Dewey's (1925) terms, I longed to "go behind the refinements and elaborations of reflective experience to the gross and compulsory things of our doings, enjoyments and sufferings" (p. 16). And this book is about my own breaking away from a worldview that has become too confining for me.

But the story is also about the consequences of academic theories and worldviews. Having different theories about cognition available may change how we carry out the practice of thinking, of perceiving, remembering, and conceptualizing our world. The proponents of any of the four worldviews would decry the narrowed, oppositional discourse that tangled my thought as I tried to extricate myself from dogmatic Lutheranism. But only contextualism honors my experience with Sandy and invites me to talk about it at the same time that it honors my intellectual struggling. Because my experience of thinking-in-relationship remained private both then and in my academic training, I always felt a real sense of loss. This sense of loss is not atypical for many women, as Belenky and her coauthors (1986) so movingly discuss in their work on women's intellectual development. Subjective and unreliable as it may have been, my voice emerged in situations that were safe against a system that excluded and silenced me. Thus, our worldviews have important implications for the ways in which we live our lives and understand our problems.

I have argued that contextualism is not only widely available in the literature of philosophy and psychology but is also an especially exciting perspective in contemporary cognitive psychology. In

admitting ordinary experience and personal knowledge as a legitimate source for investigation, it invites those who seek an alternative approach to the study of cognition. Contextualists are engaging
in lively and vigorous discussions about, for example, the role of
categorization in cognition and the role of culture in perception.
They unite in their recognition of the power and centrality of the
event—its context and integrity—for understanding cognition. In a
thoughtful piece that captures this central contextualist theme,
Asghar Iran-Nejed, Wilbert McKeachie, and David Berliner (1990)
remind us again of Bartlett's opposition to "simplification by
isolation," so characteristic of traditional psychological research,
and of his advocacy for "simplification by integration" as a better
way to conceptualize psychological inquiry. Like Bartlett, these
authors claim that "[human beings] have a natural talent for simplifying complex real-world problems by coordinating and integrating the influences of the multiple sources that simultaneously bear
on these problems" (p. 510). Systematic observation need not be
devoid of meaning to be rigorous; simplification by integration
recognizes dynamic processes.

Dogmatic mechanism eschews any contribution from other
worldviews. Often misinterpreting the contextualists' commitments
to ordinary experience and personal knowledge, such mechanists
are quick to charge others with a lack of rigor or are skeptical of
research conducted in ecologically valid contexts. As Hoffman and
Nead (1983) note in their defense of ecological research, "In recent
years, the concept of ecological validity has been misused; it has
been taken to be a necessary aspect of a piece of research in order for
that research to be ecological" (p. 532). But, as they go on to point
out, that is trivializing the contextualist's position; ultimately,
theories in psychology must be ecologically valid. That does not
mean that the laboratory or the computer simulation is never useful,
however. Recent interest in metaphor, imagination, and narrative is
similarly misinterpreted. It is not just the relevance of ordinary
experiences in narratives that is the appeal. Rather it is the recognition that the problems of cognition are not simple. Our situations in
the modern (or postmodern) world are multifaceted and complex.
Theories about cognition must be able to connect with these lived
situations, messy, contradictory, and full of conflict as they may be.
As a worldview, contextualism recognizes the ways we recreate our
surroundings: look again, it says, there is more to be seen and heard.

In spurring us to reform our perspectives, it forces us to face the ambiguities and tensions that characterize modern life, for instance, the relation between experience and knowledge, community and the individual, knowledge and power, history and freedom, and morality and technology. In defining investigation as an open-ended process in a never fully determinate situation, contextualism invites mutual dialogue and publicly shared discourse as important for responsible action. In this way, it challenges the well-entrenched, official mental set that we have inherited from the objectivist tradition, one that pushes for clarity and simplicity in its systematic, reductive programs and abandons what remains (see Dennett, 1991, for a mechanistic revision that attempts to meet this limitation). Because of the power of this canonical version of cognition, alternative perspectives about cognition have had difficulty getting a full hearing. Having them available makes better science; they produce thoughtful interactions between theorists holding different psychological premises. We need real, open-ended dialogues that connect cognitive science with experience, for as Varela, Thompson, and Rosch (1991) point out, "Neither extreme is workable for a pluralistic society that must embrace both science and the actuality of human experience" (p. 13).

The traditional approach has often been exclusionary, harsh, and sarcastic in its discourse when alternative views about knowledge challenge what it admits as legitimate scientific practice (remember that the "sacred" path leads to the heaven of science; think of the dichotomy in that metaphor). The certainty and power of its views are couched in a technical discourse that silences other worldviews, leaving new generations of students bereft of different possibilities and perspectives for conceptualizing cognitive processes. To be truthful, contextualists (including this author) may sometimes contribute to their own difficulties; the concepts *are* hard to explain: What is an "event"? Where does the situation end? (See Alexander, et al., 1991, for a related discussion of the proliferation of terms used to designate knowledge constructs; Shanon, 1990, for a discussion of problems with the term *context*.) Such vagueness has been a real disadvantage, especially when the alternatives are, for example, elaborately developed and neatly designed programs of systematic thought, constructed with mathematics, formal logic, and economic rationality. Perhaps this is why in developing Gibson's ecological theory of perception, Turvey and his

colleagues stay closely tied to biology; they turn to animal behavior
to formulate conceptions of ecological laws or "roughly, laws that
inform the relation of things perceived to actions performed"
(Turvey, et al., 1981, p. 271). Other ecological psychologists, such
as Neisser, do not stay within the natural sciences but develop
theories of language and culture and, as a result, become more open
to questioning.

In a recent, vituperative criticism of the ecological movement
in the study of memory, Banaji and Crowder (1989) seek to identify
what I have called the objectivist and mechanistic approach with the
practice of science itself. In a telling strategy, they pursue Neisser
and not Turvey since they are anxious to stand with the physical
sciences. More or less equating the ecological movement with
Neisser, they claim that the movement to study memory ecologically (i.e., in terms of ordinary experience) has reached a point of
bankruptcy: "No theories that have unprecedented explanatory
power have been produced; no new principles of memory have been
discovered; and no methods of data collection have been developed
that add sophistication or precision" (p. 1185). They claim that to
endorse ecological validity as an aim is tantamount to being opposed to science as such. To follow out Banaji and Crowder's
banking metaphor, a contextualist does not believe that scientific
practice is like making withdrawals from a fixed account in a bank.
These authors push this economic metaphor by arguing that one
must "invest" in scientific projects which are to be judged "worthy" via a "cost-benefit analysis" (p. 1188). We see here the ways
mechanists buttress their objectivist view of science by appeals to
economic rationality (see Varela, et al., 1991, pp. 245–46, for a
parallel analysis of the economic view of the mind). Such terms fuse
in a technical discourse that mirrors the language of the political and
social order. It operates to foreclose discussion by making alternatives look sloppy and sentimental. "What other science, we ask, has
established that its students should decide on the importance of
questions by checking first with Aunt Martha or the express-way
toll taker?" Banaji and Crowder ask, in their patronizing, rhetorical
tone (p. 1187).

Indeed, Neisser is their target because he openly proclaims his
ecological psychology and his revisions of it over time. These acts of
disclosure create difficult vulnerabilities. But this vulnerability, the
contextualist argues, leads to participation, openness, and height-

ened awareness of alternative perspectives. It can engender meaningful dialogue about ordinary experience and about thinking about our thinking about thinking. Vulnerability opens the possibility for mutuality in a world whose meanings constantly need to be negotiated and renegotiated. Of course, technical discourse can inform students of memory; but in predefining the conditions of intelligibility and science, Banaji and Crowder exclude alternatives: "we retain our faith that laboratory abstractions are controlled by the same laws as mundane phenomena, in psychology just as in chemistry" (p. 1190). Such appeals to official scientific discourse, however, sound beleaguered. To adapt a metaphor from Ian Hacking (1982), the contextualist's little guerilla army of unlike examples, of contextual nuances, have told against the big guns (i.e., the defenders of the canon). From outside the narrower, objectivist view Banaji and Crowder define as "legitimate" science, contextualists have made strong contributions to the study of perception, memory, and cognition.

In being open, contextualism often looks more chaotic, less disciplined, even (shudder) feminine. In a complex and uncertain world, the mechanist will always appear more real and definite (hard), the formist more cogent and structured (rational), and the organicist more integrated (systematic). The contextual persuasion offers no such grounds for certitude. Its cosmology is horizontal "in contrast to the other views, which have a vertical cosmology. There is no top nor bottom to the contextualistic world. In formism or mechanism or organicism one has only to analyze in certain specified ways and one is bound, so it is believed, ultimately to get to the bottom of things or to the top of things" (Pepper, 1961, p. 251). The insights of contextualism are often ignored. Thus, the study of memory in ecologically valid settings, Banaji and Crowder warn, "carries the potential danger of compromising genuine accomplishments of our young endeavor" (p. 1185). (Contextualists are not the only sentimental ones.) They state, for example, that ecological methodology "would lead the psychology of memory into the same stultification as studying backyard astronomy with the naked eye, chemistry in the kitchen, and biology with a walk through the forest. We have nothing against backyards, kitchens, or forests, but they are not ideal settings for the practice of science, and neither is everyday memory" (p. 1188). That is a strange way to put it, we contextualists respond. For one, it sets up the old bifurcations: real and imaginary, objective and subjective, hard and soft, beep and bop. Are not our pressing questions about how to connect our best understandings of the human mind with ordinary experience including how go back to our backyards, kitchens, and forests and make them habitats for communities? Science originates from and eventuates in ordinary experience. Contextualism does not eliminate experimentation, but it is skeptical about aims that do not recognize the historical, political, and moral dimensions of the practice of science. Such practice must engage scientists and nonscientists in dialogues that include technical and scientific as well as aesthetic and narrative reasoning. Contextualistically oriented cognitivists encourage just such a dialectic.

I acknowledge the generative power of the mechanist root metaphor in order to remain faithful to Pepper's claim that each worldview is legitimate, but characterizations such as Banaji and Crowder's make it difficult to refrain from setting up the opposition, especially since contextualism is often defined as soft, subjective, and irrational. Contextualists admit that local mechanisms and formal procedures help make sense of experience and are absolutely indispensable to our daily lives. Layers of history, culture, and personal habit are as essential to contextualism as the novelty and change it endorses; but habit, routine, and mechanical practice can enslave, which is why the contextualist always claims *this* situation is open for question, no matter how smoothly the machines may be running. Contextualists always ask how we can continue to decenter ourselves enough in our experiences so that we can see our situations anew.

I hope to have disrupted the canonical status of the mind's I of mechanism and to have presented evidence for the mind's we of contextualism. In one of its most important contributions to psychology, contextualism encourages a more critical dialogue about cognition and its situatedness. From this book, for instance, many readers may remember the stories. If so, that is not because they exemplify new principles of memory research or lead to new methods of data collection (they were not used as methodology); rather, beginning in ordinary experience, they stand out as an alternative in a field overgrown with technically rational discourse. True life stories, they are all about weaving real connections. Paradoxically, we know from laboratory experiments on memory that if the field were full of stories, mine would not stand out so much. Watchful of the ways human thought and action are always already historically situated, a contextually oriented psychology does not aim to hinder laboratory research but to understand its significance in terms of the storied and relational nature of the mind.

References
Index

References

Aanstoos, C. M. (1987). A critique of the computational model of thought: The contribution of Merleau-Ponty. *Journal of Phenomenological Psychology*, *18*, 187–200.

Alexander, P. A., Schallert, D. L., & Hare, V. C. (1991). Coming to terms: How researchers in learning and literacy talk about knowledge. *Review of Educational Research*, *61*, 315–343.

Allman, W. F. (1989). *Apprentices of wonder: Inside the neural network revolution*. New York: Bantam.

Anderson, J. R. (1980a). *Cognitive psychology and its implications*. San Francisco: W. H. Freeman.

Anderson, J. R. (1980b). Concepts, propositions, and schemata: What are the cognitive units? In J. H. Flower (Ed.), *Cognitive processes: Nebraska Symposium on Motivation* (Vol. 28, pp. 121–162). Lincoln: University of Nebraska Press.

Anderson, J. R. (1989). A rational analysis of human memory. In H. L. Roediger III & F. I. M. Craik (Eds.), *Varieties of memory and consciousness: Essays in honor of Endel Tulving* (pp. 195–210). Hillsdale, NJ: Erlbaum.

Anderson, J. R., & Bower, G. H. (1973). *Human associative memory*. Washington, DC: Winston.

Anderson, R. M. (1974). Wholistic and particulate approaches in neuropsychology. In W. B. Weimer & D. S. Palermo (Eds.), *Cognition and the symbolic processes* (pp. 389–396). Hillsdale, NJ: Erlbaum.

Attneave, F. (1959). *Applications of information theory to psychology*. New York: Holt, Rinehart, and Winston.

Bakan, D. (1967). *On method: Toward a reconstruction of psychological investigation*. San Francisco: Jossey-Bass.

Balzano, G. J., & McCabe, V. (1986). An ecological perspective on concepts and cognition. In V. McCabe & G. J. Balzano (Eds.), *Event cognition: An ecological perspective* (pp. 93–112). Hillsdale, NJ: Erlbaum.

Banaji, M. R., & Crowder, R. G. (1989). The bankruptcy of everyday memory. *American Psychologist, 44*, 1185–1193.

Bandura, A. (1977). *Social learning theory*. Englewood Cliffs, NJ: Prentice-Hall.

Barclay, J. R. (1973). The role of comprehension in remembering sentences. *Cognitive Psychology, 4*, 229–254.

Barsalou, L. W. (1987). The instability of graded structure: Implications for the nature of concepts. In U. Neisser (Ed.), *Concepts and conceptual development: Ecologic intellectual factors in categorization* (pp. 101–140). Cambridge: Cambridge University Press.

Bartlett, F. C. (1932). *Remembering*. Cambridge: Cambridge University Press.

Bechtel, W., & Abrahamsen, A. (1991). *Connectionism and the mind: An introduction to parallel processing in networks*. Oxford: Blackwell.

Belenky, M. F., Clinchy, B. M., Goldberger, N. R., & Tarule, J. M. (1986). *Women's ways of knowing: The development of self, voice, and mind*. New York: Basic Books.

Belli, R. F. (1986). Mechanist and organicist parallels between theories of memory and science. *The Journal of Mind and Behavior, 7*, 63–86.

Bem, S. L. (1974). The measurement of psychological androgyny. *Journal of Consulting and Clinical Psychology, 42*, 155–162.

Bem, S. L. (1978). Beyond androgyny: Some presumptuous prescriptions for a liberated sexual identity. In J. Sherman & F. Denmark (Eds.), *The psychology of women: Future directions in research* (pp. 1–23). New York: Psychological Dimensions.

Bem, S. L. (1981). Gender schema theory: A cognitive account of sex typing. *Psychological Review, 88*, 354–364.

Bem, S. L. (1983). Gender schema theory and its implications for child development: Raising gender-aschematic children in a gender-schematic society. *Signs: Journal of Women in Culture and Society, 8*, 598–616.

Ben-Zeev, A. (1988). The schema paradigm in perception. *The Journal of Mind and Behavior, 9*, 487–514.

Berkeley, G. (1910). *An essay towards a new theory of vision*. New York: E. P. Dutton. (Original work published 1709)

Berkeley, G. (1929). A treatise concerning the principles of human knowledge. In M. W. Calkins (Ed.), *Berkeley: Essay, princi-*

ples, dialogues. New York: Charles Scribner. (Original work published 1710)

Bernstein, R. J. (1976). *The restructuring of social and political theory*. New York: Harcourt Brace Jovanovich.

Berry, F. M. (1984). An introduction to Stephen C. Pepper's philosophical system via *World hypotheses: A study in evidence*. *Bulletin of the Psychonomic Society, 22*, 446–448.

Bobrow, D. G., & Hayes, P. J. (1985). Artificial intelligence — Where are we? *Artificial Intelligence, 25*, 375–415.

Bobrow, D. G., & Norman, D. A. (1975). Some principles of memory schemata. In D. G. Bobrow & A. Collins (Eds.), *Representation and understanding: Studies in cognitive science* (pp. 131–149). New York: Academic Press.

Boden, M. A. (1987). *Artificial intelligence and natural man* (2nd ed.). New York: Basic Books.

Boden, M. A. (1988). *Computer models of mind: Computational approaches in theoretical psychology*. Cambridge: Cambridge University Press.

Bolton, N. (1972). *The psychology of thinking*. London: Methuen.

Bolton, N. (1987). The programme of phenomenology. In A. Costall & A. Still (Eds.), *Cognitive psychology in question* (pp. 234–254). Brighton, Sussex: Harvester Press.

Bordo, S. (1986). The Cartesian masculinization of thought. *Signs: Journal of Women in Culture and Society, 11*, 439–456.

Bourne, L. (1970). Knowing and using concepts. *Psychological Review, 77*, 546–556.

Bousfield, W. A. (1953). The occurrence of clustering and the recall of randomly arranged associates. *Journal of General Psychology, 49*, 229–240.

Bower, G. (1972). Stimulus-sampling theory of encoding variability. In A. W. Melton & E. Martin (Eds.), *Coding processes in human memory* (pp. 85–125). Washington, DC: Winston.

Bower, G., & Trabasso, T. (1963). Reversals prior to solution in concept identification. *Journal of Experimental Psychology, 66*, 409–418.

Bransford, J. D. (1979). *Human cognition: Learning, understanding, and remembering*. Belmont, CA: Wadsworth.

Bransford, J. D., Barclay, J. R., & Franks, J. J. (1972). Sentence memory: A constructive versus interpretive approach. *Cognitive Psychology, 3*, 193–208.

Bransford, J. D., & Franks, J. J. (1971). The abstraction of linguistic ideas. *Cognitive Psychology*, *2*, 331–350.

Bransford, J. D., & Franks, J. J. (1972). The abstraction of linguistic ideas: A review. *Cognition*, *1*, 211–249.

Bransford, J. D., & Johnson, M. K. (1972). Contextual prerequisites for understanding: Some investigations of comprehension and recall. *Journal of Verbal Learning and Verbal Behavior*, *11*, 717–726.

Bransford, J. D., & Johnson, M. K. (1973). Considerations of some problems of comprehension. In W. Chase (Ed.), *Visual information processing* (pp. 383–438). New York: Academic Press.

Bransford, J. D., & McCarrell, N. S. (1974). A sketch of a cognitive approach to comprehension: Some thoughts about understanding what it means to comprehend. In W. Weimer & D. Palermo (Eds.), *Cognition and the symbolic processes* (pp. 189–229). Hillsdale, NJ: Erlbaum.

Bransford, J. D., McCarrell, N. S., Franks, J. J., & Nitsch, K. E. (1977). Toward unexplaining memory. In R. Shaw & J. Bransford (Eds.), *Perceiving, acting, and knowing: Toward an ecological psychology* (pp.431–466). Hillsdale, NJ: Erlbaum.

Bransford, J. D., Nitsch, K. E., & Franks, J. J. (1977). Schooling and the facilitation of knowing. In R. C. Anderson, R. J. Spiro, & W. E. Montague (Eds.), *Schooling and the acquisition of knowledge* (pp. 31–55). Hillsdale, NJ: Erlbaum.

Brewer, W. F., & Nakamura, G. V. (1984). The nature and functions of schemas. In R. S. Wyer, Jr. & R. K. Srull (Eds.), *Handbook of social cognition* (Vol. 1, pp. 263–298). Hillsdale, NJ: Erlbaum.

Britton, B. K., & Pellegrini, A. D. (Eds.). (1990). *Narrative thought and narrative language*. Hillsdale, NJ: Erlbaum.

Broadbent, D. E. (1958). *Perception and communication*. London: Pergamon.

Broadbent, D. E. (1961). *Behaviour*. London: Eyre & Spottiswoode.

Bronfenbrenner, U. (1977). Toward an experimental ecology of human development. *American Psychologist*, *32*, 513–531.

Brown, R. H. (1989). Textuality, social science, and society. *Issues in Integrative Studies*, *7*, 1–19.

Bruce, D. (1985). The how and why of ecological memory. *Journal of Experimental Psychology: General*, *114*, 78–90.

Bruner, J. (1957). On perceptual readiness. *Psychological Review*, *64*, 123–152.

Bruner, J. (1966). *Toward a theory of instruction*. Cambridge: Harvard University Press.

Bruner, J. (1986). *Actual minds, possible worlds*. Cambridge: Harvard University Press.

Bruner, J. (1987). Life as narrative. *Social Research*, *54*, 11–32.

Bruner, J., & Feldman, C. F. (1990). Metaphors of consciousness and cognition in the history of psychology. In D. E. Leary (Ed.), *Metaphors in the history of psychology* (pp. 230–238). Cambridge: Cambridge University Press.

Bruner, J., Goodnow, J. J., & Austin, G. A. (1956). *A study of thinking*. New York: John Wiley.

Capek, M. (1971). The fiction of instants. *Studium Generale*, *24*, 31–43.

Chomsky, N. (1959). Review of B. F. Skinner's *Verbal Behavior*. *Language*, *35*, 26–58.

Churchland, P. M., & Churchland, P. S. (1990). Could a machine think: Classical AI is unlikely to yield conscious machines; systems that mimic the brain might. *Scientific American*, *262*, 32–37.

Cohen, G. (1989). *Memory in the real world*. Hillsdale, NJ: Erlbaum.

Collins, A. M., & Quillian, M. R. (1969). Retrieval time from semantic memory. *Journal of Verbal Learning and Verbal Behavior*, *8*, 240–247.

Coltheart, M. (1989). Implicit memory and the functional architecture of cognition. In S. Lewandowsky, J. C. Dunn, & K. Kirsner (Eds.), *Implicit memory: Theoretical issues* (pp. 285–321). Hillsdale, NJ: Erlbaum.

Converse, P. E. (1986). Generalization and the social psychology of "other worlds." In D. W. Fiske & R. A. Shweder (Eds.), *Metatheory in social science: Pluralisms and subjectivities* (pp. 42–60). Chicago: University of Chicago Press.

Costall, A., & Still, A. (Eds.). (1987). *Cognitive psychology in question*. Brighton, Sussex: Harvester Press.

Craik, F. I. (1979). Human memory. *Annual Review of Psychology*, *30*, 63–102.

Cutting, J. E. (1982). Two ecological perspectives: Gibson versus Shaw and Turvey. *American Journal of Psychology*, *95*, 199–222.

Cutting, J. E. (1986). *Perception with an eye for motion*. Cambridge: The MIT Press.

Dallet, K. (1974). Transactional and probabilistic functionalism. In E. C. Carterette & M. P. Friedman (Eds.), *Handbook of perception* (Vol. 1, pp. 388–397). New York: Academic Press.

Davies, G. M., & Thomson, D. M. (Eds.). (1988). *Memory in context: Context in memory*. New York: John Wiley.

Deese, J. (1965). *The structure of associations in language and thought*. Baltimore: The Johns Hopkins University Press.

Dennett, D. C. (1979). *Brainstorms: Philosophical essays on mind and psychology*. Hassocks, Sussex: Harvester Press.

Dennett, D. C. (1981). Introduction. In D. R. Hofstadter & D. C. Dennett (Eds.), *The mind's I: Fantasies and reflections on self & soul* (pp. 3–16). New York: Basic Books.

Dennett, D. C. (1991). *Consciousness explained*. Boston: Little, Brown and Company.

Dewey, J. (1896). The reflex arc concept in psychology. *Psychological Review*, *3*, 357–370.

Dewey, J. (1911). Epistemological realism: The alleged ubiquity of the knowledge relation. *The Journal of Philosophy*, *8*, 99–107.

Dewey, J. (1912). Perception and organic action. *Journal of Philosophy*, *9*, 645–668.

Dewey, J. (1922). *Human nature and conduct*. New York: Henry Holt.

Dewey, J. (1925). *Experience and nature*. Chicago: Open Court.

Dewey, J. (1928). Meaning and existence. *The Journal of Philosophy*, *25*, 345–353.

Dewey, J. (1930). Conduct and experience. In C. Murchison (Ed.), *Psychologies of 1930* (pp. 409–422). Worcester, MA: Clark University Press.

Dewey, J. (1934). *Art as experience*. New York: Minton, Balch & Co.

Dewey, J. (1938). *Logic: The theory of inquiry*. New York: Henry Holt.

Dewey, J. (1951). Experience, knowledge, and value. In P. A. Schilpp (Ed.), *The philosophy of John Dewey* (pp. 515–608). New York: Tudor. (Original work published 1939)

Dewey, J., & Bentley, A. F. (1949). *Knowing and the known*. Boston: Beacon Press.

Dreyfus, H. L. (1979). *What computers can't do: The limits of artificial intelligence* (rev. ed.). New York: Harper & Row.

Dreyfus, H. L., & Dreyfus, S. E. (1986). *Mind over machine: The power of human intuition and expertise in the era of the computer*. New York: The Free Press.

Dreyfus, H. L., & Dreyfus, S. E. (1991, January/February). "Mind Games" [Letters from readers]. *The Sciences*, p. 3.

Earhard, B. (1974). Associationism (and the nativist-empiricist axis). In E. C. Carterette & M. P. Friedman (Eds.), *Handbook of perception* (Vol. 1, pp. 93–108). New York: Academic Press.

Ebbinghaus, H. (1913). *Memory: A contribution to experimental psychology* (H. A. Ruger & C. E. Bussenius, Trans.) New York: New York Teachers College, Columbia University. (Original work published 1885)

Edwards, D. (1991). Categories are for talking: On the cognitive and discursive bases of categorization. *Theory & Psychology, 1*, 515–542.

Efron, A. (Ed.). (1982). The Pepper papers, a symposium on the metaphilosophy of Stephen C. Pepper: Root metaphors theory [special issue]. *Journal of Mind and Behavior, 3* (3, 4).

Elkind, D. (1987). *Miseducation: Preschoolers at risk*. New York: Alfred A. Knopf.

Epstein, R. (1986). Bringing cognition and creativity into the behavioral laboratory. In T. J. Knapp & L. C. Robertson (Eds.), *Approaches to Cognition: Contrasts and controversies* (pp. 91–109). Hillsdale, NJ: Erlbaum.

Epstein, W. (Ed.). (1977). *Stability and constancy in visual perception*. New York: Academic Press.

Estes, W. K. (1972). An associative basis for coding and organization in memory. In A. W. Melton & E. Martin (Eds.), *Coding processes in human memory* (pp. 161–191). New York: Winston.

Estes, W. K. (1979). On the description and explanatory functions of theories of memory. In L. Nilsson (Ed.), *Perspectives on memory research: Essays in honor of Uppsala University's 500th Anniversary* (pp. 35–60). Hillsdale, NJ: Erlbaum.

Evans, R. I. (1968). *B. F. Skinner: The man and his ideas.*. New York: Dutton.

Ferguson, A. (1977). Androgyny as an ideal for human development. In M. Vetterling-Braggin, F. Elliston, & J. English (Eds.), *Feminism and philosophy* (pp. 45–69). Totowa, NJ: Littlefield & Adam.

Feyerabend, P. (1975). *Against method: Outline of an anarchistic theory of knowledge*. Atlantic Highlands, NJ: Humanities Press.

Finkleman, D. (1978). Science and psychology. *American Journal of Psychology, 91*, 179–199.

Fiske, D. W., & Shweder, R. A. (Eds.). (1986a). *Metatheory in social science: Pluralisms and subjectivities*. Chicago: University of Chicago Press.

Fiske, D. W., & Shweder, R. A. (1986b). Pluralism and subjectivities. In *Metatheory in social science: Pluralisms and subjectivities* (pp. 362–370). Chicago: University of Chicago Press.

Fodor, J. A. (1975). *The language of thought*. Cambridge, MA: Harvard University Press.

Fodor, J. A. (1983). *The modularity of mind*. Cambridge: The MIT Press.

Fodor, J. A., & Pylyshyn, Z. W. (1981). How direct is visual perception? Some reflections on Gibson's "Ecological Approach." *Cognition, 9*, 139–196.

Fodor, J. A., & Pylyshyn, Z. W. (1988). Connectionism and cognitive architecture: A critical review. *Cognition, 28*, 3–71.

Gardner, H. (1985). *The mind's new science: A history of the cognitive revolution*. New York: Basic Books.

Geertz, C. (1973). *The interpretation of culture*. New York: Basic Books.

Geertz, C. (1979). From the native's point of view: On the nature of anthropological understanding. In P. Rabinow & W. M. Sullivan (Eds.), *Interpretive social science* (pp. 225–241). Berkeley: University of California Press.

Geertz, C. (1980). Blurred genres: The refiguration of social thought. *The American Scholar, 49*, 165–179.

Geertz, C. (1983). *Local knowledge: Further essays in interpreting anthropology*. New York: Basic Books.

Gergen, K. J. (1982). *Toward transformation in social knowledge*. New York: Springer Verlag.

Gergen, K. J. (1985). The social constructionist movement in modern psychology. *American Psychologist, 40*, 266–275.

Gergen, K. J. (1986). Correspondence versus autonomy in the language of understanding human action. In D. W. Fiske & R. A. Shweder (Eds.), *Metatheory in social science: Pluralisms and subjectivities* (pp. 136–162). Chicago: University of Chicago Press.

Gergen, K. J., & Gigerenzer, G. (Eds.). (1991). Cognitivism and its discontents: An introduction to the issue. *Theory & Psychology, 1*, 403–405.

Ghiselin, M. (1987). Classification as an evolutionary problem. In A. Costall & A. Still (Eds.), *Cognitive psychology in question* (pp. 70–86). Brighton, Sussex: Harvester Press.

Gibbs, J. C. (1979). The meaning of ecologically oriented inquiry in contemporary psychology. *American Psychologist, 34*, 127–140.

Gibson, J. J. (1966). The problem of temporal order in stimulation and perception. *The Journal of Psychology, 62*, 141–149.

Gibson, J. J. (1979). *The ecological approach to visual perception.* Boston: Houghton Mifflin.

Gibson, J. J. (1980). Foreword. A prefatory essay on the perception of surfaces versus the perception of markings on a surface. In M. A. Hagen (Ed.), *The perception of pictures* (Vol. 1, pp. xi–xxi). New York: Academic Press.

Gillespie, D. (1982). An interpretation of some metatheoretical assumptions in cognitive psychology: Mechanism and contextualism. (Doctoral dissertation, University of Nebraska at Omaha). *Dissertation Abstracts International, 43*, 1957B.

Gilligan, C. (1982). *In a different voice: Psychological theory and women's development.* Cambridge: Harvard University Press.

Givón, T. (1989). *Mind, code and context: Essays in pragmatics.* Hillsdale, NJ: Erlbaum.

Gould, S. J. (1989). *Wonderful life: The Burgess Shale and the nature of history.* New York: W. W. Norton.

Greeno, J. G., James, C. T., Da Polito, F. J., & Polson, P. G. (1978). (Eds.). *Associative learning: A cognitive analysis.* Englewood Cliffs, NJ: Prentice-Hall.

Gregory, R. L. (1973). *Eye and brain: The psychology of seeing* (2nd ed.). New York: McGraw-Hill.

Gregory, R. L. (1974). Choosing a paradigm for perception. In E. C. Carterette & M. P. Friedman (Eds.), *Handbook of perception* (Vol. 1, pp. 255–283). New York: Academic Press.

Grumet, M. R. (1988). *Bitter milk: Women and teaching.* Amherst: University of Massachusetts Press.

Haber, R. N. (1974). Information processing. In E. C. Carterette & M. P. Friedman (Eds.), *Handbook of perception* (Vol. 1, pp. 313–333). New York: Academic Press.

Haber, R. N. (1985). Perception: A one hundred year perspective. In S. Koch & D. Leary (Eds.), *A century of psychology as science* (pp. 250–284). New York: McGraw-Hill.

Hacking, I. (1982). Wittgenstein the psychologist. *The New York Review of Books*, *24*, 42–44.

Harding, S. (1986). *The science question in feminism*. Ithaca: Cornell University Press.

Harding, S. (1987). The Garden in the machine: Gender relations, the process of science, and feminist epistemological strategies. In N. J. Nersessian (Ed.), *The process of science: Contemporary philosophical approaches to understanding scientific practice* (pp. 125–139). Boston: Martinus Nijhoff.

Harding, S. (1989). The instability of the analytical categories of feminist theory. In M. R. Malson, J. F. O'Barr, S. Westphal-Wihl, & M. Wyer (Eds.), *Feminist theory in practice and process* (pp. 15–34). Chicago: University of Chicago Press.

Harré, R. (1990). Vigotsky and artificial intelligence: What could cognitive psychology possibly be about? In P. A. French, T. E. Uehling, & H. K. Wettstein (Eds.), *Midwest studies in philosophy: The Philosophy of human sciences* (Vol. 15, pp. 389–399). Notre Dame: University of Notre Dame Press.

Haugeland, J. (1978). The nature and plausibility of cognitivism. *The Behavioral and Brain Sciences*, *2*, 215–260.

Haugeland, J. (1984). First among equals. In W. Kintsch, J. R. Miller, & P. G. Polson (Eds.), *Method and tactics in cognitive science* (pp. 85–99). Hillsdale, NJ: Erlbaum.

Hawkesworth, M. E. (1989). Knowers, knowing, known: Feminist theory and claims of truth. *Signs: Journal of Women in Culture and Society*, *14*, 533–557.

Hayes-Roth, B. (1977). Evolution of cognitive structure and processes. *Psychological Review*, *84*, 260–278.

Hebb, D. O. (1949). *Organization of behavior*. New York: John Wiley.

Heil, J. (1979). What Gibson's missing. *Journal for the Theory Social Behaviour*, *9*, 265–96.

Heil, J. (1981). Gibsonian sins of omission. *Journal for the Theory of Social Behaviour*, *11*, 307–311.

Hempel, C. G. (1951). Problems and changes in the empiricist criterion of meaning. *Revue Internationale de Philosophie*, *4*, 41–63.

Hempel, C. G. (1954). A logical appraisal of operationism. *Scientific Monthly*, *1*, 251–320.

Hempel, C. G. (1966). *Philosophy of natural science*. Englewood Cliffs, NJ: Prentice-Hall.

Hilgard, E. R. (1980). Consciousness in contemporary psychology. *Annual Review of Psychology*, *31*, 1–26.

Hinton, G. E., McClelland, J. L., & Rumelhart, D. E. (1986). Distributed representations. In D. E. Rumelhart, J. L. McClelland, & the PDP Research Group (Eds.), *Parallel distributed Processing: Explorations in the microstructure of cognition* (Vol. 1, pp.77–109). Cambridge: The MIT Press.

Hirst, W., & Levine, E. (1985). Ecological memory reconsidered: A comment on Bruce's "The how and why of ecological memory." *Journal of Experimental Psychology: General*, *114*, 269–271.

Hochberg, J. E. (1974). Organization and the gestalt tradition. In E. C. Carterette & M. P. Friedman (Eds.), *Handbook of perception* (Vol. 1, pp.180–210). New York: Academic Press.

Hochberg, J. E. (1978). *Perception* (2nd ed.). Englewood Cliffs, NJ: Prentice-Hall.

Hoffman, R. R. (1986). Context and contextualism in the psychology of learning. *Cahiers de Psychologie Cognitive*, *6*, 215–232.

Hoffman, R. R., & Nead, J. M. (1983). General contextualism, ecological science and cognitive research. *The Journal of Mind and Behavior*, *4*, 507–560.

Hoffman, R. R., & Palermo, D. S. (Eds.). (1991). *Cognition and the symbolic processes: Applied and ecological perspectives*. Hillsdale, NJ: Erlbaum.

Hofstadter, D. R., & Dennett, D. C. (Eds.). (1981). *The Mind's I: Fantasies and reflections on self and soul*. New York: Basic Books.

Holland, D., & Quinn, N. (Eds.). (1987). *Cultural models in language and thought*. Cambridge: Cambridge University Press.

Horgan, T. (1976). Reduction and the mind-body problem. In M. H. Marx & F. E. Goodson (Eds.), *Theories in contemporary psychology* (2nd ed., pp. 223–231). New York: Macmillan.

Horgan, T., & Tienson, J. (1990). Soft laws. In P. A. French, T. E. Uehling, & H. K. Wettstein (Eds.), *Midwest studies in philosophy: The philosophy of human sciences* (Vol. 15, pp. 256–279). Notre Dame: University of Notre Dame Press.

Horton, D. L. (1991). Retrospections on the study of memory and cognition. In R. R. Hoffman, & D. S. Palermo, (Eds.), *Cognition and the symbolic processes: Applied and ecological perspectives* (pp. 7–14). Hillsdale, NJ: Erlbaum.

Horton, D. L. & Mills, C. B. (1984). Human learning and memory. *Annual Review of Psychology, 35*, 361–394.

Hull, C. L. (1943). *Principles of behavior: An introduction to behavior theory*. New York: Appleton-Century-Crofts.

Humphrey, G. (1963). *Thinking: An introduction to its experimental psychology*. New York: John Wiley. (Original work published in 1951)

Iran-Nejad, A., McKeachie, W. J., & Berliner, D. C. (1990). The multisource nature of learning: An introduction. *Review of Educational Research, 60*, 509–515.

Izawa, C. (Ed.). (1989). *Current issues in cognitive processes: The Tulane Flowerree symposium on cognition*. Hillsdale, NJ: Erlbaum.

Izawa, C., & Hayden, R. G. (1989). Part 2. Comparisons of visual and auditory information process under two item information presentation methods. In C. Izawa (Ed.), *Current issues in cognitive processes: The Tulane Flowerree symposium on cognition* (pp. 246–278). Hillsdale, NJ: Erlbaum.

James, W. (1890). *The principles of psychology* (Vol. 1). New York: Henry Holt.

Jenkins, J. J. (1974a). Can we have a theory of meaningful memory? In R. L. Solso (Ed.), *Theories in cognitive psychology: The Loyola symposium* (pp. 1–21). Potomac, MD: Erlbaum.

Jenkins, J. J. (1974b). Remember that old theory of memory? Well forget it! *American Psychologist, 29*, 785–795.

Jenkins, J. J. (1981). Can we have a fruitful cognitive psychology? In J. H. Flowers (Ed.), *Cognitive processes Nebraska symposium on motivation*, (Vol. 28, pp. 211–238). Lincoln: University of Nebraska Press.

Jenkins, J. J., Wald, J., & Pittenger, J. B. (1986). Apprehending pictorial events. In V. McCabe & G. J. Balzano (Eds.), *Event cognition: An ecological perspective* (pp. 117–133). Hillsdale, NJ: Erlbaum.

Johansson, G. (1973). Visual perception of biological motion and a model for its analysis. *Perception & Psychophysics, 14*, 201–211.

Johansson, G. (1979). Memory functions in visual event perception. In L. Nilsson (Ed.), *Perspectives on memory research: Essays in honor of Uppsala University's 500th Anniversary* (pp. 93–103). Hillsdale, NJ: Erlbaum.

Johansson, G., von Hofsten, C., & Jansson, G. (1980). Event perception. *Annual Review of Psychology, 31*, 27–63.

Johnson, G. (1990, July/August). New mind, no clothes. [Review of Penrose, *The emperor's new mind*] *The Sciences*, 44–49.

Johnson, M. (1987). *The body in the mind: The bodily basis of meaning, imagination, and reason.* Chicago: University of Chicago Press.

Johnson, M. K., Doll, T. J., Bransford, J. D., & Lapinski, R. (1974). Context effects in sentence memory. *Journal of Experimental Psychology, 103*, 358–360.

Johnston, T., & Turvey, M. T. (1980). A sketch of an ecological metatheory for theories of learning. In G. Bower (Ed.), *The psychology of learning and motivation* (pp. 147–205). New York: Academic Press.

Joynson, R. B. (1970). The breakdown of modern psychology. *Bulletin of the British Psychological Society, 23*, 261–269.

Kantor, J. R. (1968). Behaviorism in the history of psychology. *The Psychological Record, 18*, 151–166.

Keller, E. F. (1985). *Reflections on gender and science.* New Haven: Yale University Press.

Kelly, G. A. (1955). *The psychology of personal constructs* (2 vols.). New York: W. W. Norton.

Kendler, H. H., & Kendler, T. S. (1962). Vertical and horizontal processes in problem solving. *Psychological Review, 69*, 1–16.

Kendler, H. H., & Spence, J. T. (1976). In M. H. Marx & F. E. Goodson, (Eds.), *Theories in contemporary psychology* (2nd ed., pp. 502–521). New York: Macmillan.

Kerlinger, F. N. (1973). *Foundations of behavioral research* (2nd ed.). New York: Holt, Rinehart and Winston.

Kestenbaum, V. (1977). *The phenomenological sense of John Dewey: Habit and meaning.* Atlantic Highlands, NJ: Humanities Press.

Kintsch, W. (1974). *The representation of meaning in memory.* Hillsdale, NJ: Erlbaum.

Kintsch, W., Miller, J. R., & Polson, P. G. (Eds.). (1984). *Method and tactics in cognitive science.* Hillsdale, NJ: Erlbaum.

Kirkland, J., & Anderson, R. (1990). Invariants, constructs, afforances, analogies. *International Journal of Personal Construct Psychology*, *3*, 31–39.

Knapp, T. J. (1986). The emergence of cognitive psychology in the latter half of the twentieth century. In T. J. Knapp & L. C. Robertson (Eds.), *Approaches to cognition: Contrasts and controversies* (pp. 13–35). Hillsdale, NJ: Erlbaum.

Koch, S. (1961). Psychological science versus the science-humanism antinomy: Intimations of a significant science of man. *American Psychologist*, *16*, 629–639.

Koch, S. (1964). Psychology and emerging conceptions of knowledge as unitary. In T. W. Wann (Ed.), *Behaviourism and phenomenology* (pp. 1–42). Chicago: University of Chicago Press.

Koch, S. (1981). The nature and limits of psychological knowledge: Lessons of a century qua "Science." *American Psychologist*, *36*, 257–269.

Koch, S. (Ed.). (1959). *Psychology: A study of a science* (Vol. 3). New York: McGraw-Hill.

Koffka, K. (1930). Some problems of space perception. In C. Murchison (Ed.), *Psychologies of 1930* (pp. 161–188). Worchester, MA: Clark University Press.

Köhler, W. (1930). Some tasks of gestalt psychology. In C. Murchison (Ed.), *Psychologies of 1930* (pp. 143–160). Worchester, MA: Clark University Press.

Kugler, P. N., Shaw R., Kim, V. J., Jeffrey, K. (1991). The role of attractors in the self-organization of intentional systems. In R. R. Hoffman & D. S. Palermo (Eds.), *Cognition and the symbolic processes: Applied and ecological perspectives* (pp. 387–431). Hillsdale, NJ: Erlbaum.

Kuhn, T. S. (1970). *The structure of scientific revolutions* (2nd ed.). Chicago: University of Chicago Press. (Original work published 1962)

Lakoff, G. (1987a). Cognitive models and prototype theory. In U. Neisser (Ed.). *Concepts and conceptual development: Ecological intellectual factors in categorization* (pp. 63–100). Cambridge: Cambridge University Press.

Lakoff, G. (1987b). *Women, fire, and dangerous things: What categories reveal about the mind*. Chicago: University of Chicago Press.

Lakoff, G., & Johnson, M. (1980). *Metaphors we live by*. Chicago: University of Chicago Press.

Langacker, R. W. (1987). *Foundations of cognitive grammar* (Vol. 1). Palo Alto: Stanford University Press.

Lashley, K. S. (1951). The problem of serial order in behavior. In L. A. Jeffress (Ed.), *Cerebral mechanisms in behavior* (pp. 112–136). New York: John Wiley.

Laszlo, E. (1972). *The systems view of the world.* New York: Braziler.

Leary, D. E. (1990a). Psyche's muse: The role of metaphor in the history of psychology. In D. E. Leary (Ed.), *Metaphors in the history of psychology* (pp. 1–77). Cambridge: Cambridge University Press.

Leary, D. E. (Ed.). (1990b). *Metaphors in the history of psychology.* Cambridge: Cambridge University Press.

Levin, D. N. (1986). The forms and functions of social knowledge. In D. W. Fiske & R. A. Shweder (Eds.), *Metatheory in social science* (pp. 271–283). Chicago: University of Chicago Press.

Levine, M. (1975). *A cognitive theory of learning.* Hillsdale, NJ: Erlbaum.

Lewin, K. (1935). *A dynamic theory of personality.* New York: McGraw-Hill.

Locke, J. (1959). *An essay concerning human understanding* (Vol. 1, collated and annotated, A. C. Fraser). New York: Dover. (Original work published 1690)

Lockhart, R. S. (1989). The role of theory in understanding implicit memory. In S. Lewandowsky, J. C. Dunn, & K. Kirsner (Eds.), *Implicit memory: Theoretical issues* (pp. 3–13). Hillsdale, NJ: Erlbaum.

Loftus, G. R., & Loftus, E. F. (1976). *Human memory: The processing of information.* Hillsdale, NJ: Erlbaum.

Lombardo, T. J. (1987). *The reciprocity of perceiver and environment: The evolution of James J. Gibson's ecological psychology.* Hillsdale, NJ: Erlbaum.

McCabe, V. (1986a). Introduction: Event cognition and the conditions of existence. In V. McCabe & G. J. Balzano (Eds.), *Event cognition: An ecological perspective* (pp. 3–23). Hillsdale, NJ: Erlbaum.

McCabe, V. (1986b). Memory for meaning: The ecological use of language. In V. McCabe & G. J. Balzano (Eds.), *Event cognition: An ecological perspective* (pp. 175–191). Hillsdale, NJ: Erlbaum.

McCabe, V., & Balzano, G. J. (Eds.). (1986). *Event cognition: An ecological perspective*. Hillsdale, NJ: Erlbaum.

McClelland, J. L., Rumelhart, D. E., & Hinton, G. E. (1986). The appeal of parallel distributed processing. In D. E. Rumelhart, J. L. McClelland, & the PDP Research Group (Eds.), *Parallel distributed processing: Explorations in the microstructure of cognition* (Vol. 1, pp. 3–44). Cambridge: The MIT Press.

McCorduck, P. (1979). *Machines who think: A personal inquiry into the history and prospects of artificial intelligence*. San Francisco: W. H. Freeman.

MacCorquodale, K., & Meehl, P. E. (1948). On a distinction between hypothetical constructs and intervening variables. *Psychological Review*, *55*, 95–107.

Mace, W. M. (1974). Ecologically stimulating cognitive psychology: Gibsonian perspectives. In W. B. Weimer & D. S. Palermo (Eds.), *Cognition and the symbolic processes* (pp. 137–164). Hillsdale, NJ: Erlbaum.

Mace, W. M. (1977). James J. Gibson's strategy for perceiving: Ask not what's inside your head, but what your head's inside of. In R. Shaw & J. D. Bransford (Eds.), *Perceiving, acting, and knowing: Toward an ecological psychology* (pp. 43–65). Hillsdale, NJ: Erlbaum.

McGuire, W. J. (1983). A contextualist theory of knowledge: Its implications for innovation and reform in psychological research. In L. Berkowitz (Ed.), *Advances in experimental social psychology* (Vol. 16, pp. 1–47). New York: Academic Press.

Malcolm, N. (1977). *Memory and mind*. Ithaca: Cornell University Press.

Maltzman, I. (1955). Thinking: From a behaviorist point of view. *Psychological Review*, *62*, 275–286.

Mandler, G. A. (1962). From association to structure. *Psychological Review*, *69*, 415–427.

Mandler G. A. (1967). Organization and memory. In K. W. Spence & J. T. Spence (Eds.), *The psychology of learning and motivation: Advances in research and theory* (pp. 327–372). New York: Academic Press.

Mandler, G. A. (1979). Organization, memory, and mental structures. In C. R. Puff (Ed.), *Memory, organization, and structure* (pp. 303–319). New York: Academic Press.

Manicas, P. T., & Secord, P. F. (1983). Implications for psychology of the new philosophy of science. *American Psychologist, 38,* 399–413.

Markova, I. (1982). *Paradigms, thought, and language.* Chichester, England: John Wiley.

Marr, D. (1982). *Vision: A computational investigation into the human representation and processing of visual information.* San Francisco: W. H. Freeman.

Marshall, J. C. (1977). Minds, machines and metaphors. *Social Studies of Science, 7,* 475–488.

Marshall, J. C., & Fryer, D. M. (1978). Speak memory!: An introduction to some historic studies of remembering and forgetting. In M. M. Gruneberg & P. Morris (Eds.), *Aspects of memory* (pp. 1–25). London: Methuen.

Massaro, D. W. (1987). *Speech perception by ear and eye: A paradigm for psychological inquiry.* Hillsdale, NJ: Erlbaum.

Massaro, D. W. (1988). Some criticisms of connectionist models of human performance. *Journal of Memory and Language, 27,* 213–234.

Mead, G. H. (1934). *Mind, self, and society* (C. M. Morris, Ed.). Chicago: University of Chicago Press.

Medin, D. L., & Schaffer, M. M. (1978). Context theory of classification learning, *Psychological Review, 85,* 207–238.

Medin, D. L., & Wattenmaker, W. D. (1987). Category cohesiveness, theories, and cognitive archeology. In U. Neisser (Ed.), *Concepts and conceptual development: Ecological intellectual factors in categorization* (pp. 25–62). Cambridge: Cambridge University Press.

Meehl, P. E. (1986). What social scientists don't understand. In D. W. Fiske & R. A. Shweder (Eds.), *Metatheory in social science: Pluralisms and subjectivities* (pp. 315–338). Chicago: University of Chicago Press.

Merleau-Ponty, M. (1962). *Phenomenology of perception* (C. Smith, Trans.). New York: Humanities. (Original work published 1945)

Merleau-Ponty, M. (1963). *The structure of behavior.* (A. L. Fisher, Trans.). Boston: Beacon Press. (Original work published 1942)

Merleau-Ponty, M. (1964a). *Signs* (R. C. McCleary, Trans.). Chicago: Northwestern University Press. (Original work published 1960)

Merleau-Ponty, M. (1964b). The primacy of perception and its philosophical consequences. In J. M. Edie (Ed. and Trans.), *The primacy of perception* (pp. 12–42). Evanston, IL: Northwestern University Press. (Original work published 1947)

Michaels, C. F., & Carello, C. (1981). *Direct perception*. Englewood Cliffs, NJ: Prentice-Hall.

Miller, G. A. (1956). The magical number seven, plus or minus two: Some limits on our capacity to process information. *Psychological Review*, *63*, 81–96.

Miller, G. A., Galanter, E., & Pribram, K. H. (1960). *Plans and the structure of behavior*. New York: Holt, Rinehart & Winston.

Minsky, M. (1969). Matter, mind, and models. In M. Minsky (Ed.), *Semantic information processing* (pp. 425–431). Cambridge: The MIT Press.

Minsky, M. (1975). A framework for representing knowledge. In P. H. Winston (Ed.), *The psychology of computer vision* (pp. 211–277). New York: McGraw-Hill.

Minsky, M. (1981). K-Lines: A theory of memory. In D. A. Norman (Ed.), *Perspectives on cognitive science* (pp. 87–105). Hillsdale, NJ: Erlbaum.

Minsky, M. (1986). *The society of mind*. New York: Simon and Schuster.

Mishler, E. G. (1979). Meaning in context: Is there any other kind? *Harvard Educational Review*, *49*, 1–19.

Mishler, E. G. (1986). *Research interviewing: Context and narrative*. Cambridge: Harvard University Press.

Morrison, T. (1987). *Beloved*. New York: Alfred A. Knopf.

Murdock, B. B., Jr. (1961). The retention of individual items. *Journal of Experimental Psychology*, *62*, 618–625.

Murphy, G. L., & Medin, D. L. (1985). The role of theories in conceptual coherence. *Psychological Review*, *92*, 289–316.

Murray, D. J. (1976). Research on human memory in the nineteenth century. *Canadian Journal of Psychology*, *30*, 201–220.

Nagel, T. (1991: Nov. 7). What we have in mind when we say we're thinking [review of *Consciousness explained*]. *Wall Street Journal*, p. A14.

Neisser, U. (1967). *Cognitive psychology*. New York: Appleton-Century-Croft.

Neisser, U. (1976). *Cognition and reality: Principles and implications of cognitive psychology*. San Francisco: W. H. Freeman.

Neisser, U. (Ed.). (1982). *Memory observed: Remembering in natural contexts*. San Francisco: W. H. Freeman.

Neisser, U. (Ed.). (1987a). *Concepts and conceptual development: Ecological and intellectual factors in categorization*. Cambridge: Cambridge University Press.

Neisser, U. (1987b). From direct perception to conceptual structure. In U. Neisser (Ed.), *Concepts and conceptual development: Ecological and intellectual factors in categorization* (pp. 11–24). Cambridge: Cambridge University Press.

Neisser, U. (1987c). Introduction: The ecological and intellectual bases of categorization. In U. Neisser (Ed.), *Concepts and conceptual development: Ecological and intellectual factors in categorization* (pp. 1–10). Cambridge: Cambridge University Press.

Neisser, U. (1988). What is ordinary memory the memory of? In U. Neisser & E. Winograd (Eds.), *Remembering reconsidered: Ecological and traditional approaches to the study of memory* (pp. 356–373). Cambridge: Cambridge University Press.

Neisser, U., & Winograd, E. (Eds.). (1988). *Remembering reconsidered: Ecological and traditional approaches to the study of memory*. Cambridge: Cambridge University Press.

Nelson, K. (1986). *Event knowledge: Structure and function in development*. Hillsdale, NJ: Erlbaum.

Nelson, K. (1988). The ontogeny of memory for real events. In U. Neisser & E. Winograd (Eds.), *Remembering reconsidered: Ecological and traditional approaches to the study of memory* (pp. 244–276). Cambridge: Cambridge University Press.

Newell, A. (1973). You can't play 20 questions with nature and win: Projective comments on the papers of this symposium. In W. G. Chase (Ed.), *Visual information processing* (pp. 283–311). New York: Academic Press.

Newell, A., & Simon, H. A. (1961). The simulation of human thought. In W. Dennis (Ed.), *Current trends in psychological theory* (pp. 152–179). Pittsburgh: University of Pittsburgh Press.

Newell, A., & Simon, H. A. (1963). GPS, A program that simulates human thought. In E. A. Feigenbaum & J. Feldman (Eds.), *Computers and thought* (pp. 279–293). New York: McGraw-Hill.

Newell, A., & Simon, H. A. (1972). *Human problem solving*. Englewood Cliffs, NJ: Prentice-Hall.

Newell, A., Shaw, J. C., & Simon, H. A. (1958). Elements of a theory of human problem solving. *Psychological Review*, 65, 151–166.

Nilsson, L. (1979). Functions of memory. In L. Nilsson (Ed.), *Perspectives on memory research: Essays in honor of Uppsala University's 500th Anniversary* (pp. 3–15). Hillsdale, NJ: Erlbaum.

Noble, W. (1981). Gibsonian theory and the pragmatist perspective. *Journal for the Theory of Social Behaviour*, 11, 65–85.

Norman, D. A. (1979). Perception, memory, and mental processes. In L. Nilsson (Ed.), *Perspectives on memory research: Essays in honor of Uppsala University's 500th Anniversary* (pp. 121–144). Hillsdale, NJ: Erlbaum.

Norman, D. A. (1980). What goes on in the mind of the learner? In W. J. McKeachie (Ed.), *New directions for teaching and learning: Learning, cognition and college teaching* (Vol. 2, pp. 37–49). San Francisco: Jossey-Bass.

Olson, D. R. (1990). Thinking about narrative. In B. K. Britton & A. D. Pellegrini (Eds.), *Narrative thought and narrative language* (pp. 99–111). Hillsdale, NJ: Erlbaum.

Overton, W. F., & Reese, H. W. (1973). Models of development: Methodological implications. In J. R. Nesselroade & H. W. Reese (Eds.), *Life-span developmental psychology: Methodological issues* (pp. 65–86). New York: Academic Press.

Palermo, D. S. (1971). Is a scientific revolution taking place in psychology? *Science Studies*, 1, (135–155).

Palmer, A. (1987). Cognitivism and computer simulation. In A. Costall & A. Still (Eds.), *Cognitive psychology in question*. Brighton, Sussex: Harvester Press.

Palmer, S. E., & Kimchi, R. (1986). The information processing approach to cognition. In T. J. Knapp & L. C. Robertson (Eds.), *Approaches to cognition: Contrasts and controversies* (pp. 37–77). Hillsdale, NJ: Erlbaum.

Parker, I. (1989). *The crisis in modern social psychology and how to end it*. London: Routledge.

Peirce, C. S. (1931). *Collected writings* (Vol. 1). Cambridge: Harvard University Press.

Penrose, R. (1989). *The emperor's new mind: Concerning computers, minds, and the laws of physics*. New York: Oxford University Press.

Pepper, S. C. (1956). *The basis of criticism in the arts*. Cambridge: Harvard University Press.

Pepper, S. C. (1961). *World hypotheses: A study in evidence*. Berkeley: University of California Press. (Original work published in 1942)

Polanyi, M. (1958). *Personal knowledge*. New York: Harper & Row.

Polanyi, M. (1966). *The tacit dimension*. Garden City, New York: Doubleday.

Popper, K. R. (1963). *Conjectures and refutations: The growth of scientific knowledge*. New York: Harper & Row.

Putnam, H. (1981). *Reason, truth and history*. Cambridge: Cambridge University Press.

Quillian, M. R. (1968). Semantic memory. In M. Minsky (Ed.), *Semantic information processing* (pp. 227–271). Cambridge: The MIT Press.

Quillian, M. R. (1969). The teachable language comprehender. *Communications of the Association for Computing Machinery*, *12*, 459–475.

Redner, H. (1987). *The ends of science: An essay in scientific authority*. Boulder: Westview Press.

Reed, E. S. (1987a). James Gibson's ecological approach to cognition. In A. Costall & A. Still (Eds.), *Cognitive psychology in question* (pp. 142–173). Brighton, Sussex: Harvester Press.

Reed, E. S. (1987b). Why do things look as they do? The implications of James Gibson's *The ecological approach to visual perception*. In A. Costall & A. Still (Eds.), *Cognitive psychology in question* (pp. 90–114). Brighton, Sussex: Harvester Press.

Reed, E. S. (1988). *James J. Gibson and the psychology of perception*. New Haven: Yale University Press.

Reed, E. S., & Jones, R. K. (1981). Is perception blind? A reply to Heil. *Journal for the Theory of Social Behaviour*, *11*, 87–91.

Reese, H. W., & Overton, W. F. (1970). Models of development and theories of development. In L. R. Goulet & P. B. Baltes (Eds.), *Life-span developmental psychology: Research and theory* (pp. 115–145). New York: Academic Press.

Reynolds, A. G., & Flaggs, P. W. (1977). *Cognitive psychology*. Cambridge: Winthrop.

Robertson, L. C. (1986). From Gestalt to Neo-Gestalt. In T. J. Knapp & L. C. Robertson (Eds.), *Approaches to cognition: Contrasts and controversies* (pp. 159–188). Hillsdale, NJ: Erlbaum.

Robinson, E. S. (1932). *Association theory today: An essay in systematic psychology*. New York: Century.

Rock, I. (1975). *An introduction to perception*. New York: Macmillan.

Rock, I. (1977). In defense of unconscious inference. In W. Epstein (Ed.), *Stability and constancy in visual perception* (pp. 321–376). New York: John Wiley.

Rock, I. (1984). *Perception*. New York: Scientific American Books.

Roediger, H. L. (1980). Memory metaphors in cognitive psychology. *Memory and Cognition*, *8*, 231–246.

Rosch, E. H. (1973). Natural categories. *Cognitive Psychology*, *4*, 328–325.

Rosch, E. H. (1975). Cognitive reference points. *Cognitive Psychology*, *7*, 532–547.

Rosch, E. H. (1978). Principles of categorization. In E. H. Rosch & B. B. Lloyd (Eds.), *Cognition and categorization* (pp. 27–48). Hillsdale, NJ: Erlbaum.

Rosch, E. H. (1988). Coherences and categorization: A historical view. In F. Kessel (Ed.), *The development of language and language researchers: Essays in honor of Roger Brown* (pp. 373–392). Hillsdale, NJ: Erlbaum.

Rosch, E. H., & Lloyd, B. B. (Eds.). (1978). *Cognition and categorization*. Hillsdale, NJ: Erlbaum.

Rosch, E. H., & Mervis, C. B. (1975). Family resemblances: Studies in the internal structure of categories. *Cognitive Psychology*, *7*, 573–605.

Rosch, E. H., Mervis, C. B., Gray, W. D., Johnson, D. M., & Boyes-Braem, P. (1976). Basic objects in natural categories. *Cognitive Psychology*, *8*, 382–439.

Rosenfield, I. (1988). *The invention of memory: A new view of the brain*. New York: Basic Books.

Rosmarin, A. (1989). The narrativity of interpretive history. In J. Phelan (Ed.). *Reading narrative: Form, ethics, ideology* (pp. 12–26). Columbus: Ohio State Press.

Royce, J. R. (1974). Cognition and knowledge: Psychological epistemology. In E. C. Carterette & M. P. Friedman (Eds.), *Handbook of perception* (Vol. 1, pp. 149-176). New York: Academic Press.

Rumelhart, D. E., Lindsay, P. H., & Norman, D. A. (1972). A process model for long-term memory. In E. Tulving & W. Donaldson (Eds.), *Organization of memory* (pp. 197–246). New York: Academic Press.

Rumelhart, D. E., McClelland, J. L., & the PDP Research Group (Eds.). (1986). *Parallel distributed processing: Explorations in the microstructure of cognition* (Vol. 1). Cambridge: The MIT Press.

Rumelhart, D. E., & Ortony, A. (1977). The representation of knowledge in memory. In R. C. Anderson, R. J. Spiro, & W. E. Montague (Eds.), *Schooling and the acquistion of knowledge* (pp. 99–135). Hillsdale, NJ: Erlbaum.

Rychlak, J. F. (1977). *The psychology of rigorous humanism*. New York: John Wiley.

Sacks, O. (1990). Neurology and the soul. *The New York Review of Books, 37* (18), 44–50.

Sampson, E. E. (1981). Cognitive psychology as ideology. *American Psychologist, 36*, 730–743.

Sampson, E. E. (1983). Deconstructing psychology's subject. *The Journal of Mind and Behavior, 4*, 135–164.

Sarbin, T. R. (1977). Contextualism: A world view for modern psychology. In A. W. Landfield (Ed.), *Current theory and research in motivation: Nebraska symposium on motivation* (Vol. 24, pp. 1–41). Lincoln: University of Nebraska Press.

Sarbin, T. R. (Ed.). (1986a). *Narrative psychology: The storied nature of human conduct*. New York: Praeger.

Sarbin, T. R. (1986b). The narrative as a root metaphor for psychology. In T. R. Sarbin (Ed.), *Narrative psychology: The storied nature of human conduct* (pp. 3–21). New York: Praeger.

Schacter, D. L. (1987). Implicit memory: History and current status. *Journal of Experimental Psychology: Learning, Memory and Cognition, 13*, 501–518.

Schacter, D. L., & Graf, P. (1986). Effects of elaborative processing on implicit and explicit memory for new associations. *Journal of Experimental Psychology: Learning, Memory, and Cognition, 12*, 432–444.

Schank, R. C. (1981). Language and memory. In D. A. Norman (Ed.), *Perspectives on cognitive science* (pp. 105–147). Hillsdale, NJ: Erlbaum.

Schank, R., & Abelson, R. (1977). *Scripts, plans, goals and understanding: An inquiry into human knowledge structures*. Hillsdale, NJ: Erlbaum.

Schmidt, R. A. (1982). The schema concept. In J. A. S. Kelso (Ed.), *Human motor behavior* (pp. 219–235). Hillsdale, NJ: Erlbaum.

Schnaitter, R. (1986). A coordination of differences: Behaviorism, mentalism, and the foundations of psychology. In T. J. Knapp & L. C. Robertson (Eds.), *Approaches to Cognition: Contrasts and controversies* (pp. 291– 315). Hillsdale, NJ: Erlbaum.

Schneider, W. (1987). Connectionism: Is it a paradigm shift for psychology? *Behavior Research Methods, Instruments, & Computers, 19*, 73–83.

Scriven, M. (1957). A study of radical behaviorism. In H. Feigl & M. Scriven (Eds.), *Minnesota studies in the philosophy of science* (Vol. 1, pp. 88–130). Minneapolis: University of Minnesota Press.

Searle, J. (1983). *Intentionality*. Cambridge: Cambridge University Press.

Searle, J. (1990). Is the brain's mind a computer program? *Scientific American, 262*, 26–31.

Secord, P. F. (1986). Explanation in the social sciences and in life situations. In D. W. Fiske & R. A. Shweder (Eds.), *Metatheory in social science: Pluralisms and subjectivities* (pp. 197–221). Chicago: University of Chicago Press.

Segal, E., & Lachman, R. (1972). Complex behavior or higher mental process. *American Psychologist, 27*, 46–55.

Shanon, B. (1988). Semantic representation of meaning: A critique. *Psychological Bulletin, 104*, 70–83.

Shanon, B. (1990). What is context? *Journal for the Theory of Social Behaviour, 20*, 157–166.

Shaw, R., & Bransford, J. (Eds.). (1977). *Perceiving, acting, and knowing: Toward an ecological psychology*. Hillsdale, NJ: Erlbaum.

Shaw, R., & Hazelett, W. M. (1986). Schemas in cognition. In V. McCabe & G. J. Balzano (Eds.), *Event cognition: An ecological perspective* (pp. 45–58). Hillsdale, NJ: Erlbaum.

Shaw, R., & Pittenger, J. (1977). Perceiving the face of change in changing faces: Implications for a theory of object perception. In R. Shaw & J. D. Bransford (Eds.), *Perceiving, acting and knowing: Toward an ecological psychology* (pp. 103–132). Hillsdale, NJ: Erlbaum.

Sherif, C. W. (1979). Bias in psychology. In J. A. Sherman & E. T. Beck (Eds.), *The prism of sex: Essays in the sociology of knowledge* (pp. 93–133). Madison: University of Wisconsin Press.

Shimp, C. P. (1976). Organization in memory and behavior. *Journal of the Experimental Analysis of Behavior*, *26*, 113–130.

Shotter, J. (1975). *Images of man in psychological research*. London: Methuen.

Shotter, J. (1987). Cognitive psychology, "Taylorism," and the manufacture of unemployment. In A. Costall & A. Still (Eds.), *Cognitive psychology in question* (pp. 44–52). Brighton, Sussex: Harvester Press.

Shweder, R. (1986). Divergent rationalities. In D. W. Fiske & R. A. Shweder (Eds.), *Metatheory in social science: Pluralisms and subjectivities* (pp. 163–196). Chicago: University of Chicago Press.

Shweder, R., & Fiske, D. W. (1986). Introduction: Uneasy social science. In D. W. Fiske & R. A. Shweder (Eds.), *Metatheory in social science: Pluralisms and subjectivities* (pp. 1–18). Chicago: University of Chicago Press.

Simon, H. A. (1980). Cognitive science: The newest science of the artificial. *Cognitive Science*, *4*, 33–46.

Simon, H. A. (1990). Invariants of human behavior. *Annual Review of Psychology*, *41*, 1–19.

Simon, H. A., & Newell, A. (1958). Heuristic problem solving: The next advance in operations research, *Operations Research*, *6*, 6.

Simon, H. A., & Newell, A. (1964). Information processing in computers and man. *American Scientist*, *52*, 281–300.

Simon, H. A., & Newell, A. (1971). Human problem solving: The state of the theory in 1970. *American Psychologist*, *26*, 145–159.

Skinner, B. F. (1950). Are theories of learning necessary? *Psychological Review*, *57*, 193–216.

Skinner, B. F. (1956). A case history in scientific method. *American Psychologist*, *11*, 221–233.

Skinner, B. F. (1976). A science of behavior. In M. H. Marx & F. E. Goodson (Eds.), *Theories in contemporary psychology* (2nd ed., pp. 522–534). New York: Macmillan.

Skinner, B. F. (1989). The origins of cognitive thought. *American Psychologist*, *44*, 13–18.

Smith, E. E., & Medin, D. L. (1981). *Categories and concepts*. Cambridge: Harvard University Press.

Smith, K. (1987). Fodor on language comprehension as inferential process: A phenomenological critique. *Journal of Phenomenological Psychology*, *18*, 143–186.

Solso, R. L. (1989). Prototypes, schemata, and the form of human knowledge: The cognition of abstraction. In C. Izawa (Ed.), *Current issues in cognitive processes: The Tulane Floweree symposium on cognition.* (pp. 345–368). Hillsdale, NJ: Erlbaum.

Spence, K. W. (1957). The empirical basis and theoretical structure of psychology. *Philosophy of Science*, *24*, 97–108.

Spiro, R. J., Vispoel, W. P., Schmitz, J. G., Samarapungavan, A., & Boerger, A. E. (1987). Knowledge acquisition for application: Cognitive flexibility and transfer in complex context domains. In B. K. Britton & S. M. Glynn (Eds.), *Executive control processes in reading* (pp. 177–199). Hillsdale, NJ: Erlbaum.

Squire, L. R. (1986). Mechanisms of memory. *Science*, *232*, 1612–1619.

Stephens, S. S. (1976). Operationism and logical positivism. In M. H. Marx & F. E. Goodson (Eds.), *Theories in contemporary psychology* (2nd ed., pp. 2–30). New York: Macmillan. (Original work published in 1939)

Sternberg, S. (1966). High-speed scanning in human memory. *Science*, *153*, 652–654.

Still, A., & Costall, A. (1987). Introduction: In place of cognitivism. In A. Costall & A. Still (Eds.), *Cognitive psychology in question* (pp. 1–12). Brighton, Sussex: Harvester Press.

Sullivan, E. V. (1984). *A critical psychology: Interpretation of the personal world.* New York: Plenum Press.

Swartz, R. J. (1956). *Perceiving, sensing, and knowing.* Garden City, NY: Anchor Books.

Sweetser, E. (1990). *From etymology to pragmatics: Metaphorical and cultural aspects of semantic structure.* Cambridge: Cambridge University Press.

Thomson, D., & Davies, G. (1988). Introduction. In G. M. Davies & D. M. Thomson (Eds.), *Memory in context: Context in memory* (pp. 1–10). New York: John Wiley.

Thorndyke, P. W. (1984). Applications of schema theory in cognitive research. In J. Anderson & S. Kosslyn (Eds.), *Tutorials in learning and memory: Essays in honor of Gordon Bower* (pp. 167–192). San Francisco: W. H. Freeman.

Tiberghien, G. (1986). Context and cognition: Introduction. *Cahiers de Psychologie Cognitive*, *6*, 105–119.

Tolman, E. C. (1932). *Purposive behavior in animals and men*. New York: Appleton-Century-Crofts.

Tulving, E. (1962). Subjective organization in free recall of "unrelated" words. *Psychological Review*, *69*, 344–354.

Tulving, E. (1964). Intratrial and intertrial retention: Notes toward a theory of free recall verbal learning. *Psychological Review*, *71*, 219–237.

Tulving, E. (1967). The effects of presentation and recall of material in free-recall learning. *Journal of Verbal Learning and Verbal Behavior*, *6*, 175–184.

Tulving, E. (1972). Episodic and semantic memory. In E. Tulving & W. Donaldson (Eds.), *Organization of memory* (pp. 381–403). New York: Academic Press.

Tulving, E. (1979). Memory research: What kind of progress? In L. Nilsson (Ed.), *Perspectives on memory research: Essays in honor of Uppsala University's 500th Anniversary* (pp. 19–34). Hillsdale, NJ: Erlbaum.

Tulving, E. (1984). Relations among components and processes of memory. *The Behavioral and Brain Sciences*, *7*, 257–263.

Tulving, E. (1985). How many memory systems are there? *American Psychologist*, *40*, 385–398.

Tulving, E., & Thomson, D. M. (1973). Encoding specificity and retrieval processes in episodic memory. *Psychological Review*, *84*, 67–88.

Tulving, E., & Wiseman, S. (1975). Relation between recognition and recognition failure of recallable words. *Bulletin of the Psychonomic Society*, *6*, 79–82.

Turvey, M. T. (1977). Contrasting orientations to the theory of visual information processing. *Psychological Review*, *80*, 67–88.

Turvey, M. T., & Shaw, R. (1979). The primacy of perceiving: An ecological reformulation of perception for understanding memory. In L. Nilsson (Ed.), *Perspectives on memory research: Essays in honor of Uppsala University's 500th Anniversary* (pp. 167–222). Hillsdale, NJ: Erlbaum.

Turvey, M. T., Shaw, R., Reed, E. S., & Mace, W. M. (1981). Ecological laws of perceiving and acting: In reply to Fodor and Pylyshyn. *Cognition*, *9*, 237–304.

Tyler, L. E. (1981). More stately mansions—Psychology extends its boundaries. *Annual Review of Psychology, 32,* 1–20.

Underwood, B. J. (1963). Stimulus selection in verbal learning. In C. N. Cofer & B. S. Musgrave (Eds.), *Verbal behavior and learning: Problems and processes* (pp. 33–47). New York: McGraw-Hill.

Underwood, B. J. (1972). Are we overloading memory? In A. W. Melton & E. Martin (Eds.), *Coding processes in human memory* (pp. 1–25). Washington, DC: Winston.

Underwood, B. J., Ham, M., & Ekstrand, B. (1962). Cue selection in paired-associate learning. *Journal of Experimental Psychology, 64,* 405–409.

Valsiner, J. Construction of the mental: From the "cognitive revolution" to the study of development. *Theory & Psychology, 1,* 477–494.

Varela, F. J., Thompson, E., & Rosch, E. (1991). *The embodied mind: Cognitive science and human experience.* Cambridge: The MIT Press.

von Helmholtz, H. (1884). *Popular lectures on scientific subjects* (E. Athinson, Trans.). New York: Longman, Green.

Walls, J. (1982). The psychology of David Hartley and the root metaphor of mechanism: A study in the history of psychology. *The Journal of Mind and Behavior, 3,* 259–274.

Wallston, B. S., & Grady, K. E. (1985). Integrating the feminist critique and the crisis in social psychology: Another look at research methods. In V. E. O'Leary, R. K. Unger, & B. S. Wallston (Eds.), *Women, gender, and social psychology* (pp. 7–33). Hillsdale, NJ: Erlbaum.

Warren, N. (1971). Is a scientific revolution taking place in psychology?— Doubts and reservations. *Science Studies, 1,* 407–413.

Watkins, M. J. (1978). Theoretical issues. In M. M. Gruneberg & P. Morris (Eds.), *Aspects of memory* (pp. 40–61). London: Methuen.

Watkins, M. J., & Tulving, E. (1975). Episodic memory: When recognition fails. *Journal of Experimental Psychology: General, 104,* 5–29.

Watson, J. B. (1913). Psychology as a behaviorist views it. *Psychological Review, 20,* 158–177.

Watson, J. B. (1924). *Behaviorism.* New York: W. W. Norton.

Wechsler, D. B. (1963). Engrams, memory storage, and mnemonic coding. *American Psychologist, 18,* 149–153.

Weimer, W. B. (1977). A conceptual framework for cognitive psychology: Motor theories of the mind. In R. Shaw & J. Bransford (Eds.), *Perceiving, acting, and knowing: Toward an ecological psychology* (pp. 267–311). Hillsdale, NJ: Erlbaum.

Wertheimer, M. (1974). The problem of perceptual structure. In E. C. Carterette & M. P. Friedman (Eds.), *Handbook of perception* (Vol. 1, pp. 75–91). New York: Academic Press.

Wertz, F. J. (1987). Cognitive psychology and the understanding of perception. *Journal of Phenomenological Psychology, 18,* 103–142.

Westland, G. (1978). *Current crises of psychology.* London: Heinemann.

Wilcox, S., & Katz, S. (1981a). A direct realistic alternative to the traditional conception of memory. *Behaviorism, 9,* 227–239.

Wilcox, S., & Katz, S. (1981b). What Gibson isn't missing after all: A reply to Heil. *Journal for the Theory of Social Behaviour, 11,* 313–317.

Winograd, E. (1988). Continuities between ecological and laboratory approaches to memory. In U. Neisser & E. Winograd (Eds.), *Remembering reconsidered: Ecological and traditional approaches to the study of memory* (pp. 11–20). Cambridge: Cambridge University Press.

Winograd, T. (1976). Artificial intelligence and language comprehension. In *Artificial intelligence and language comprehension.* Washington, DC: National Institute of Education.

Winograd, T. (1980). What does it mean to understand language? *Cognitive Science, 4,* 209–241.

Winograd, T., & Flores, F. (1986). *Understanding computers and cognition: A new foundation for design.* Norwood, NJ: Ablex.

Winston, P. H. (1975). Learning structural descriptions from examples. In P. H. Winston (Ed.), *The psychology of computer vision* (pp. 157–210). New York: McGraw-Hill.

Wittgenstein, L. (1953). *Philosophical investigation* (G. E. M. Anscombe, Trans.). New York: Macmillan.

Wittig, M. A. (1985). Metatheoretical dilemmas in the psychology of gender. *American Psychologist, 40,* 800–811.

Woods, W. A. (1975). What's in a link: Foundations for semantic networks. In D. G. Bobrow & A. Collins (Eds.), *Representation and understanding: Studies in cognitive science* (pp. 35–82). New York: Academic Press.

Wyer, R. S., Jr., & Srull, T. K. (1989). *Memory and cognition in its social context*. Hillsdale, NJ: Erlbaum.

Zimbardo, P. G. (1969). The human choice: Individuation, reason, and order versus deindividuation, impulse, and chaos. In W. J. Arnold & D. Levine (Eds.), *Nebraska symposium on motivation* (Vol. 17, pp. 237–307). Lincoln:University of Nebraska Press.

Index

231

Diane Gillespie is an associate professor in the Goodrich Scholarship Program at the University of Nebraska at Omaha. She is one of the original faculty members of this program, which has received national recognition for its retention of economically disadvantaged students. The winner of several teaching awards, including the 1992 all-university Outstanding Teaching and Instructional Creativity Award, she has contributed to the American Association of Higher Education's Forum on Exemplary Teaching at the association's 1990 and 1991 annual conferences. Her research focuses on contemporary issues in the social sciences, especially in relationship to women's studies. She has published articles in *Affilia: Journal of Women in Social Work*, *Gender & Society*, and *Women & Politics*.